Birmingham Archaeology Monograph Series 5

The Great Hall, Wolverhampton:
Elizabethan Mansion
to Victorian Workshop

Archaeological Investigations at Old Hall Street,
Wolverhampton, 2000–2007

Christopher Hewitson, Eleanor Ramsey, Michael Shaw, Malcolm Hislop and Richard Cuttler

with

Steven Allen, Robert Bracken, John Crowther, James Greig, Emma Hancox, Rob Ixer, Yvonne Jones, Erica Macey-Bracken, Richard MacPhail, Quita Mould, Stephanie Rátkai, David Smith, Wendy Smith, Emma Tetlow, and Richard Wisker

Illustrations by Nigel Dodds, John Halsted, and Bryony Ryder

BAR British Series 517
2010

Published in 2016 by
BAR Publishing, Oxford

BAR British Series 517

Birmingham Archaeology Monograph Series 5
The Great Hall, Wolverhampton: Elizabethan Mansion to Victorian Workshop

ISBN 978 1 4073 0702 2

© Birmingham Archaeology and the Publisher 2010

BAR Publishing is the trading name of British Archaeological Reports (Oxford) Ltd.
British Archaeological Reports was first incorporated in 1974 to publish the BAR
Series, International and British. In 1992 Hadrian Books Ltd became part of the BAR
group. This volume was originally published by Archaeopress in conjunction with
British Archaeological Reports (Oxford) Ltd / Hadrian Books Ltd, the Series principal
publisher, in 2010. This present volume is published by BAR Publishing, 2016.

Printed in England

BAR
PUBLISHING

BAR titles are available from:

BAR Publishing
122 Banbury Rd, Oxford, OX2 7BP, UK
EMAIL   info@barpublishing.com
PHONE +44 (0)1865 310431
FAX   +44 (0)1865 316916
www.barpublishing.com

CONTENTS

Figures

Plates

Tables

SUMMARY

This report outlines the results of archaeological investigations at Old Hall Street, Wolverhampton, West Midlands (NGR SO 916984), carried out between 2000 and 2007. The results of the archaeological work have been combined with documentary, cartographic and genealogical studies, together with finds and scientific analyses, to present a broad interpretation of the history of settlement in the area and the motives behind it.

The site was the location of a moated Elizabethan mansion house, the Great Hall, which lay at the edge of the then settled area of Wolverhampton in an area that had once been part of the town fields. A documentary reference suggests that there was an earlier house on the site, but there is only limited archaeological evidence to support this.

The building of the Great Hall was intended to make a clear statement about the status, wealth and prestige of its owners, the Leveson family, who were prominent Wolverhampton merchants, also involved in the early industrialisation of the Black Country. The aspirations of the family are clearly demonstrated by their construction of one of Staffordshire's most significant early brick buildings

The later history of the Great Hall mirrors that of the Black Country, for towards the end of the 18th century it was converted for use as a japanning factory, known as the Old Hall Works, artefacts from which were exhibited in the Great Exhibition of 1851. A large-scale map of 1852 gives a detailed insight into the layout of the japanning factory, which was finally demolished in 1883, an Adult Education College being built on the site in 1899.

The archaeological excavations took place ahead of the redevelopment of the college. The foundations of the northwest portion of the Great Hall and the subsequent Old Hall Works were located and recorded and several sections were excavated across the moat. This proved to have been backfilled in the mid-18th to mid-19th centuries and important finds assemblages of this period were recovered. The results of the excavations and associated analyses trace the history of the site through the various stages of its development, including its medieval function as part of the open field system around Wolverhampton, the 16th-century construction of a prestigious dwelling house, and its later adaptation as an industrial complex; in doing so show the report shows something of the process by which the Black Country attained its distinctive personality.

CHAPTER 1: INTRODUCTION

Richard Cuttler and Eleanor Ramsey

INTRODUCTION

The Great Hall was one of Elizabethan Wolverhampton's most important domestic buildings. Subsequently, it was taken over for use as industrial premises known as the Old Hall Works, before being demolished at the end of the 19th century. Accordingly, when redevelopment of the Adult Learning College, which now occupies the site, was proposed in 2000 a programme of archaeological investigation was planned and subsequently undertaken, ahead of and during the building works, in order to recover evidence of the history of the Great Hall site. The following report brings together the results of these archaeological investigations, along with historical, genealogical and cartographic research.

The site lies at NGR SO 916984 on the southeastern edge of the medieval town of Wolverhampton, bisected by Old Hall Street, a late 19th-century addition to the street plan (Figs 1 and 2). The underlying subsoil is a thin layer of glacial till, comprising pebbly clay, which overlies Permian deposits of the Clent Formation. This formation comprises mudstone and breccia with thin beds of sandstone. The mudstone can be used for brick clay (Powell *et al* 1992, figs 2B, 3B, 20, 28).

An initial desk-based assessment of the site had been carried out in 1996 (White 1996). When development proposals became clearer in 2000 Birmingham Archaeology were commissioned by Wolverhampton City Council to undertake a more detailed assessment, which included geo-rectification of the historic mapping in order to plot the position of the hall and its surrounding moat more accurately (Watt 2000). Archaeological evaluation was undertaken in 2000 (Williams 2001) and 2002. This led to an open area excavation in 2003 of those parts of the hall and its surrounding moat affected by the development proposals. Subsequent to the excavation a watching brief and salvage excavation were conducted over the remainder of the site between 2003 and 2004 (Cuttler and Ramsey 2005). A section was also excavated across the line of the moat to the south of Old Hall Street ahead of the construction of a public square in 2003. A further watching brief was conducted in 2007 as part of the refurbishment of an existing structure as a proposed school and library facility (Breeze 2007).

AIMS, OBJECTIVES AND METHODOLOGY

The objectives of the archaeological work were to define the survival, nature, extent and significance of archaeological deposits pertaining to the Great Hall, and to enable appropriate archaeological sampling and recording to be undertaken in advance of the development.

The expectation was that both the northern and southern edges of the moat would be identified beneath the modern cellaring, and that evidence relating to the hall might survive under the remains of the demolished pottery workshop of the Adult Education College.

The aims for the archaeological investigations can be summarised as follows:

- To establish a plan of the moat and its width, depth, date of excavation and phases of infill and recutting.

- To recover environmental information pertaining to the economy, diet, etc, of the inhabitants of the area.

- To establish the plan of the hall, its date and any phases of rebuilding.

- To establish the plan and phases of additions, alterations and extensions to the hall during its subsequent use as a japanning factory.

- To establish whether there were earlier buildings (eg, remains of an earlier hall, remains of garden wall or turrets) within the moated area.

- To establish the plan, nature and date of the ancillary buildings to the southwest of the moated area.

- To establish whether there was earlier occupation outside the moated area.

Recording was by means of pre-printed *pro formas* for contexts and features, supplemented by plans (at 1:20 and 1:50), sections (at 1:10, 1:20 and 1:50), and by monochrome, colour print, colour slide and digital photography. Feature numbers discussed in the text and illustrated on plans are three figure numbers with an 'F' prefix. Context numbers all have four figures commencing with 1000 for the evaluation, 5000 for the excavation and 8000/ 9000 for the watching brief.

THE ARCHAEOLOGICAL INVESTIGATIONS (Fig. 3)

Desk-Based Assessment, 2000

Initially, a desk-based assessment (Watt 2000) was conducted to assess the potential for survival of the Great Hall beneath the current urban landscape. As part of the desk-based assessment, Taylor's 1750 plan of Wolverhampton (Fig. 4), was geo-rectified and superimposed over a present-day plan, confirming that the Great Hall and the northern arm of the moat lay within the site.

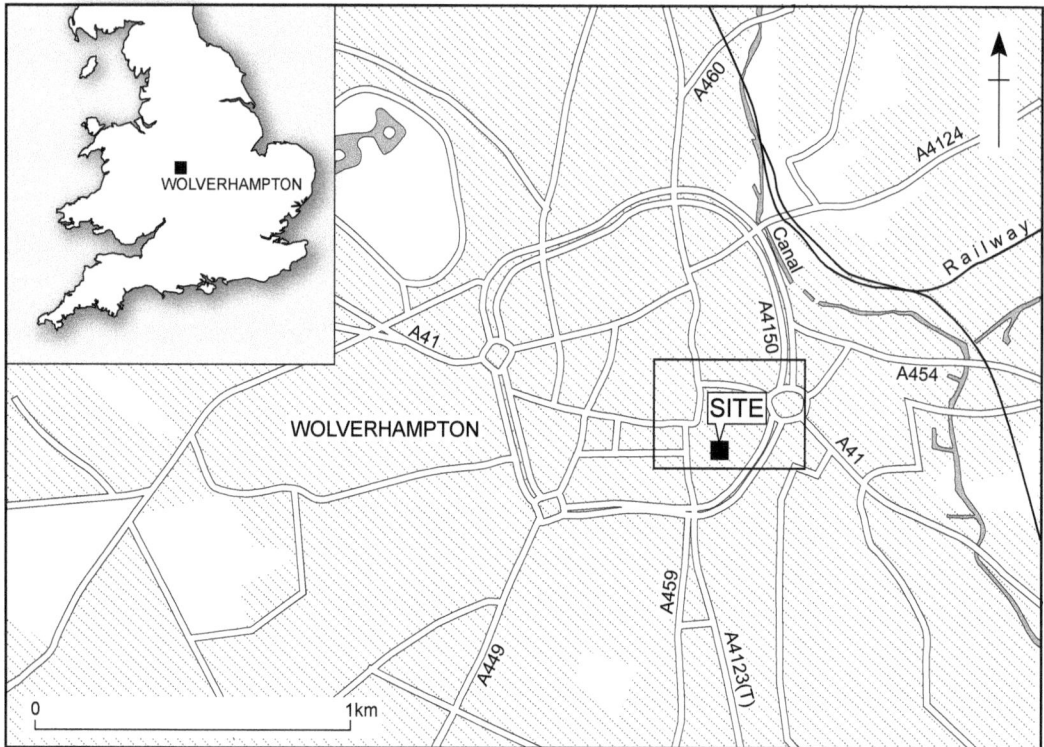

FIGURE 1 LOCATION OF WOLVERHAMPTON OLD HALL

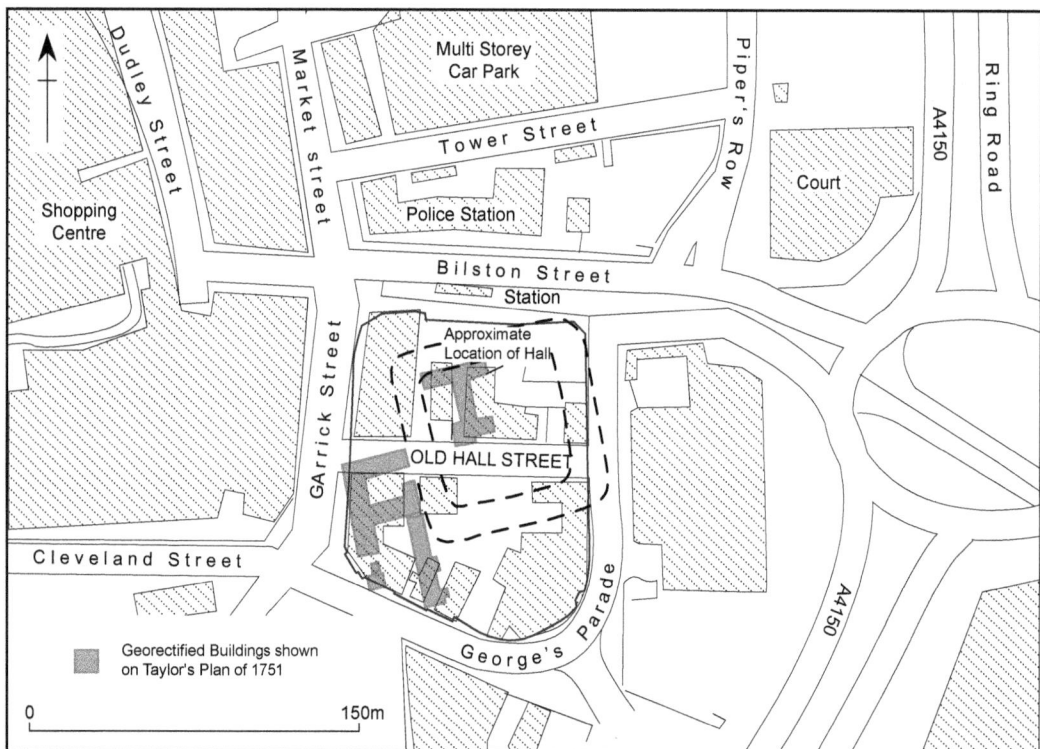

FIGURE 2 SITE PLAN

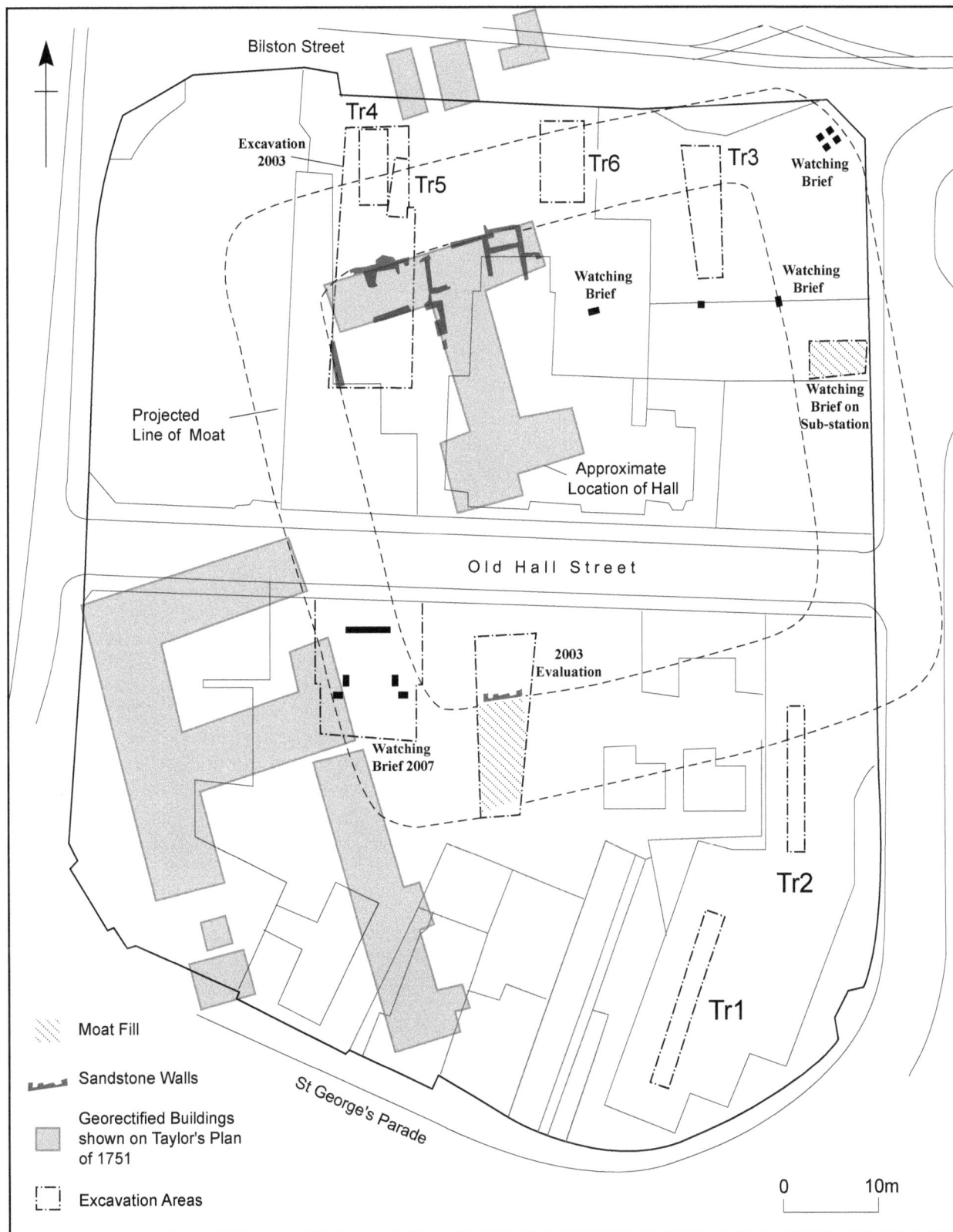

FIGURE 3 LOCATION OF INVESTIGATED AREAS

Evaluation, 2000

The results of the desk-based assessment led to evaluation of the site (Williams 2001). Four trenches were excavated in the 2000 evaluation. The upper fills of the moat were identified in Trench 3, enabling the location of the northern arm of the moat to be securely identified. However, the western extent of the moat and the precise location of the Great Hall could not be determined.

Trench 1 was located in the St George's Parade car park. It was excavated to a depth of *c* 0.6m until the natural subsoil was uncovered. At the northern end of the trench a machine-cut red-brick cellar was excavated containing 18th- and 19th-century white glazed pottery. The cellar was sealed by layers of brick rubble and the formation of the tarmac car park surface.

Likewise, Trench 2 was located in the St George's Parade car park on a north–south alignment. The natural sub-soil was recorded at a depth of 0.3m below the ground level. Two machine-cut red-brick cellars, which were recorded in the trench, were back-filled with brick rubble. The whole trench was sealed by formation layers and by the tarmac surface of the car park.

Trench 3 was located on derelict ground in the northeast corner of the site. The natural subsoil was located at a depth of 0.5m below the current ground level. The moat was recorded in the northern extent of the trench, orientated east–west and was excavated to a depth of 1.5m. South of the moat was an ironstone structure consisting of a north–south and an east–west aligned ironstone wall. Both walls were capped with concrete and bricks probably of a later rebuild. A small channel, which ran beneath the wall, was filled with brick, tile and 18th- to 19th-century pottery. In the southeast corner of the trench was a square brick cellar. The trench was sealed by a formation layer and tarmac.

Trench 4 was located in the northwestern corner of the car park of the Adult Education College and was orientated in a north–south alignment. The natural subsoil, red-brown sand (4001), was recorded at a depth of 1.2 to 1.7m at the southern end of the trench. A single post-medieval pit (F400) was located in the northwestern corner of the trench. This was sealed by a layer of yellow-orange clay silt (4003) containing post-medieval pottery and bottle glass. Layer 4003 was sealed by a deep layer of brick rubble (4002) that was, in turn, sealed by the tarmac of the car park.

Evaluation, 2002

Two further trenches were excavated as part of the evaluation of the site in April and May 2002. These revealed the moat to its full depth (Trench 6), demonstrating that sections of the infilled moat survived below the car park of the Adult Education College, despite severe truncation of the upper fills by 19th-century cellars. Importantly, the evaluation also showed that the northern arm of the moat extended to the western edge of the site, and that its western arm lay outside the site, under the former cinema complex on the corner of Bilston Street and Garrick Street.

Trench 5 was located in the northwest corner of the present car park directly adjacent to, and about 1m to the south of Trench 4 on a north–south orientation. The trench was excavated by machine over the upper fills of the moat. The natural subsoil was uncovered at a depth of 1.2m below the modern ground surface at the northern extent. The moat was hand dug to a depth of 2.2m below the modern ground level.

Trench 6 was located in the northeast corner of the former car park and was aligned north–south. The trench was excavated by machine until the upper moat fills were uncovered and the moat was subsequently excavated by hand. At the northern extent of the trench the natural subsoil was encountered at a depth of 0.7m but the moat was excavated to a full depth of 3.5m below the modern ground surface. The moat was filled by lower layers of sand, clay and silt over which lay a thick layer of black coal-rich material (1006). The upper 1.5m was truncated by brick cellars that had been backfilled with brick rubble.

The Excavation Trench, 2003

From the location of the moat, as determined by the evaluation and from cartographic evidence, it was suggested that the remains of the Great Hall might be located under the former pottery workshop of the Adult Education College and that these remains would be affected by the proposed development. Accordingly, excavation was mounted in this area after the recording and demolition of the pottery workshop in December 2003.

The excavation constituted an area 8m by 26m that was cleared of modern debris and cellaring by a JCB excavator under direct archaeological supervision. The first archaeological horizon was identified at approximately 0.2m below the modern ground surface at the southern end of the site. The cellaring present at the northern end of the site was removed to a depth of approximately 1.5m for the whole width of the area. The machined horizon was then cleaned by hand, which defined the archaeological features and deposits present at their uppermost horizons. Excavation by hand comprised 50% of all discrete archaeological features, and an appropriate section through all linear features. Context number 5000 was allocated as a general cleaning layer.

The excavations revealed a medieval ploughsoil that was sealed by a sterile layer of re-deposited clay. This clay appeared to have resulted from the digging of a moat, prior to the construction of the Great Hall. The Hall itself, therefore, was constructed over a medieval ploughsoil, perhaps indicating its initial location within the town's fields. The upcast from the moat was deposited on the island formed by the moat to create a platform onto which the Hall was constructed. Whilst there were no features suggesting the presence of an earlier hall, architectural fragments from an earlier building or buildings were incorporated into the walls and foundations (see below).

Important information regarding the chronology and development of the Great Hall was revealed, the ground plan of the northwest wing was exposed (see Figs 16, 17 and 19), and the excavations demonstrated that during its last phase of use the Great Hall was sub-divided into smaller units, possibly when the building was used as a japanning factory in the 19th century (see above). To the north of the main building many of the later deposits had been disturbed by later brick cellars, particularly in the area of the former moat.

Watching Brief, 2003

The watching brief also revealed the northern extent of the main building, along with parts of the moat and stone walls, which were interpreted as the remains of a curtain wall located around the inside of the moat, which is depicted on earlier drawings (see above). Further construction work in advance of the building piling was monitored. As additional remains of the Great Hall were encountered archaeological remains were excavated and recorded to the full depth of the disturbance. The moat was also recorded in areas where the proposed dig depth disturbed archaeological remains. These included the construction of an electricity sub-station within the eastern arm of the moat. Further structural remains of the Hall were recorded to the east of the excavation trench (see Figs 16, 17, 18 and 20). The watching brief on the groundworks continued until July 2004.

Evaluation South of Old Hall Street, 2003

Further evaluation was undertaken in advance of a second development to the south of Old Hall Street. The evaluation was conducted prior to the construction of a public square which included the provision of a water feature, seating and paving. This work identified the location of the southern arm of the moat, again revealing the presence of a curtain wall (Fig. 21).

The archaeological evaluation to the south of Old Hall Street demonstrated that the southern arm of the moat, and its associated curtain wall, survived as below ground archaeology within the site boundaries. While similarities between the lower fills of both the northern and southern arm were noted, differences in the middle and upper fills of the moat suggest they were filled in at different times and for different purposes. A later sandstone wall and brick drains that may relate to the later japanning factory were also identified. No evidence for an earlier phase of moat or earlier structure was identified during the evaluation.

Watching Brief, 2007

A watching brief was undertaken during development works undertaken within the Alan Garner Centre, Old Hall Street, in advance of refurbishment of an existing structure as a proposed school and library facility. The groundworks comprised the excavation of four trenches for mass concrete bases and the underpinning of existing walls. One further trench, measuring 2.10m x 5m was excavated for the emplacement of a lift shaft.

Archaeological observation and recording demonstrated the presence of preserved lower fills of the western arm of the moat in the area of the lift shaft and subsequent later moat infilling in two (potentially three) of the foundation trenches. Additionally, material possibly associated with the curtain wall was identified, and the stratigraphic sequence associated with the construction of the current 20th-century building observed.

ARRANGEMENT OF THE PUBLICATION

Chapters 2, 3 4 are concerned largely with the historical evidence, Chapter 2 being devoted to the general history, and sources for the development of the site, Chapter 3 to the history of the Leveson family, the builders of the Great Hall, and Chapter 4 to the japanning and enamelling factory known as the Old Hall Works. Chapters 5, 6 and 7 describe the results of the archaeological work, Chapter 5 narrating the phased development, and chapters 6 and 7 encompassing specialist reports on the finds and environmental evidence respectively. Chapter 8 comprises discussion and interpretation of the evidence. The main text is followed by the acknowledgements and references.

In the report the hall is referred to the Great Hall during its phase as a private house but as the Old Hall during its subsequent phase as industrial premises. This reflects usage at the time, although it has also been referred to as Turton's Hall after its tenants in the 18th century.

CHAPTER 2: THE HISTORICAL BACKGROUND

Michael Shaw

INTRODUCTION

The documentary evidence for the Great Hall is relatively extensive, although there are significant gaps still to be filled. The evidence comprises written documents (primary documentary evidence) and books (secondary documentary evidence), early maps and plans, drawings, and photographs. In addition, extensive information regarding the Leveson family has been drawn together (see Wisker below).

The earliest probable evidence for a hall on the site comes from John Leland's *Itinerary*. Leland, writing in the late 1530s to early 1540s, refers to the ancient house of the 'Luson' family at the town's end of Wolverhampton (Toulmin Smith 1964, II, 170). This attribution to the Leveson family (still pronounced Luson) and the location of the building on the edge of Wolverhampton would suggest that the Great Hall is the building that is being referred to. However, the Great Hall as excavated is extremely unlikely to date as far back as 1530s–40s and certainly would not have been described as ancient at this date. One explanation may be that there was an earlier building on the site at this time which was cleared away to make way for the building we now know as the Great Hall. Indeed one source specifically states that the hall was built on earlier foundations (Garner 1844, 177). The presence of the moat may provide further evidence for an earlier building. Moated sites are generally of medieval date, most commonly 13th to early 14th century (Le Patourel and Roberts 1978, 51). They were, however, often reused as garden features.

OWNERS AND TENANTS OF THE GREAT HALL

Most accounts of the Great Hall date it to the Elizabethan period (see Jones 1900, 27, Barford and Hewitt, 1871, 16) and although it has been suggested that it dates from an earlier period – to the reign of Queen Mary (1553–4, Mander and Tildesley 1960, 53) and other accounts put it later – in the reign of James I (Niven, 1882, 26), there can be little doubt that the majority view is correct. Stylistically, a date of around the 1570s is most consistent with the surviving drawings (Malcolm Airs pers. comm.) and this fits best with the genealogical evidence, for this was when the Leveson family were at their most powerful. The most likely candidate for the builder, and the man traditionally associated with the Great Hall's construction is John Leveson (Barford and Hewitt, 1871, 16), who succeeded to the Leveson estate on the death of his brother in 1563, and who died in 1575. The other chief candidates are Thomas Leveson, John's older brother, who succeeded to the Leveson estate on the death of his father in 1512 and

died in 1563; or John's son, also Thomas Leveson, who succeeded his father in 1575 and died in 1594. All three would be looking to display their status by the construction of a prestigious building such as the Great Hall.

An idea of the wealth of the Leveson family can be gained from the Lay Subsidy of 1541. Although he was the younger son, John appears to have been the wealthier of the two brothers, for he paid 40s, while Thomas paid 30s (Mander 1916a, 189–90). The only person in Wolverhampton to pay more was Thomas's and John's arch rival, James Leveson, of the senior branch of the Leveson family, who paid a massive £11 13s 4d (Wisker 1995–6, 126–9).

Details of John Leveson's landholdings and his connections with the wool trade are discussed by Wisker below. Another source of wealth appears to have stemmed from his involvement in the early industrialisation of the Black Country. In 1563 he was granted a licence to cut down wood for use in ironmaking (Mander and Tildesley 1960, 52), while in 1564 references were made to his coal mines in Wednesbury (King 2007, 37). In his will he left his coal mines to one of his sons (Mander and Tildesley 1960, 52).

The 17th-century hearth tax emphasises the massive size of the hall. In 1665–6 the then owner, Robert Leveson, paid tax on eleven hearths, presumably at the Great Hall. By 1673 he paid tax on twelve hearths and on eleven hearths 'for his ould house' suggesting that he had moved out of the Great Hall at this time, probably to the other major family residence, Ashmores, which lies around 5km northeast of Wolverhampton. The figure of eleven hearths for the Great Hall is one of the largest for a building in Wolverhampton, the only significantly larger building being the Deanery with 15–16 hearths (Mander 1916b).

The Leveson family's interest in the Great Hall ceased in 1702 when Robert Leveson sold his Wolverhampton estate, including the Great Hall, to the Earl of Bradford, from whom it later descended to the Dukes of Cleveland. The hall then became the residence of the Turton family. Although it is stated in Mander and Tildesley (1960, 115) that they purchased the property, it would appear that the Turtons were in fact tenants. Hence, Shaw describes them as tenants (Shaw 1801, 163) and in a letter of around 1793 Dr John Turton says that his ancestors lived in the hall as tenants (WSL S. MS 478/20/77). Mander and Tildesley (1960, 115) say that the hall was occupied by either Joseph Turton senior (d 1709), possibly before the end of the 17th century, or his son, Joseph Turton jnr (1671–1729). They also suggest that two subsequent generations of the Turton family were born here, Dr John Turton (1700–64), the younger Joseph Turton's son, and his grandson, also Dr John Turton (1735–1806). If this is the case they may have moved out soon after 1735, as the younger Dr John Turton, in his letter of around 1793, states that his grandfather lived there, but makes no mention of his father or himself residing there.

Like the Levesons, the Turtons were a family of some wealth and status. The two Joseph Turtons were wealthy ironmongers and Joseph Turton senior was a churchwarden in 1681 and a High Constable for the Hundred in 1690. The younger Dr John Turton was Physician in Ordinary to the King and the Prince of Wales. The family were nonconformists and the hall was licensed as a place of worship for a short time in 1715 under the Toleration Act, after a chapel in John Street had been burnt down in anti-Presbyterian riots (Mander and Tildesley 1960, 115).

The Turtons may have made significant changes to the Great Hall. Mander and Tildesley say that the building was ruinous before the Turton's took up residence and that they 'restored it [the hall] in the fashion of the day' by inserting sash windows and removing the upper storey (Mander and Tildesley 1960, 115), while Shaw (1801, 163) also states that Joseph Turton took off the upper storey early in the 18th century. Hence the removal of an original pitched roof and its replacement by a flat roof is often ascribed to the Turtons. However, Taylor's map of 1750 shows the Great Hall as having a pitched roof. If correct this would imply that the roof was lowered after 1750, possibly after the Turtons left, and as part of the conversion of the building into a factory.

As we have seen the Turtons perhaps left the hall in the late 1730s. Jones (1900, 4) says that the hall was empty for a long time afterwards and became the resort of coiners, although Barford and Hewitt suggest that it was in commercial use by 1745 (Barford and Hewitt 1871, 18).

The Turtons were sufficiently associated with the hall in the public mind for it to become known as Turton's Hall well into the 19th century. Eventually, however, this name was superseded and the hall became known as the Old Hall. For simplicity, the building will be referred to as the Old Hall when referring to its life as a japanning works.

OWNERS OF THE OLD HALL WORKS

Sometime, by the end of the 1770s to the early 1780s, the hall was given over to japanning, and it was to continue to be used as such for over a century. Japanning is a process of covering a material with a hard, black lacquer in imitation of Japanese lacquer work. It was originally introduced into the British Isles around 1665 from the continent and was principally manufactured in South Wales, especially Pontypool. Wolverhampton succeeded Pontypool as the centre of the japanning industry in the 18th century (Burritt 1869, 171). Most commonly, metal goods were japanned, but other materials were also experimented with. The most successful was papier mâché, which became a particular speciality of the Old Hall works from the 1820s (see Hewitson and Jones below). The original japanning works was set up by Taylor and Jones, but William and Obadiah

Ryton had taken over by 1805 (Jones 1900). The history of the japanning works at the Old Hall can be pieced together from the various trade directories held in Wolverhampton Archives and Local Studies. Jones and Taylor do not appear in a Wolverhampton trade directory of 1770 (Sketchley and Adams 1770) but are entered in one of 1780 (Pearson and Rollason) as Jones and Taylor, Japanners and Merchants, Bilston Street, and in one of 1783 (Bailey) as Jones and Taylor, Merchants and Japanners, Turton's Hall. Barford and Hewitt (1871, 18) state that the hall had been in the hands of Taylor, Jones and Badger, the first japanners in Wolverhampton. Jones was the craftsman – he had been a foreman at the Pontypool Japan Works, while Taylor and Badger were businessmen (DeVoe 1971, 55–6). The schedule accompanying Godsons' map of 1788 gives the occupier as William B Taylor, and the proprietor as William Pulteney (although Pulteney had in fact died in 1764; pers. comm. Richard Wisker).

Although DeVoe states that William and Obadiah Ryton moved their japanning business from Tinshop Yard in North Street to the Old Hall in 1775 this seems to be a mistake for as we have seen above Taylor and Jones are mentioned as tenants of the Old Hall in records down to 1788. Barney and Ryton, Japanners, occur in the 1783 directory on Stafford Street. Obadiah and William Ryton, japanners, Bilston Street, do occur in a directory of 1805 (Holden 1805) so they had moved to the Old Hall by this time. Jones, (1900, 28) says that the Rytons lived in part of the building and used the remainder as a factory. Obadiah died in 1810 and William Ryton was joined by Benjamin Walcot. A directory of 1833 (Bridgen) describes them as Ryton and Walton, general japanners and iron and tin plate works, manufacturers of paper trays, improved patent dish covers, etc. William Ryton retired in 1842 and Benjamin became sole proprietor. A lawsuit and business problems affected Benjamin's health and he was declared bankrupt before his death in 1847 (Post Office Directory 1847). The business was, however, re-established by Benjamin's eldest son Frederick, and the Old Hall Works continued to hold a leading position in the japanning industry. Frederick exhibited at the Great Exhibition in 1851 (Jones 1900, 55). DeVoe says that the business ended in 1874 (DeVoe 1971, 56). A directory of 1879–80 (Hulley), however, still lists Walton, Frederick and Co, japanned ware manufactures, of Garrick Street. At any rate, the hall was demolished shortly afterwards in 1883, and the site was then derelict until the Adult Education College was built in 1899.

DESCRIPTIONS OF THE OLD HALL

A number of sources add detail to our impression of the Old Hall, at least during its time as a japanning works. Jones (1900) has published a detailed description of the Old Hall as it was in 1839 when he commenced work there.

> …[The building] had the appearance of a decayed Elizabethan mansion, with large stone mullioned windows, and a square tower in front over the entrance porch…Before the hall stretched a large green paddock surrounded with a high wall and iron gates; a broad

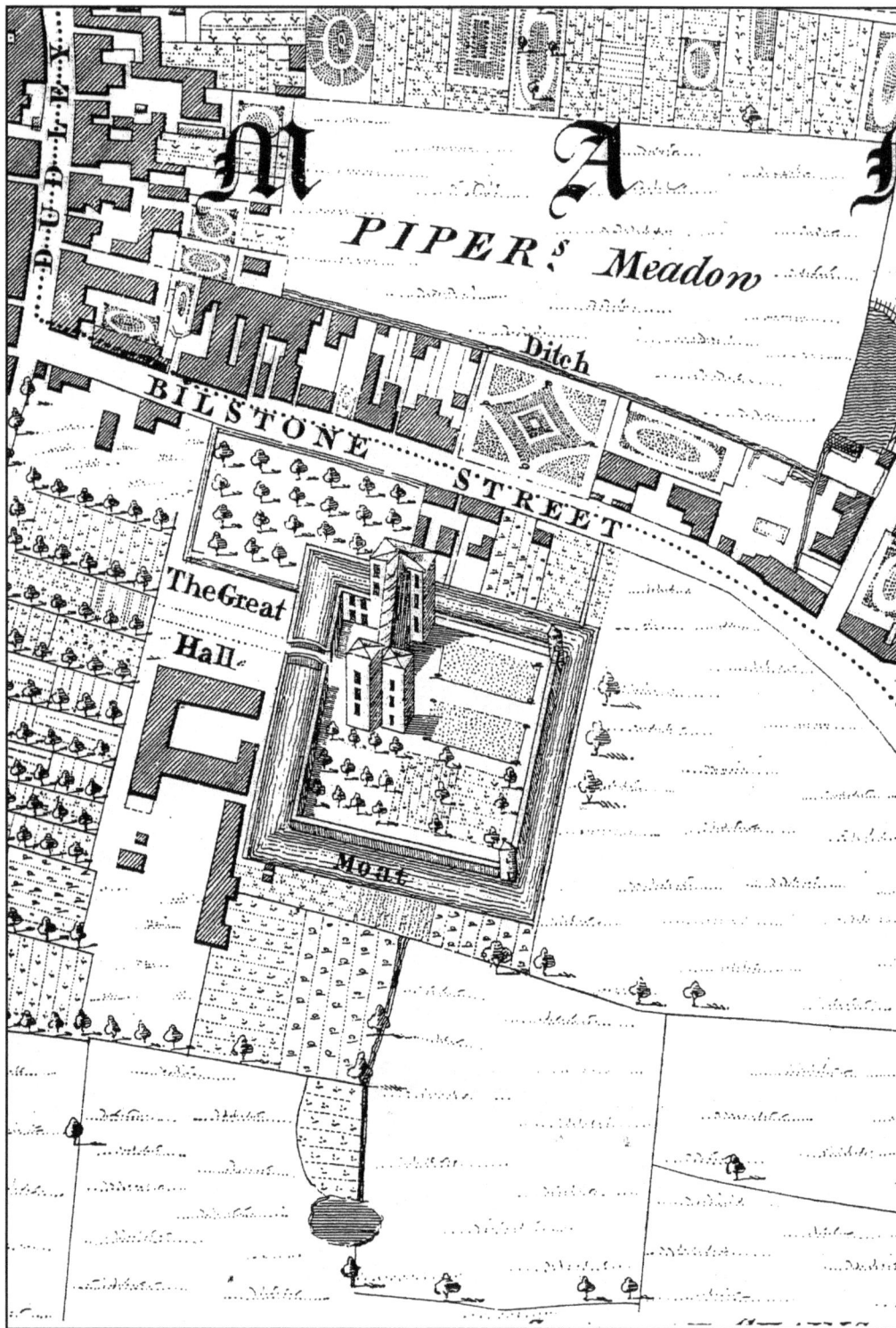

FIGURE 4 TAYLOR'S MAP OF 1750

pathway led through the green paddock to the porch, while behind the hall was a nicely kept garden laid out with flower beds, and fishponds filled with gold fish. Outside the boundary wall at the back was a part of the old moat filled with water...Adjoining the hall stood several large barns, formerly used for receiving flocks of sheep and storing wool. A small part of the front of the main building was used as a dwelling house, the remainder being devoted to business. In the interior a strange transformation was apparent. The grand oak staircase with its dark balustrades, instead of leading to the state ballroom, now led into warehouses where women and girls were employed wrapping up goods, and the bedrooms were used as storerooms. On the ground floor the change was equally great. The large open kitchen fireplace, instead of providing feasts for the great personages who resided at the hall, was utilised for tinning the goods; vans of molten metal and grease stood under the great fireplace, and the kitchen floor was strewn with pans and dish covers in the process of tinning. All of the other rooms in the Old Hall were degraded to

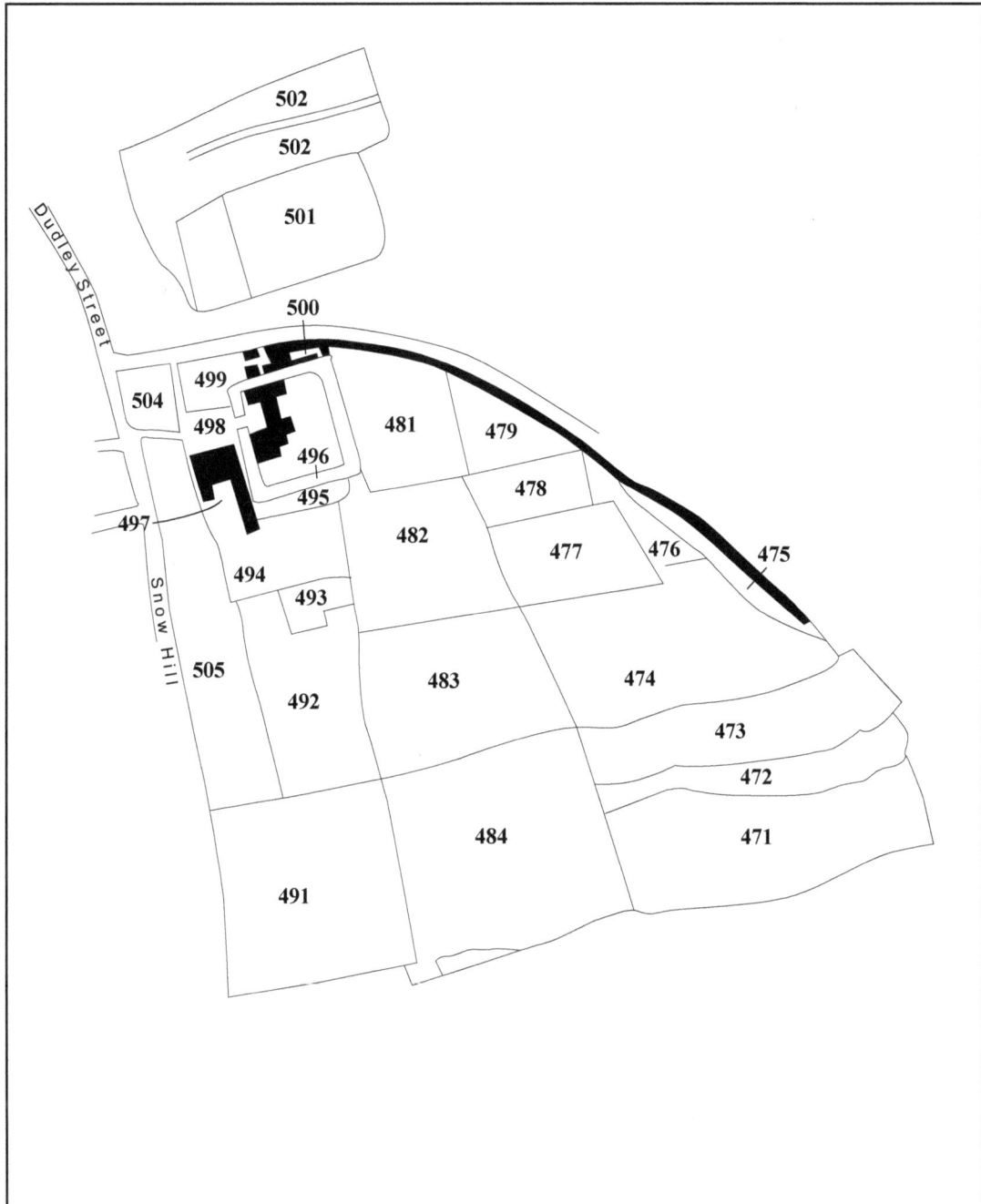

FIGURE 5 GODSONS' MAP OF 1788

trade purposes of one sort or the other... (Jones 1900, 5, 27f).

He also describes the later addition of new workshops and stores:

...at various times new workshops and japanning stores were erected adjoining the old mansion, till it was surrounded with busy hives of industry. Even the old barns were converted into workshops...the large open space around the hall was covered with signs of industry and enterprise... (Jones 1900, 54).

An account of 1871 says that:

...the building was of great strength, the walls, in part, being five feet in thickness – not of ordinary brickwork but between the inner and outer surfaces are filled with concrete of extraordinary hardness. A deep moat surrounded the Hall on all sides, of great depth and width, which was capable of being filled with water in a short time from an artificial reservoir. This moat was spanned by a moveable drawbridge which was raised at sunset by the warder. The banqueting room ran the whole length of the building, with small withdrawing rooms, partly let into the thickness of the walls, on either side. Several of the rooms were oak panelled... (Barford and Hewitt 1871, 17).

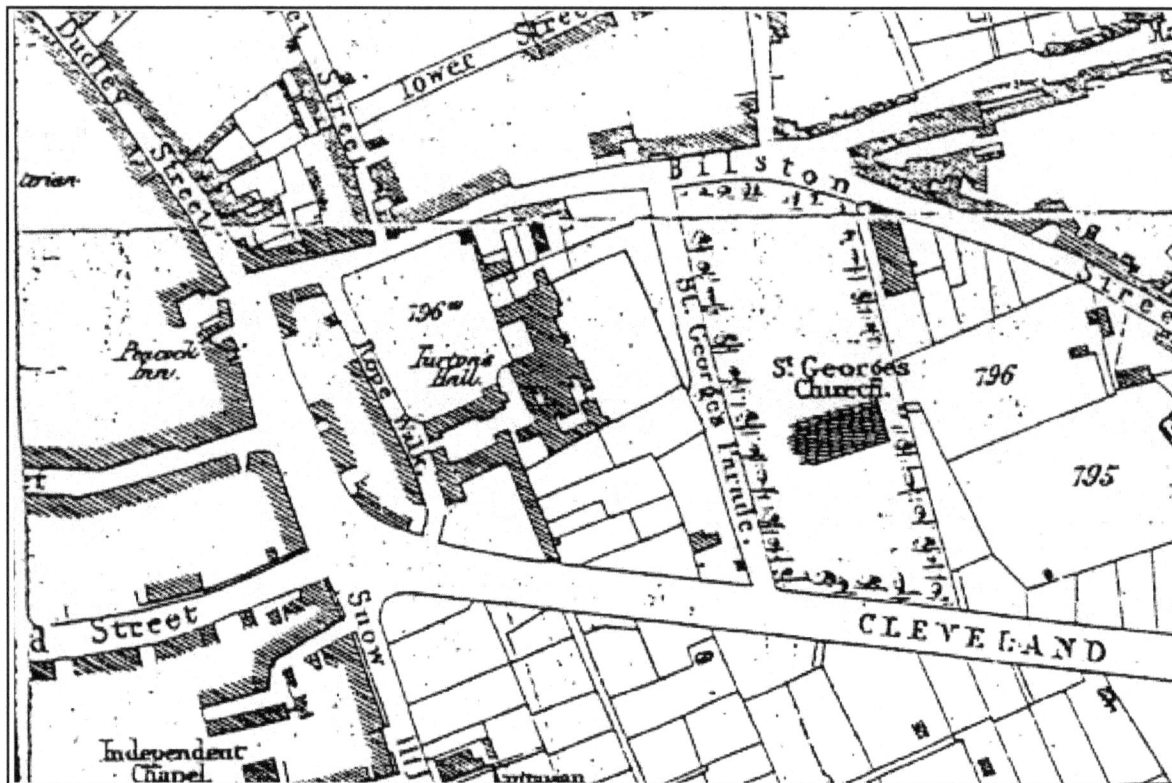

FIGURE 6 TURTON'S HALL ON TITHE MAP OF 1842

A footnote in the same publication says that the drawbridge had been cut down, probably during the Civil War, and had been discovered some years before during some excavations.

Another account, published in 1882, talks of Turton's Hall as:

> ...large and lofty, two storeys above ground floor, central portion with wings projecting back and front; porch entrance in the centre...brick with stone quoins and window dressings, mullioned and transomed windows...formerly surrounded by a moat which remained within living memory of the present occupants... (Niven 1882, 26).

CARTOGRAPHIC EVIDENCE

Our best cartographic evidence comes from the earliest map of Wolverhampton, Isaac Taylor's superb plan of the town in 1750 (Fig. 4). 'The Great Hall' is shown in an isolated position on the southern edge of the town; it is shown in detail in a bird's eye view, itself an indication of its importance as only seven buildings are shown thus. The main building is three storeys and aligned north–south. At either end there appear to be projecting wings, giving the building the appearance of an H-plan, typical of the Elizabethan period. The northern wing is of three storeys, with a further two-storey building attached to its west side. The southern wing is less clearly delineated. It appears to comprise two separate buildings, slightly offset, but, given

the small scale of the original, this is not necessarily an accurate depiction.

The Great Hall is set within a large moat which encloses a square area of around 0.45ha (1.1 acres), each arm being 60m (196 feet) in length. A curtain wall runs round the inside of the moat with turrets at its northeast and southeast corners. The Great Hall is not set centrally within the moat but occupies its northwestern quarter. Its northeast quarter contains two rectangular areas of lawn, its southwest quarter comprises an orchard, while its southeast quarter is a kitchen garden.

The moat is crossed by a bridge towards the northern end of the western side, possibly a replacement for one cut down in the Civil War. A pond around 100m to the south of the moat is presumably the reservoir referred to in the 1871 account (see above) as a leat leads off from the pond towards the moat. A second pond to the northeast of the moat feeds a feature called the Ditch on the north side of Bilston Street but the lie of the land falls from south to north so that the northern pond is unlikely to be the source for the moat.

Outside the moat a further series of large buildings is shown immediately to the west, set around a courtyard. They measure around 36m east–west by 30m north–south; to the southwest were two small outhouses, while to the southeast was a long narrow building around 48m by 4m. These are the buildings identified as barns by Jones (see above). One possibility to be borne in mind, given their

Phase 3a

Phase 3b

Phase 3c

Phase 4a
(Godson Map 1788)

Phase 4b
(Tithe Map 1842)

Phase 4c
(Board of Health
Map 1852)

Bilston Street

Garrick Street

The Town Hall

Police Barracks

Tin Shop

Old Hall

Lodge

Polishing Room

Stamp Shop

Polishing Shop

Iron Stores

Sand Room

Packing House

Store Room

Tin Room

Tin Shop

Stove

Delivery →

Removal

Stores

Store

Tin Shop

Stamp Shop

Wheeling Shop

Stores

Tin Shop

Theatre Royal

Tinning Shop

Engine House

Furnace for Enameling

Burnish Mill

Boiler

Mill

Engine House

Scouring Room

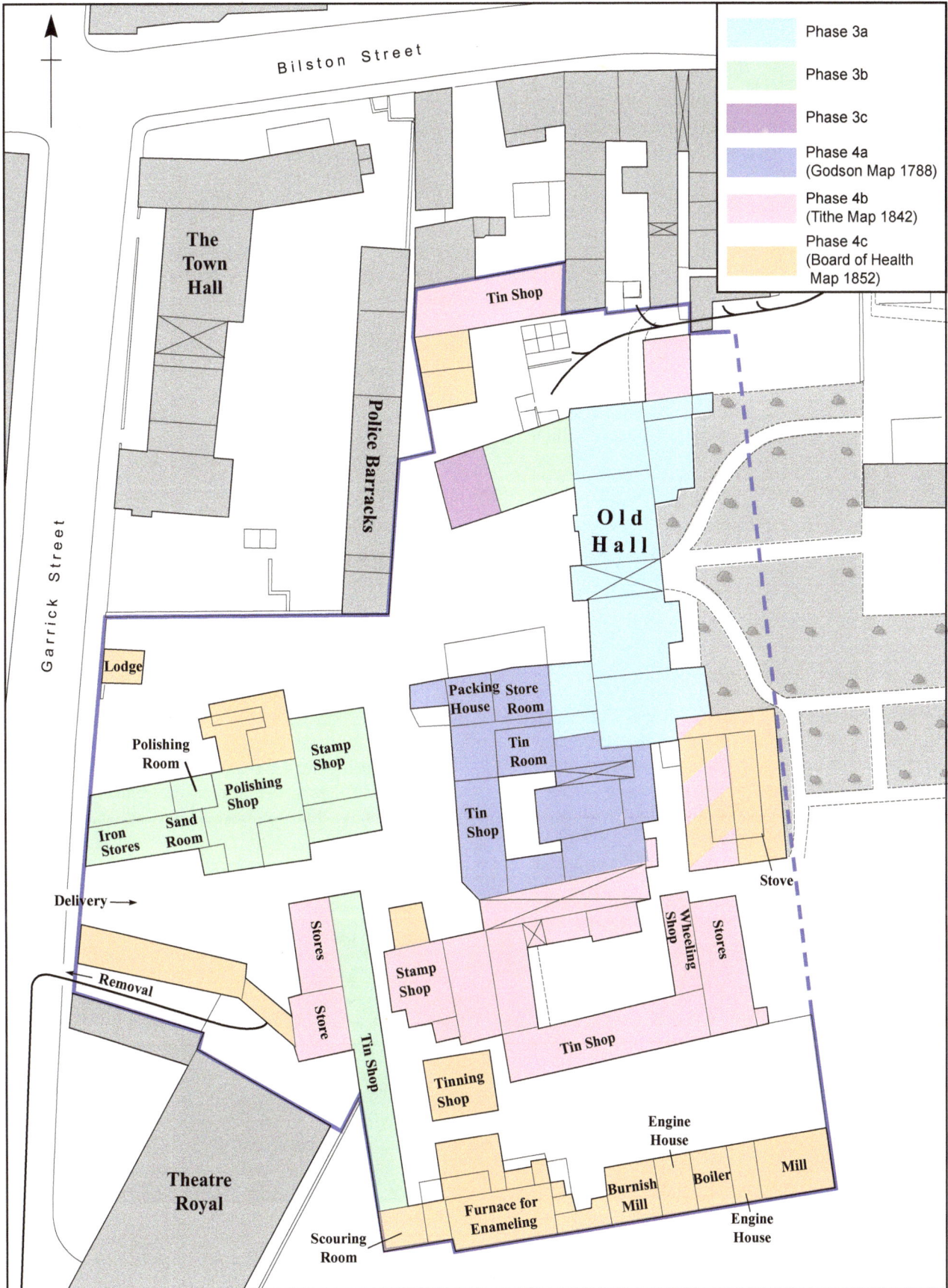

FIGURE 7 THE OLD HALL AS DEPICTED ON THE HEALTH OF TOWNS MAP OF 1852 (REDRAWN)

large size, is that these buildings formed the nucleus of the original hall and were only later converted to use as barns. It must be admitted, however, that none of the later accounts suggest that these buildings show signs of having been part of a major building. A path leads from the moat bridge to the west, but appears to terminate against a series of allotments which front on to Dudley Street to the west. To the north, a series of buildings, orchards and allotments front on to Bilston Street.

The next oldest map, Godsons' map of 1788 (Fig. 5) is of less value, as it is at a smaller scale. Nevertheless, it does show some additional features of interest, and has a valuable accompanying schedule. In particular, pathways leading towards the moat are shown from both the Bilston Street and Dudley Street frontages. The map is also useful in showing that the hall is little altered (though there may have been accretions against the south wing), and that the moat and barns outside it are still present and unaltered.

There are a number of small-scale early 19th-century maps (Wallis 1827, Bliss 1828 and Dewhirst 1836, not illustrated). Given their small scale, however, and the possibility that they may be copied from other maps rather than original surveys, caution needs to be exercised, and it is better to move on to the larger-scale tithe map of 1842 (Fig. 6) which shows the early 19th-century changes better. The hall is shown, marked as Turton's Hall, and additional buildings have been added to its southern end. The western side of the moat has been filled in but the line of the northeastern corner of the moat is still demarcated by property boundaries, and the moat itself may still survive here. It certainly appears to have survived down to around 1837 for it appears on a drawing of this date (see below). The barns outside the moat are also shown. New roads have been added to the west (The Rope Walk), south (Cleveland Road) and east (St George's Parade).

A small-scale map of 1850 (Bridgen, not illustrated) shows that the Rope Walk had been replaced by a new street on a slightly different alignment, marked on later maps as Garrick Street. It is also of interest in being the first map to name the hall as the Old Hall.

We are fortunate in having a large-scale Health of Towns Act map of 1852 (Haggar, Fig. 7) which not only shows the Old Hall works in detail but gives the use of the rooms. The original Old Hall is shown in the centre with some surviving gardens behind it to the east but this has all been swamped by a mass of new buildings to the north, south and west. The building of Garrick Street has impinged upon the barn buildings and there has been some demolition of these but the remainder have been adapted for use as part of the japanning works.

There is another detailed plan of 1871 (Steen and Blackett, not illustrated). The only new build has been a small amount to the east of the hall in the former garden area and at the southeast corner of the complex. The next detailed plan is of 1886 (Ordnance Survey 1:500) after the demolition of 1883. It shows the site as a cleared space.

The Ordnance Survey 1:2500 1st revision of 1903 shows the Adult Education College, marked as a school.

DRAWINGS

Five views of the hall offer further insights into the hall and its surrounds.

A view of the Old Hall from the east (Fig. 8, Wolv ALS N2/OLD/E1) which dates to the 1820s to 1830s shows the upper two storeys of the hall with the ground floor obscured by the surrounding wall. The roof is flat and almost down to the level of the tops of the windows of the upper storey, perhaps supporting the idea that there had originally been a further storey. The surrounding wall and turret at the northeast corner are shown. The surrounding wall is of coursed stone with frequent small buttresses on top. Lower down, the wall is of large stone blocks with large buttresses. The moat is still present and filled with water.

A drawing of 1837 (Buckler, Fig. 9, WSL SV XII 123a) shows the hall from the southeast. The details shown are similar to those of the previous view, but the entire roof can be seen and five banks of chimneys can be identified, and the southeast corner turret is shown in addition to the turret at the northeast corner.

A drawing of 1845, (Buckler, Fig. 10, WSL SV XII 124) shows the west front of the hall. All three storeys can be seen. A two-storey entrance porch is centrally placed along the west front. On top is a distinctive bell turret. To the south (right on the drawing) is a projecting three-storey wing, to which is attached a two-storey building, whose upper storey is approached from an outer staircase. To the north (left on the drawing) is a chimney with diaper work. Beyond this is a two-storey projecting wing; this is of a different character to the main building' suggesting a later building. There is no sign of the moat, which had been filled in by this date, certainly on this west side. A paved path leads up to the entrance porch.

An undated view, possibly c 1838 (Wood, Fig. 11), again shows the west front of the hall, but from the northwest rather than the west and slightly further back. This drawing has been attributed to c 1838 but there is some evidence that it is later than Figure 10 as a clock has been added to the second storey of the porch, and the bell turret above has been castellated. On the other hand the two-storey building with an exterior access stair to the south, evident on Figure 10, is no longer shown. Had it been demolished? Or was it left off for aesthetic reasons? It is in any case a reminder that we do need to be careful in using evidence from drawings. What is clear is that the two-storey northwest wing is of a quite different architectural character and its roof is hipped rather than flat. Buildings have also been added to the south side of the hall. St George's church tower and spire, built 1830, have been sketched in.

A further view, (Fig. 12, Wolv ALS DX/6/76) is similar to the above but this time is drawn directly from the west.

FIGURE 8 DRAWING OF THE EAST FRONT OF THE OLD HALL FROM THE NORTHEAST, 1820S–30S

FIGURE 9 BUCKLER'S DRAWING OF THE EAST FRONT OF THE OLD HALL
FROM THE SOUTHEAST, 1837

FIGURE 10 BUCKLER'S DRAWING OF WEST FRONT
OF THE OLD HALL, 1845

FIGURE 11 DRAWING OF THE WEST FRONT
OF THE OLD HALL, UNDATED

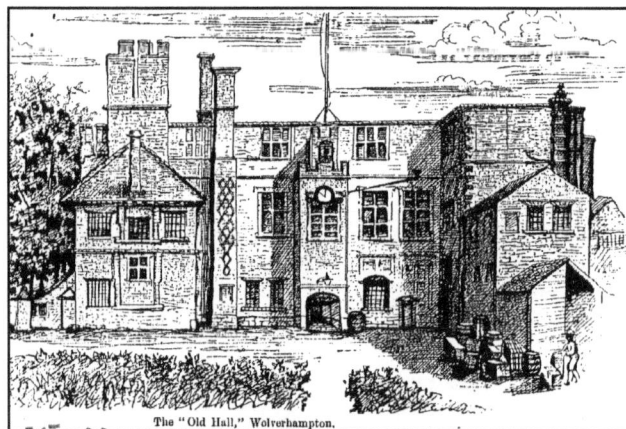

FIGURE 12 DRAWING OF THE WEST FRONT
OF THE OLD HALL, UNDATED

FIGURE 13 PHOTOGRAPH OF THE DEMOLITION OF THE HALL FROM THE NORTHWEST, 1883

FIGURE 14 PHOTOGRAPH OF THE DEMOLITION OF THE HALL FROM THE SOUTHWEST, 1883

The main changes are that two windows on the ground floor of the main range to the south of the entrance porch have been replaced by a smaller window and a doorway and a new building has been added to the south, replacing the building with an external stair shown on Figure 10.

PHOTOGRAPHS

There are two photographs showing the hall during demolition in 1883; both provide useful information. One (Fig. 13, Wolv ALS N2/OLD/E/11) shows the west front of the hall from the northwest. The main building survives but the later north wing has been removed. This reveals the large chimney stack, which can itself be seen to have been placed against the main building, partially obscuring a window which has been bricked up.

The other (Fig. 14, Wolv ALS N2/OLD/E/10) shows the southwest corner of the hall at a more advanced stage of the demolition. The main hall has been reduced to ground- and first-floor levels. The south wing survives to roof level but buildings against its west and south sides have been removed. Chimney stacks can be seen set against the west and south sides of the south wing.

CHAPTER 3: THE LEVESON FAMILY

Richard Wisker

The Leveson family were owners of the hall from at least the 16th century down to 1702 (Fig. 15). They were an important local family entrenched in the upper echelons of society. At the time of the Great Hall's construction, they were an Elizabethan merchant family with an eye to increasing their wealth and branching out into new enterprises. These were the people who were to pioneer the new industries, which were eventually to lead to the heavily industrialised Black Country of the 18th and 19th centuries.

The documentary evidence for the family goes back to the 1200s. Richard Leveson of Willenhall married Margery, daughter and heiress of Henry, son of Clement of Wolverhampton, late in the 13th century (Staff RO D 593 B/1/26/6/9/6). While John, the eldest son, inherited his father's estate, Richard, the second son, was endowed in 1311 with substantial property in Wolverhampton. This included a messuage, perhaps with a substantial house, four bovates (about 72 acres), five acres of moor, five acres of meadow and 38 shillings of rents in Wolverhampton (SHC 1911, 76–7). Richard's family lived and flourished in Wolverhampton.

Descendants of the family make their appearance again in the early 15th century. After the battle of Shrewsbury (1403), Henry IV granted (another) Richard Leveson £10 a year '....for his good service at the battle ... when he was maimed (SHC 1908, 275) .....'. Richard's son, William, was involved in the rebuilding of St Peter's church, Wolverhampton, from 1439. A major part of the plan was to replace the tower and steeple at a cost of £120; in the event the fine existing tower was built without a steeple (Staff RO D593 B/1/26/6/26/11).

Walter, grandson of William, inherited in 1492. He and his two sons, Thomas and John, who succeeded him, were all important landowners. The number of court cases in which they are cited indicates their quarrelsome natures. In 1498 Walter was accused of leading a party of over 100, armed with bows and bills, to Walsall because of a dispute at Willenhall Fair. Walter deposed that he went escorted by two of his servants to enquire about someone who had been detained (SHC 1907 80–2). Thomas, who succeeded in 1512, supported by his brother John, was involved in disputes which kept the Court of Star Chamber busy in the reign of Henry VIII. No one gave the Leveson brothers more trouble than their distant cousins Nicholas and James Leveson, descended from John Leveson, eldest son of Richard and Margery. James, a merchant of the Staple, had made a massive fortune in the wool trade which enabled him to build up a great estate in Staffordshire and Shropshire. The Dissolution of the Monasteries finally gave him the opportunity to become the possessor of an estate of between 35,000 and 37,000 acres (Wisker 1995–6, 126–9).

Leveson v. Leveson in 1529 indicated the atmosphere between the two sides. James had cut down and driven through hedges belonging to Thomas who, in retaliation, cut down a gate. James had also complained of his enemies (including Thomas) plotting against him. Relations reached boiling point on 10 June 1534, market day in Wolverhampton. Thomas had complained that James had appointed his brother Nicholas' servant, Robert Welbe, to the office of bellman when it had become vacant '...of his own mind as he is wont to do in suchlike matters...' To remonstrate, he went accompanied by quite a large party to James's house, High Hall on High Green (near the present-day site of Prince Albert's statue). James, alarmed at the size of the party, would not come out. Both sides, after abusing each other, submitted declarations to the Star Chamber that they wished to negotiate (SHC 1912, 34–5, 63–79).

These violent quarrels were full of sound and fury but did not, in the end, amount to much. The same family members who took part in them were ready to act for each other in property transactions (Staff RO D593 B/1/26/6/31/4). John Leveson, like James Leveson, a member of the Staple prospered. He inherited the family estate as well when his brother Thomas died aged about 64 in 1563. He had previously bought out Jane, his brother's daughter, married to Richard Poultney. When John died in 1575, he held about 3,750 acres (1517.6 ha.) in and around Wolverhampton. He also held a lease of six of the seven prebendal manors of the church in Wolverhampton. The prebendal manors consisted of a town house and with it a plot of land sufficient to support the prebendary either in Wolverhampton or elsewhere in Staffordshire (Mander 1945, 103–7; Shaw 1801, 154–5, 167–8).

John Leveson was High Sheriff of Staffordshire in 1561–2. He obtained a grant of arms from Lawrence Dalton, Norrey King at Arms, in November 1562. On his shield were three couped hands in armour to distinguish him from the luces on the arms of members of the senior branch like James (SHC 1883, 106). The battered remains of his tomb can still be seen in St Peter's church, Wolverhampton.

His son, Thomas (1535–94), who succeeded him, was also a merchant of the Staple, and Sheriff of Staffordshire. Both in his time, and that of his son Sir Walter (1567–1621), the family became more significantly Catholic. At the Reformation Staffordshire was largely Catholic with few supporters of the reformed religion. Most people were prepared to settle down under the Elizabethan settlement

```
                                    Fulk            Walter = Elizabeth Archer
                                                    d.1512


                             Thomas = Ann Wrottesley      John = Joyce Ashfield
                             d.1563                       1493-1575


                                  Jane = Richard Pulteney


                                       Thomas = Mary Brooke          4 other Children
                                       c 1535-1594


                             Edward        Walter = Dorothy Giffard  Thomas          9 other Children
                             1563-1602     1567-1621                 1576-1643
                                           Later Sir Walter
                                                                     Levesons of
                                                                     Willenhall


                                       Thomas = Frances Paulet  Magdalen      5 other Children
                                       1615-1652                1616-1692
                                                                Carmelite


                                  Robert = Sarah Povey
                                  c 1636-1709


                             Richard = Penelope       Sarah = Charles Fowler   6 other Children
                             1659-1699    d.1697


                                                          Richard Fowler


                                                              Issue
```

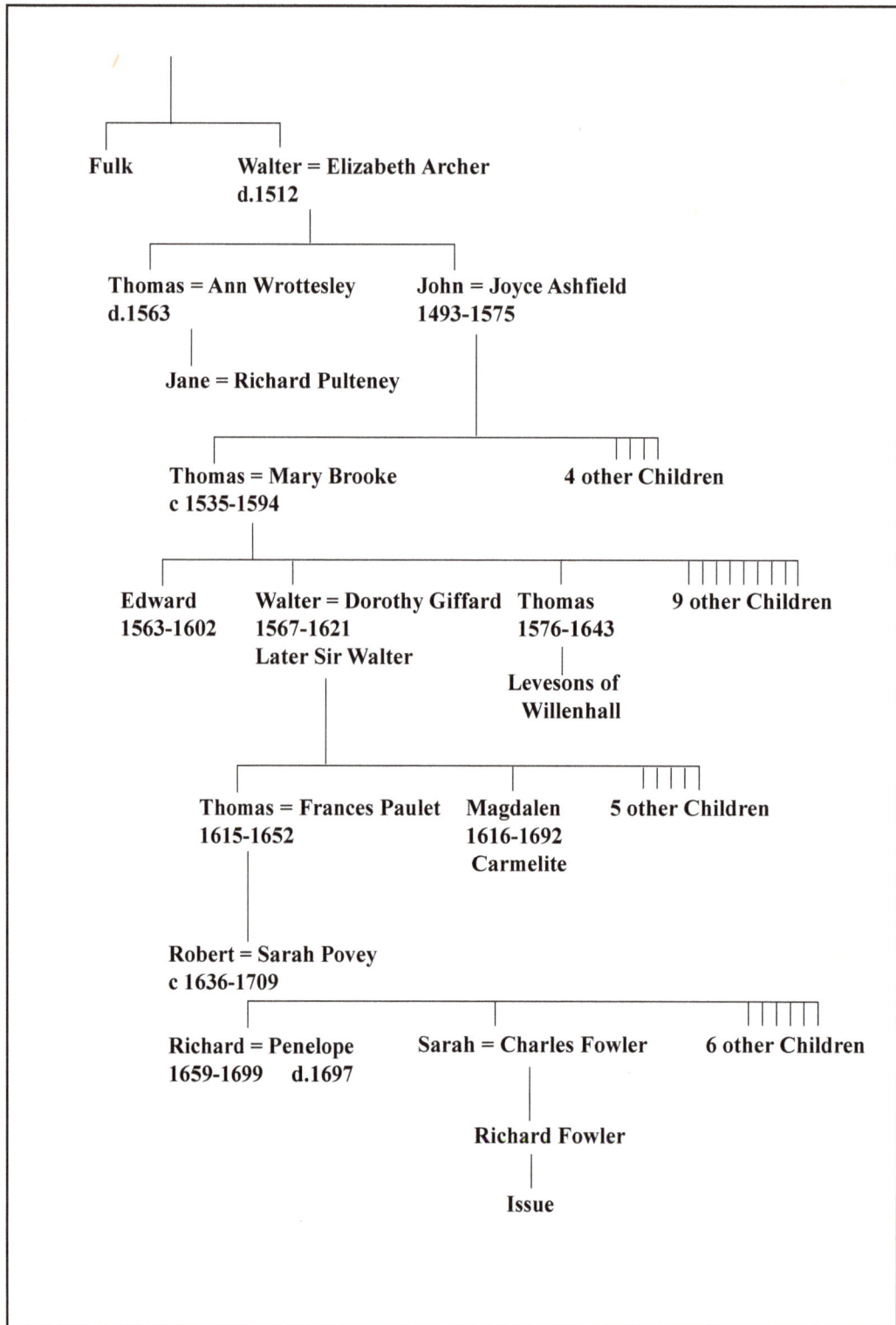

FIGURE 15 THE LEVESON FAMILY TREE

18

from 1560. Those who, like the Wolverhampton Levesons, clung to the old faith, found their positions becoming more and more difficult as Catholic missionaries came to England and the Popes denounced Elizabeth as a usurper. The senior branch, the much wealthier Levesons of Trentham, Staffordshire, and Lilleshall, Shropshire, had no problem in conforming and got their share of public offices.

Thomas was succeeded by his son Edward, regarded as of weak mind, who died in 1602. His brother Walter followed him, while a younger brother Thomas (1576–1643) founded a junior branch based in Willenhall. Sir Walter determined to attach himself to the fortunes of the most successful member of the senior Leveson family, Admiral Sir Richard Leveson (1570–1605). It was a profitable connection, for the generous Admiral gave him a trunk filled with pearls which Walter kept in his house at Ashmores. This came from the great carrack, the St Valentine, which the Admiral had taken on its return to Portugal from the East Indies in Cezimbra bay in 1602. Unfortunately the Admiral died young and all Walter could do was to entertain some of the mourners in the Great Hall when the Admiral was buried in St Peter's church on 2 September 1605 (Staffs RO, D593 C/9/3; Shaw 1801, 167–8).

The Admiral left his estate in great confusion, which his cousin Sir John Leveson had to settle on behalf of the heir, his young son Richard. Sir Walter had high hopes of inheriting the Admiral's estates of Lower and Upper Penn, Oxley and Bushbury, but a later conveyance had cancelled this bequest and kept all his estates together for his heir. Sir Walter threatened to claim, but Sir John reminded him of the many benefits he had received from Sir Richard. On reflection, Walter realised the danger of antagonising so powerful a man with many great friends at court, including the Chief Minister, the Earl of Salisbury, who also had the favour of the King. He was able to add to his lands in and near Wolverhampton when Sir John was obliged to sell a great part of the Admiral's estate in 1614. After Sir John's death in 1615, Sir Walter decided to try again, but proceedings were interrupted in 1621 by his own death.

His executors continued with the action on behalf of his young son, Thomas, aged eight in 1623. Richard Leveson, now 25, defended his possession. He explained how the conveyance under which the claim was brought had been cancelled. He conceded that Sir John had promised Sir Walter the reversion of Seawell (Bushbury) only, but this was before he knew the extent of the claims upon the estate. Having to spend over £18,000 over and above the income received from the estate, Sir John, and Richard after him, regarded all the estate as well and truly bought and at their disposition; the Court supported Richard. Four years later the executors tried again. This time the benefits Sir Walter had received from Sir Richard were described in court. John Terrick, an associate of Sir Richard and Michael Nicholls, who had served under him at sea, gave evidence. Terrick remembered paying £300 to Sir Walter. Nicholls remembered a rich jewel, originally given to the Admiral by Philip III of Spain, which he had presented to Sir Walter

who wore it in his hat. Later it was sold, he believed for £1,000. Most valuable of all was the gift of the lease of the Deanery manor. Originally granted to James Leveson, the Admiral's great grandfather, at a rent of £38 in 1516, the lease was still held at the same figure, though the profits from it were now considerably in excess of £38. By 1660 it was worth over £300 annually (Staffs RO D868 1/67, Staffs RO D593E/6/12, Shaw 1801, 168). Once again the executors failed.

Thomas Leveson (1615–52) was brought up as a Catholic; in 1634 he was reported as a recusant who did not attend church and in the next year a small school for Catholics was reported to be on his property (SHC 1941, 137; Roberts 1963, 18). When the Civil War came, like other Catholics, he supported the King. In April 1642 Parliament had issued an order to seize the arms of Roman Catholics. Thomas went to the shop of John Tanner, an armourer in Wolverhampton, to demand why Tanner had not sent him the arms he had ordered. When Tanner tried to explain that this was by the order of the deputy lieutenants naming Mr Wrottesley as one, Thomas exploded, characterising Wrottesley as a fool and a rogue, and Tanner as a stinking rogue. He then beat Tanner about the head with his cane raising a great lump. The King's peace had certainly been breached in Wolverhampton (Mander and Tyldesley 1960, 77). When he got arms, Thomas garrisoned the Great Hall and was appointed Governor of Dudley Castle by the King. The castle was the major royalist base in this area, being also a convenient place to detain prisoners. The King had great problems supplying and maintaining his forces, which was why '…our trusty and well beloved Thomas Leveson…', now a colonel, was given permission in July 1643 to levy contributions in the hundreds of Seisdon and Cutteslowe which would hardly make either him or the royalist cause popular. By this time the Great Hall had been given up as a garrison; it was too low lying and exposed to be held easily. Thomas contrived to obtain permission from the parliamentary leaders for his wife, Frances, to live there. In September 1643 he regained Chillington Hall, which the parliamentarians had taken; later in December he supplied 40 musketeers for the defence of Aston Hall which, however, was forced to surrender on 28 December 1643. The roundheads were growing stronger, as the Earl of Denbigh showed, besieging Dudley Castle in June 1644. He raised the siege hurriedly on the approach of a royalist relieving force, not without a skirmish with Lord Wilmot's men as he withdrew. In May 1645 the King called a meeting of the governors of royalist garrisons at Dudley Castle on his way to Lichfield. Later the Dudley garrison supplied some troops to the King's army at the battle of Naseby. After this disastrous defeat, Thomas Leveson found it increasingly difficult to carry on. He could not raise more troops and was plagued with deserters. Above all money was lacking (SHC 1958, 90 and 157; Mander and Tydesley 1960, 87; Dore 1990, Letter 707, note 1). He surrendered Dudley Castle on terms to Sir William Brereton on 10 May 1646. He had hoped to save his estate, but Parliament treated him as a recusant and confiscated his property. He was forced to go into exile. There was a last glimpse of him enjoying the hospitality of the Prince de Conti and living in some style, with servants and horses, but when he died in Bordeaux aged 37 in September 1652, he was penniless (SHC 1941, 147).

In the 1650s Thomas' sister Magdalen entered the Carmelite Order to become a nun; spending the rest of her life at Lierre in Belgium, she died there in 1692 (Catherine 1961, 19). His son Robert survived the Commonwealth and Protectorate apart from a brief period of detention during Booth's rebellion in 1659 (SHC 1958b, 22). At the Restoration he regained all his father's lands including the valuable lease of the Deanery manor. The estate which, before the Civil War, had been valued at £1,000 per annum, was considerably reduced from what it had been at John Leveson's death in 1575. Now, Robert's estate was reckoned at £600–£700 per annum. An estate had been detached at Willenhall for the benefit of Thomas Leveson, younger brother of Sir Walter, there had been large families to provide for, and the ravages of the Civil War to contend with. Robert did inherit the estate of Seawell (Showell) at Bushbury on the death of Sir Richard Leveson in 1661, which marked the end of the senior line (Shaw 1801, 187). Robert conformed to the Church of England and did not appear in the lists of Catholics recorded in Staffordshire. His son Richard made a career for himself in the army rising to the rank of lieutenant colonel under James II. He also sat as a Member of Parliament. At the Revolution of 1688, he switched sides and served William III, rising to be a major general and Governor of Berwick. His death in March 1699, when he left £4,500 to his two illegitimate sons, precipitated a crisis in Leveson affairs

(Watson 2002, 618). Robert Leveson determined to sell the Wolverhampton estate in the same year. By the time the sale was completed in 1702, Robert had become a widower and had one surviving grandchild – Richard Fowler – by his daughter Sarah who had married Charles Fowler. The estate consisted of rent and tithes in Wolverhampton, the house, as the Great Hall was termed, with its lands being estimated at £54 per annum and the tithes at £100 per annum. There were many other properties in Broad Meadow, Blakenhall, Monmore and Ablow Field making a total of £599 5s 6d. Outside Wolverhampton, the second house, Ashmores, was assessed with its lands at £114, but the main income came from the tithes of Wednesfield, Willenhall, Bilston, Pelsall, Coton, Hatherton and Hilton, which, together with rents from lands at Showell, Cheslyn Hay and Pool Hayes, amounted to a further total of £508 10s 0d. The grand total was £1,107 15s 6d (Mander 1934, 57–9).

The estate was finally sold in 1702 to Francis, First Earl of Bradford, for £22,000 (Mander 1921, 212). There was a complicated descent from him to the dukes of Cleveland, today represented by Lord Barnard.

Robert Leveson retired to Cheshire and died there in 1709. His cousins, the Levesons of Willenhall, still survived. They had supplied priests to the Catholic church, but they were to die out within 50 years. The Fowler heiress of Robert then sold their lands. First the Levesons, and then their Great Hall, became only a distant memory in the history of Wolverhampton.

CHAPTER 4: THE OLD HALL WORKS, AND THE 18TH AND 19TH CENTURY JAPANNING AND ENAMELLING TRADE

Christopher Hewitson and Yvonne Jones

The Great Hall was converted to a japanning works possibly as early as 1767 and was certainly established as such by the 1770s (Jones 1982, 19). The expansion and development of the works can be traced to some extent through the cartographic evidence of the late 18th and 19th centuries as well as archaeological and historical evidence.

The historical map evidence suggests the hall developed gradually from that visible on Taylor's Map of 1750 (Fig. 4). This includes the buildings to the southwest interpreted as possible barns. An initial phase of expansion is visible on Godsons' map (1788, Fig. 5) with the addition of a number of buildings to the south and southwest of the hall (Figs 5 and 16). These are depicted in a number of 19th century illustrations (Figs 8, 10, 11 and 12) as brick-built one- and two-storey warehouses and factories, and may have represented the heavier industrial manufacturing processes, including enamelling, tinning and burnishing. This expansion may have been associated with the early years of the works in the 1760s–1770s and its subsequent adaptation to the japanning process. Subsequent expansion occurred gradually between the late 18th century and the mid-19th century. By the time of the 1842 Tithe map the works had expanded to the south and west with the addition of a series of square and linear blocks (Fig. 6). A single block was added to the northeast of the house and the western wing was elongated. A further building was located north of the hall. Expansion to the southwest of the hall may have begun after Benjamin Walton joined William Ryton in partnership in 1820. If, as appears likely, they were the first to manufacture papier mâché at the Old Hall, then it is likely that they would have needed extra workshops. Since Jones (1900) makes no mention of papier mâché being made in the Hall in 1839, it is possible only to speculate that any new workshops would, initially, have been devoted to that manufacture.

It is unlikely there was much expansion after *c* 1845, when, as sole proprietor, Benjamin Walton saw the factory slide from flourishing prosperity into bankruptcy. Thus the major expansion evident on the 1852 map must have occurred either prior to *c* 1845 or post 1847, when Walton's son Frederick re-established the firm and added new workshops and converted old barns, most likely before Walton's death in 1861. The map shows that by 1852, these newer workshops focused on the manufacture and japanning of tinned iron goods; this corresponds with the main thrust of their trade at the time.

By the time of the 1852 Board of Health map, expansion had continued to the south, and buildings had been added to the north of the hall up to the line of Bilston Street (Fig. 7). A stove for baking the japanned wares appeared to have

been constructed southeast of the hall, though this may have been expansion to a pre-existing stove.

In order to grasp how different areas of the site were used it is important to understand the processes at work. The Old Hall works were known to have produced tin ware, both plated and japanned, as well as japanned papier mâché wares. From its beginning, the Old Hall produced tin-plated iron goods of all qualities. In 1847, Walton patented a method of enamelling wrought iron and other metals, and decorating them in the style of japanned goods. It became a sufficiently important part of their trade to be shown, alongside other goods, at major exhibitions.

The tin plate industry involved the coating of iron or steel objects with a thin layer of tin in order to prevent corrosion. It is unlikely the iron or steel objects were manufactured on site but they may have been brought in from elsewhere and subsequently plated. Papier mâché was produced in several ways. The two most frequently used were 'common' made from paper pulp formed into moulds, and 'best' made from sheets of paper pasted together into several layers.

At the works, the two products were treated by two different processes; until the mid-19th century this was exclusively japanning, with enamelling being undertaken in the later period. Japanning involved several processes. The initial stage was undertaken in the Blacking Shop which involved the application of a base coat of tar varnish followed by a second coat of varnish to seal this. Japan varnish was a sticky tar-like substance, the main ingredients of which were asphaltum and linseed oil. In order for the wares to dry thoroughly and to harden, they had to be slowly baked in an oven or stove at temperatures in the region of 120–140°C. A series of decorative effects was then applied to the varnished piece; this may have included the application of pearl decoration, bronze gilding, gold leaf and painted designs. Each of these applications would be undertaken at a different department of the factory. Finally, a pure clean varnish was applied in the varnish shop and the pieces were heavily polished. Japanning and enamelling were two wholly different processes. Only the metal goods were enamelled. Enamel glazes included glass among other inorganic materials which, when quickly heated at between 750–850°C, fused to formed a vitrified surface.

Initially, the works appeared to specialise in tin-manufactured oval tea trays (Jones 1900, 6). The manufacture of patterns was originally done by hand. It was not until the mid-19th century that tin began to be stamped using an adapted version of Nasmyth's steam hammer (*ibid*, 42). The use of papier mâché was seen as a specialism of the Old Hall Works but this was not until the later period from the 1820s onwards when the Walton family became involved (*ibid,* 14). Papier mâché was always a smaller part of their business, something that was common among Wolverhampton japanners, Birmingham being the leading centre for this manufacture. Economic pressure in the mid-1840s led to the temporary closure of the works after the death of Benjamin Walton (Jones 1900, 47).

As the industry declined in the 1880s, japanners, and associated tradesmen such as tin-plate workers, turned their skills to other manufactures, eg, beaten copper and other sheet-metal trades, bicycles and, later, the newly emergent motor-car industry. The larger and more prestigious japanning factories did not embrace galvanising, unlike those at the more utilitarian end of the trade. It would not, therefore, have impacted upon the likes of the Old Hall Works.

The 1852 map provides an important insight into the processes involved with the Old Hall Works. The commercialisation of the works from the 1840s led to the infilling of the moat and expansion of the premises. The date for this is unclear, but it had begun to occur by the time of the Tithe map of 1842 and was largely complete by the time of the Health of Towns map of 1852. The buildings outside the moat were incorporated into the japannery (Jones 1900), and it is possible that these correlate with those on the map. By 1852, many processes would have been fully mechanised; one of the last men to have been apprenticed as a japanner at the Wolverhampton factory of Henry Loveridge and Co, in the early 20th century, related that there, as machines took over, so less and less of the factory was used. The same was almost certainly true at the Old Hall Works.

Taking the 1852 map at face value, the process would have begun in the block that abutted Garrick Street where the presence of an 'iron store' is recorded. This indicated the need for black-iron at the beginning of the process. Moreover, the existence of a nearby lodge indicates that some, if not all, raw materials may have been delivered to this end of the factory. The 'polishing shop' and 'stamping room' would have been where the iron was cleaned and stamped into various shapes prior to being tinned. The contents of the adjoining 'sand room' may have been required for these purposes or, indeed, for catching oil, solder, etc, in later manufacturing processes, or for the enamelling technique which Walton had patented in 1847, or for sand-blasting the iron moulds used for making papier mâché trays.

Thereafter, the procedural order becomes less clear because of the duplication of workshops - possibly as a result of piecemeal expansion as and when needs arose.

Logically, one would expect the goods to have passed to the 'tinning shop', which, according to the 1852 map, was an independent building situated amidst the complex of factory buildings to the south of the Old Hall, and from there to the 'stores' in the workshop across the yard to

the south of the polishing shop. That the tinning shop is closer to the workshops adjoining the Hall suggests that it was built initially to serve only those, and that as trade increased, was pressed into service for the additional tin-shops. Another possibility is that the workshops linked to the Hall were associated with japanning, and those in the 'L-shaped' building to the south and west of the tinning shop, were devoted to the manufacture of 'common tin' (ie, un-japanned) goods,. Certainly, the presence of the Burnish Mill would support this.

The two stamp shops would have housed the various steam and fly presses for shaping the tin. It is noticeable that the stamp shops both saw low blocks constructed adjacent to them between 1842 and 1852, the date that roughly corresponds with the acquisition of the engine-powered adaptations of Naysmyth's steam hammer for the works (Jones 1900), and these may indicate the engine houses designed to support the stamp shops.

The tin shops were where the black-iron was applied to the tin products in bulk to protect against rust. Tinning would occur prior to the japanning process. The Tin Shop was a long linear building with open light windows for fine workmanship on the tin products as part of the finishing process. The wheeling shop was where metal shapes were formed on chucks and lathes. The Burnish Mill was likewise part of the finishing process prior to baking of the product.

The location of the stoves next to the Great Hall again indicates historical piecemeal development rather than design. Stoves were large constructions: those at H Loveridge and Co, for example, were arranged in rows of eight, each stove measuring approximately 15ft long, 5–6ft wide, and 6–8ft high, heated from underground. Their replacement therefore would have been a costly procedure. Japanning stoves would be large walk-in rooms with metal cages for the japanned wares, and have been described as lion cages at the London Zoo (Jones 2009). The rooms would be stoked from underground and exterior to the room and the lining would be kept air tight to prevent air escaping from the room. The initial stoves may have been located in the Old Hall utilising existing fireplaces.

Papier mâché continued to be produced at the Old Hall Works, certainly until well into the 1860s, if not until the end. It must therefore be assumed that its manufacture was carried out in the Hall itself. This would accord with the pattern at H Loveridge and Co., where papier mâché manufacture was necessarily conducted at some distance from the dirtier processes associated with the tin shops (Jones 2009). Gentlemen artists were kept away from the remainder of the works and were not associated with the workforce. A possible location for this part of the process may have been on the upper floors in the Hall.

The final expansion of the works to the south corresponded closely with the patent for a new enamel process (see earlier) and the buildings along the southern edge of the site may correspond to this process. These include a scouring room, a burnish mill, a further mill, two engine houses and a boiler, as well as a further independent tinning shop in the yard. Several buildings are unnamed and it is possible to speculate that one of these housed the furnace for enamelling. The 'scouring room' was where surfaces were cleaned after tinning. Maybe in earlier times or still in 1852 one of the unidentified rooms nearer the Hall was used for a similar purpose.

The expansion of buildings to the north of the site is unnamed on the 1852 map (Fig. 7) except for a single tin shop that pre-dated the 1842 Tithe map. It is unclear whether all the buildings were associated with the Old Hall Works.

CHAPTER 5: RESULTS OF THE ARCHAEOLOGICAL INVESTIGATIONS

Richard Cuttler and Eleanor Ramsey

Based on archaeological investigations, the chronological development of the site at Old Hall Street can be broken down into five distinct phases. These phases are outlined below under the following headings:

Phase 1 Pre-medieval
Phase 2 Medieval
Phase 3 Late medieval to early post-medieval
Phase 4 Late post-medieval
Phase 5 Late 19th to 20th century

PHASE 1: PRE-MEDIEVAL

The earliest phase of activity recorded at the site comprised several undated features that cut the natural subsoil (5048/ 9031) at the southwestern end of the excavation trench (Fig. 16). These were characterised by shallow scoops (unlikely to be of anthropogenic origin) and five small linear/ curvilinear gullies (F533, F543, F544, F547 and F548, Figs 16, 17 and 19). Although none of these features contained datable artefacts, they were sealed by medieval ploughsoil (see Phase 2). No features or deposits predating the medieval period were encountered during the watching brief.

PHASE 2: MEDIEVAL AGRICULTURE

The medieval phase of the site was characterised by a layer of grey sandy silt with occasional coke/ charcoal inclusions (5001, Fig. 18; 5015, not illustrated; 9015, not illustrated; 9035, not illustrated), interpreted as a former ploughsoil. Where it was exposed during the excavations, the soil displayed morphological evidence of ridge and furrow. Micromorphological analysis of the soil confirmed this identification (see McPhail and Crowther below). A few fragments of degraded 13th- to 15th-century pottery were recovered from this layer, mostly represented by iron-poor wares (see Rátkai below). No evidence for structures was identified from this period, though a fragment of late 14th- to early 15th-century window tracery was identified, incorporated into a later wall.

PHASE 3: THE HALL AND MOATED SITE, LATE MEDIEVAL TO EARLY POST-MEDIEVAL

Phase 3 features and deposits relate to the construction of the moat and island, and the foundations of the hall. Unfortunately, the dating evidence is rather imprecise owing both to the paucity of dateable pottery and other artefacts uncovered and the removal of stratigraphic deposits by later activity. The foundations of the hall were so massive that they tended to survive later activity, but few early layers remained.

The Moat

During the course of works, sections across the moat were excavated in a number of areas (Fig. 15), including a machine-excavated section during the excavation (5029, not illustrated) and a hand-excavated section (F526, Figs 16 and 19). Adjacent to Bilston Street the northern arm of the moat was recorded in trenches 3, 5 and 6. The moat was dug into the medieval plough soil and underlying red clay. At its deepest point, the moat was approximately 3m in depth and would have been up to 10m wide with a flat base (see F526, Figs 16 and 19; Trench 5, F105, 1025, not illustrated; Trench 6, F100, 1002–1011, not illustrated). Only the lower fills remained undisturbed by 19th-century cellars. Four 1m x 1m pits, excavated by machine in the northeast corner of the site during the development, recorded the natural subsoil, which was cut by the eastern edge of the moat, at approximately 1m below the modern ground surface. The easternmost arm of the moat was recorded during the construction of an electricity sub-station at the eastern edge of the site and during the laying of services. Further evaluation to the south of Old Hall Street recorded the southern arm of the moat (F103). The moat was also recorded in five trenches during the watching brief in 2007. An overview of the various moat sections and fills ensues.

The moat cut was similar in all areas, having an asymmetrical profile that was shallower on the outer edge of the moat than the inner edge. A series of small gullies (F107, F109, F110 and F111) was present at the base of the moat to the south of Old Hall Street, as were drains (F104 and F105, Fig. 21) that were not identified in the other sections.

The stratigraphy of the lower moat fills was similar, comprising grey-brown sand sealed by a layer of black organic silt. For example, the earliest moat fills within F526 (5033 and 5046, Fig. 18) comprised grey and brown sand, and produced no pottery or artefacts. Sealing these fills was a layer of dark black organic silt (5031), which produced a large amount of artefacts including pottery. Environmental samples were taken from layers 5031 and 5033, and from the lower levels of the southern arm of the moat (F103, 1018) for environmental analysis (see below).

The pottery from the various lower sections of the moat had different make-ups. Although the same four wares were present (creamware, coarseware, white salt-glazed stoneware and slip-coated ware were dominant), their relative proportions were not the same (see Rátkai below). The pottery from F100 (Trench 5, not illustrated) was dominated by formal dining wares and tea wares, while the pottery from moat section F526 had coarseware as the

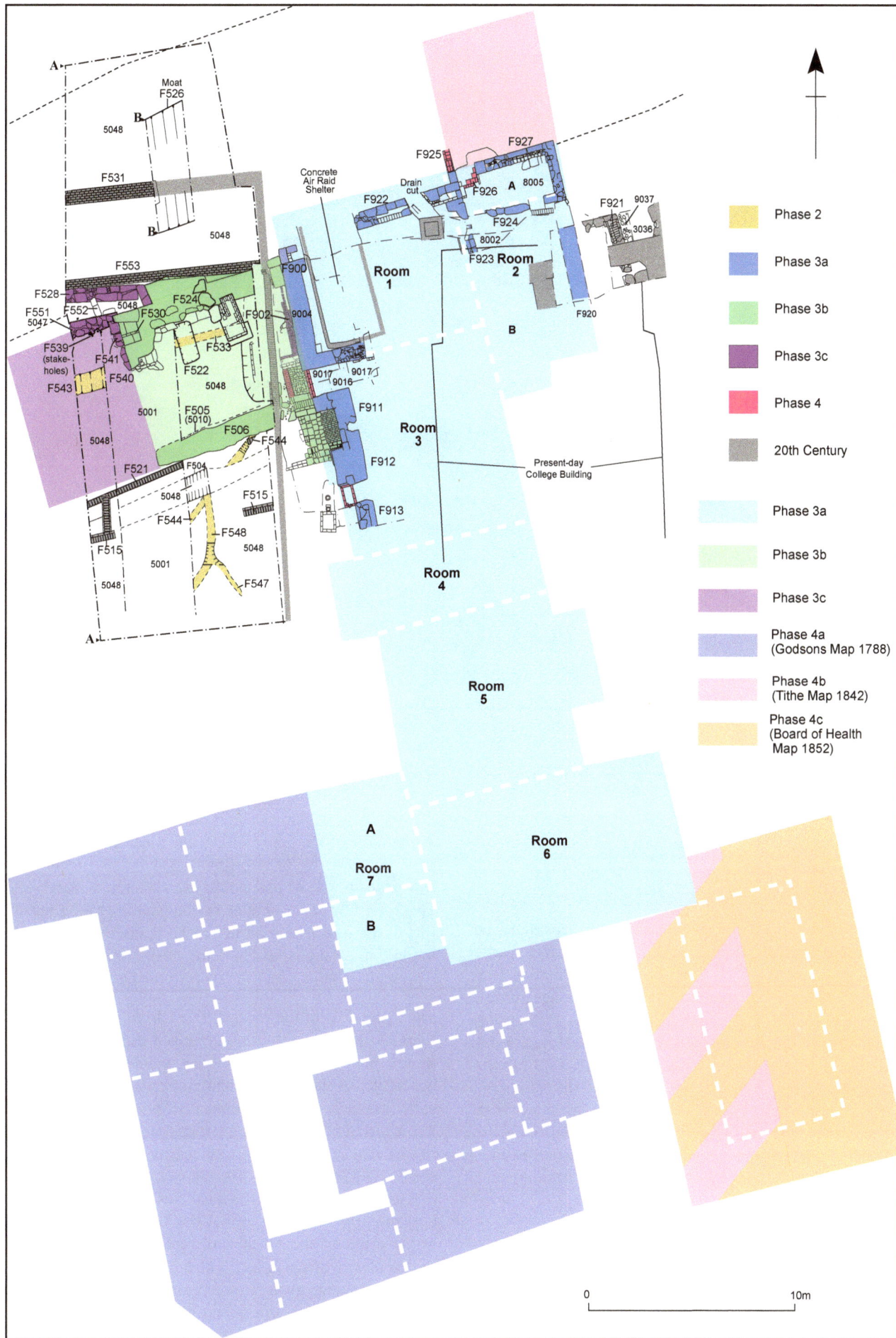

FIGURE 16 OVERALL PLAN AND BUILDINGS (BY PHASE)

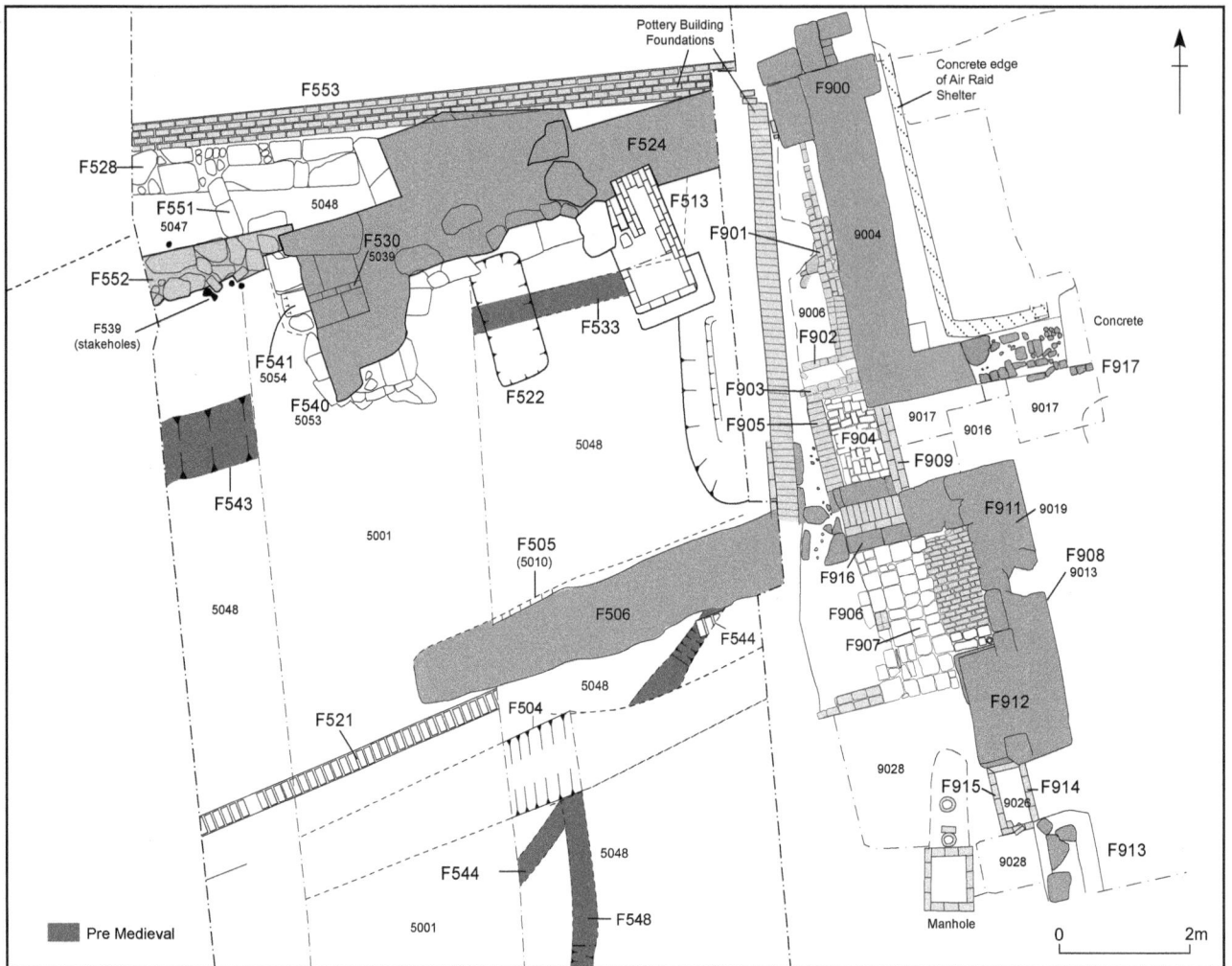

Figure 17 Detail plan of western annexe and west front of building

most frequent type. There was little pottery from either section that pre-dated *c* 1725, with the latest pottery dating to the early 19th century.

Unlike the pottery, the glass assemblage recovered from the lower moat fills also contained items that were earlier in date. Fragments of 17th-century wine bottles were recovered from the machine-excavated sondage through the moat (5029), and from F100, as well as 18th-century vessels (see Bracken below). An intact phial, and a near complete phial, possibly dating to the late 18th century, were recovered from F100. It is possible that the earlier glass assemblage reflects longevity of use, as we know that bottles were reused and refilled (see Bracken below). Organic artefacts, including a tropical hardwood bowling ball and leather shoes, were also recovered from the moat fills.

Within the excavated area, the lowest fills of moat section F526 were sealed by a layer of brick and sandstone rubble (5032), which also produced large quantities of pottery and other artefacts such as three conjoining fragments of window glass with graffiti etching (see Bracken below).

While most of the upper fills of the moat in this location were truncated by later cellars (F531, F553 and F554), two deposits (5037 and 5038, not illustrated) survived. These deposits were similar in composition to the upper fills of the moat recorded in Trench 6, consisting mainly of sand, silt, charcoal and building rubble, and are likely to represent the same phase of late post-medieval deposition.

The upper fills of the moat differed from north to south. Those of the southern arm comprised deposits of brown topsoil and redeposited red clay natural, whereas the upper fills of the northern and eastern arms of the moat comprised lenses of coke, metal residues and brick rubble. These differences would suggest that the moat was infilled in different areas for differing reasons, a theory that is corroborated by the cartographic evidence, which shows that the southern arm of the moat was infilled prior to the northern arm. This also implies that the japanning factory to the south of the Great Hall reclaimed land over the southern arm of the moat, which was therefore infilled before the factory was in use. The clay and topsoil fills within the southern arm of the moat may indicate rapid backfilling prior to the expansion of the factory. The

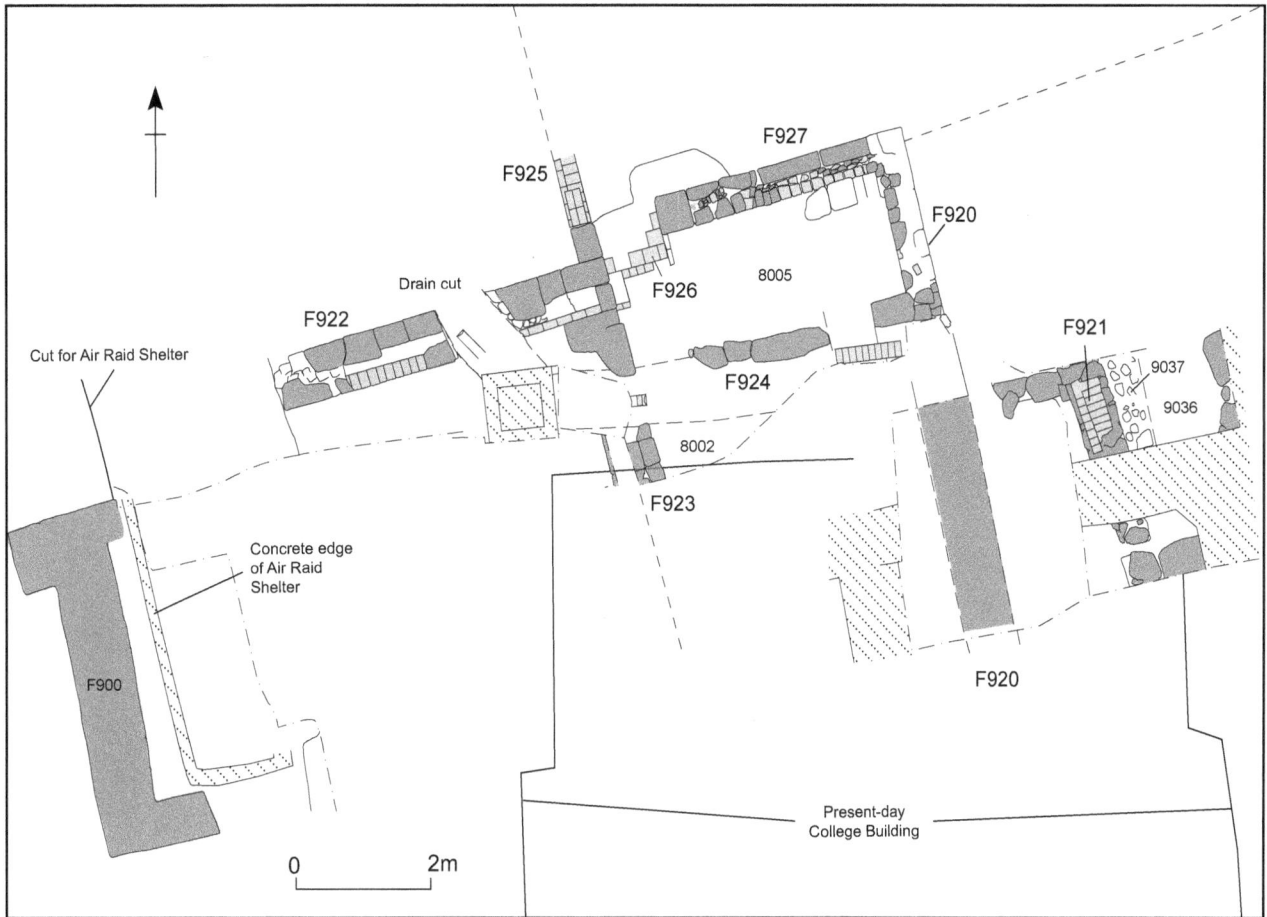

FIGURE 18 DETAIL PLAN OF MAIN WATCHING BRIEF AREA

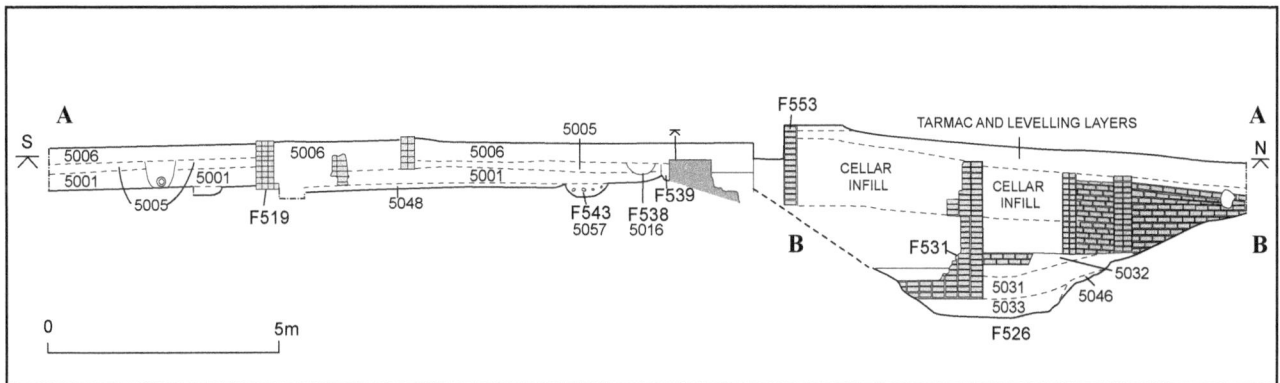

FIGURE 19 SECTION THROUGH EXCAVATION AREA AND MOAT

industrial fills identified within the northern and eastern arms of the moat perhaps represent a gradual infilling of the moat with waste deposits from the japanning factory.

The House Platform

The late medieval plough soil (5001) was sealed by a sterile layer of pink-red clay (5005, Fig. 18; 9036, Fig. 19) forming a house platform. This layer was presumably the result of the deposition of clay excavated during the

digging or cleaning out of the moat. Foundations for the main house cut the clay. Layer 5005 contained pottery of 15th- or 16th-century date, and a few brick fragments.

The Main Building

The foundations of the Great Hall were exposed to a depth of 1.2m and comprised several walls constructed from substantial sandstone blocks. Most of these measured approximately 0.8 to 0.9m in width. Three north–south

27

aligned walls (F900, F911 and F913, Figs 16, 17 and 20) formed the west-facing front of the hall, with a 1.2m wide entrance or passage between the return of F900 and F911. An opening between F911 and F913 appeared to form part of a second entrance. The southern extent of wall F911 was bonded with a large stone block F912 (Fig. 17), a chimney foundation approximately 1.6m in width, and evidently identifiable with the small external chimney depicted in 19th-century drawings of the west front (Figs 10–12). It is likely that wall F911 was at some stage truncated and rebuilt, as the top of the wall comprised mortar, along with fragments of stone, brick and tile (9019). A fragment of glass from 9019 was dated to 1780–90, and another from a wine bottle was dated to 1800–10. Beer bottle fragments were also present, dating to the late 19th to early 20th century (see Bracken below) and some of the worked stone incorporated into the build may also be earlier (see below). In addition, an air raid shelter that abutted F900 to the east had destroyed the relationship between F900 and east–west aligned wall F922 (Fig. 16). The relationship of wall F900 with east–west aligned wall F524 to the west had also been destroyed by a later brick wall and associated cut.

From the frontage of the hall, the foundations extended to the east. Two east–west aligned walls (F922 (west) and F927 (east), Figs 16 and 18) formed the northern extent of the building and also part of the curtain wall, which ran adjacent to and parallel with the moat (see above). Both were faced with dressed stone on the northern side, and contained a sandstone and brick core. While the two walls were on the same alignment, F927 lay a little further to the north, so that the line of the north wall was staggered, and, at the point of juncture, there was a gap in the upper courses providing an opening to the north about 0.94m wide, either a doorway, or, perhaps, a drain discharging into the moat. As the upper courses of the opening were faced with dressed stone, it seems likely that this gap was an original feature of the curtain wall, although it is, perhaps, possible that the opening was created after the moat had been abandoned.

The return of F927 towards the south (F920, Fig. 19), is likely to represent the eastern wall of the hall. The foundations of F920 comprised a cut through the house platform, into which rubble and mortar had been poured. The return of F922 to the south (F923, Fig. 19) formed a north–south aligned internal wall. A second internal wall (F924, Fig. 19) was on an east–west alignment between F920 and F923 forming a room in the northeast corner of the building.

Layers and Features in the Main Building

Within the building, a series of layers abutted the sandstone walls. Layers 8012, 8011 and 8010 (not illustrated) included lenses of brick, tile, charcoal, silt and sand, and were located between walls F927 and F924, sealed by layer 8005 (Fig. 19). Layer 8010 contained one fragment of 15th- to 16th-century pottery, while layer 8005 contained a few fragments of medieval pottery, also mostly dating to the 15th to 16th century. These are

likely to be residual, as the majority of the pottery from this layer was post-medieval in date. This pottery included coarsewares, earlier in date than those recovered from the moat, and similar in form to pottery found in deposits relating to Civil War destruction deposits at Dudley Castle (see Rátkai below). Other pottery from this layer included sherds dating to the later 17th to early/ mid-18th centuries amongst which was a waster fragment.

To the south of F924 was a layer of sandy clay with a high concentration of charcoal (9039, not illustrated) which was sealed by a layer containing brick, tile and mortar fragments (9040, not illustrated). Also to the south of F924 and abutting sandstone wall F923 was a thin mixed layer of coke and charcoal with clay, sand, silt and pottery (8002, Fig. 19). This was possibly the remains of an industrial layer, sealed by a layer of grey brown clay (8001, not illustrated). The pottery recovered from 8002 was medieval in date, and 8001 contained a mixed group of pottery, including medieval wares, as well as sherds from the 16th and 17th centuries, and a waster fragment. It is likely that 8001 dates to the 17th century (see Rátkai below).

Immediately to the west of wall F923 was a layer of grey-brown sandy clay with a high concentration of charcoal (9041, not illustrated). This is likely to be the same layer as 9039 to the east of F923. Sealing layer 9041 was a thin layer of white mortar (9042, not illustrated). These layers did not extend to the walls comprising the west face of the Great Hall (F900, F911 and F913). This may be due to severe truncation and alteration by later brick walls and features in this area.

Cutting these layers within the building footprint were three pits and a ditch. To the west of wall F923, layer 9041 was cut by a pit (F800, not illustrated) approximately 1.2m wide and 0.5m deep, which was filled with grey brown mixed sandy silty clay with much charcoal (8000), and sealed by mortar layer 9042. Immediately to the north was a second pit (F801, not illustrated), approximately 1.8m wide and 0.5m deep, which cut both layers 9041 and 9042. The fill (8006) was a mixed deposit of grey silty clay with mortar, charcoal and brick fragments with a couple of fragments of 15th- to 16th-century pottery.

Further to the east, located to the south of F924 and cutting layers 8002 and 8001, a third pit was identified (F802, not illustrated). Approximately 1.4m wide and 0.5m deep, it was filled with lenses of red sand, grey-brown silty sand and charcoal and mortar (8009).

Between walls F927 and F924 was a ditch (F803, not illustrated), which cut layers 8012, 8011 and 8010. This feature was sealed by layer 8005 and was possibly associated with drainage.

The Western Annexe

The alignment of the curtain wall defined by F922 and F927 continued to the west of F900 as F524 (Figs 16 and

17). This wall was approximately 1.2m wide but increased to 2.1m wide to account for the base of a rectangular buttress which extended northwards. A drain (F530/ 5039, Fig. 17), which was incorporated into the western end of wall F524, contained pottery and glass dating to the second half of the 18th century; another fragment of glass from this context was dated to 1810–20 (see Bracken below). The foundation cut for wall F524 (F541, 5054, Fig. 17) produced one fragment of 18th-century pottery, although due to severe truncation by later activity, it is possible that this pottery is intrusive. To the west of the northern wall (F524) a smaller wall (F552, Figs 16 and 17) continued on a slightly offset alignment beyond the western extent of the excavation. The southern edge of F524 displayed evidence of possible partial collapse and rebuilding, though the northern face did not. A series of small, circular voids (F539) within the natural subsoil to the west of F524 and south of F552 were interpreted as stakeholes, and may represent the impressions of scaffolding holes (Figs 16 and 17). A short north–south aligned wall (F540, 5053, Figs 16 and 17), roughly constructed and incorporated worked stone within its build, abutted the southern edge of F524. A broken off end of a dagger blade was also found associated with this structure. The fill of the construction cut (F536, 5052, not illustrated) produced one fragment of pottery, dating to the 16th or 17th century.

Approximately 5m to the south of F524, and parallel with it, was a second sandstone wall (F506, Fig. 17) and foundation cut (F505, 5010), extending as far west as the line of wall F540. Again, the relationship between walls F911 and F506 had been truncated by later activity. These walls (F506, F524 and F540) formed a western annexe to the Great Hall, which appears to have been a later addition to the main building.

At right angles to F524 was a narrow sandstone wall (F551, Figs 16 and 17), which abutted the northern face of F552 (Figs 16 and 17). To the west of wall F551 was a deposit of sand and sandstone fragments (5047, Figs 16 and 17) which may relate to a period of demolition, specific to the main wall F524. The pottery recovered from deposit 5047 included two jars which were very similar to jars found in Civil War deposits at Dudley Castle (see Rátkai below).

Other features associated with the hall included a set of steps (F916) and two brick surfaces (F904 and F905, Figs 17 and 20, and F907, Fig. 17) that were located to the west of wall F911. One of the brick surfaces (F904) appeared to relate to the entrance between walls F900 and F911. From this level three steps constructed from firebrick and stone (F916) led upwards to a later stone and brick surface (F907) that abutted F911 and F912 (see below). A north–south aligned brick wall (F901, Fig. 17) abutted wall F900 to the west.

Layers and Features

To the south of the western annexe south wall (F506) was a ditch (F504/, 5009/, 5062/, 5069, Fig. 17) cutting the medieval ploughsoil (5001). This was on a similar

alignment to the annexe walls (F506 and F524) and had a 'V' shaped profile. A possible brick wall or drain (F521, Fig. 17) was located between the ditch (F504) and the wall (F506), although only one course of bricks survived. A small linear feature (F538, 5016, Fig. 18) on an east–west alignment also cut the medieval ploughsoil and overlying red clay layer (5001 and 5005).

The Curtain Wall

As is evidenced by the drawings and photographic records of the Great Hall, the moat platform was bounded by a curtain wall constructed above the inner face of the moat. The curtain wall was identified to the north, south, east and west of the site, though the quality of construction and level of survival differed in each area. The curtain wall identified in the excavation (F524, Figs 16 and 17) along the northern arm of the moat was well constructed from large dressed sandstone blocks bonded together with very hard mortar. The continuation of the curtain wall in this area to the east, recorded during the watching brief (F922, F927), was slightly narrower, and was also constructed from large faced sandstone blocks. In these areas the curtain wall also formed the north wall of the Great Hall, and survived to a depth of over 1m.

Evidence for the curtain wall was also identified during watching briefs to the east and west of the main area of investigation (Fig. 15). At the western edge of the excavation, similar sized, dressed sandstone blocks were recorded though not in situ, suggesting that the moat lay immediately to the west and that truncation had occurred during the construction of the adjacent building. The watching brief at the eastern edge of the development site identified the remains of a sandstone wall along the edge of the moat, though this was not as well constructed as the wall to the west. It was roughly faced and bonded with red clay and sand, and survived to a depth of one to three courses. The evaluation to the south also produced evidence of a sandstone curtain wall F102 (Figs 15 and 21), though again, this was not as well made as the curtain wall recorded along the northern arm. This wall (F102) was built from large rectangular blocks and smaller sub-rounded stones, and survived to a depth of 0.3m. It was sealed by a layer of mixed soil and brick rubble (1012). The watching brief in 2007 identified masonry fragments that in position, cross-section, and alignment suggest a remnant of the inner curtain wall of the western arm of the moat, although the fabric differed markedly from that recorded elsewhere, being roughly-fired, hand-made brick as opposed to ashlar sandstone.

Features to the East of the Main Building

To the east of the main building was a foundation composed of two courses of irregular sandstone blocks. These were not bonded with mortar and were laid directly on top of the redeposited red clay of the house platform (9036, Fig. 19). The remains of a brick wall, possibly part of a garden wall (F921, Fig. 19), overlay the blocks. Immediately to the east of this foundation was a layer of sub-rounded cobbles and

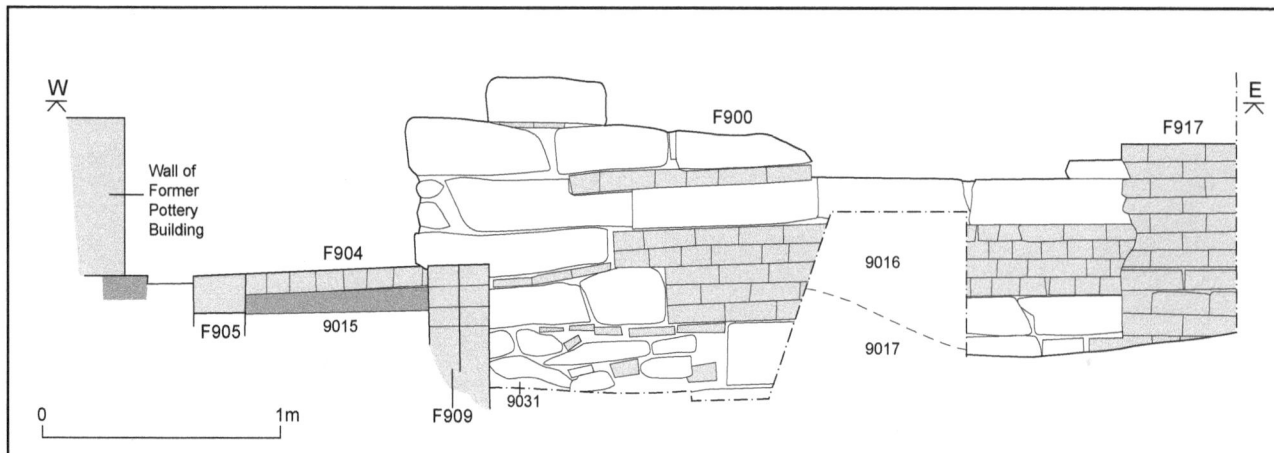

FIGURE 20 SOUTH-FACING ELEVATION OF WALL F900 AND ASSOCIATED STRUCTURES

sandstone blocks (9037, Fig. 19) which directly overlay the re-deposited red clay (9036) of the house platform.

PHASE 4: THE JAPANNING FACTORY, LATE 19TH CENTURY

Although the documentary and cartographic evidence indicated that the hall was used as a factory from roughly 1770, the alterations and additions to the main sandstone walls are likely to be associated with the continued use of the hall as a japanning factory in the latter part of the 19th century.

The Main Building

Two entrances within the main north–south wall of the hall (F900, F911 and F913) were blocked with brick (F909 and F914, Figs 17 and 20). A brick wall (F917, Figs 17 and 20) abutting the east–west arm of F900 exceeded the depth of the stone foundations for F900, and also the depth of the surface F904 and steps F916 (Fig. 20). This appeared to be a wall for a cellar that had been excavated after the original foundations had been built. Bonded with this wall (F917), and with a similar brick construction, was the wall F909 that served to block off the entrance between F900 and F911. The three internal faces of these walls had evidence of plaster still attached, as did the three internal faces of the blocked off entrance to the south (F911, F913, F914). Two clay and rubble deposits, 9016 and 9017, were identified abutting F909 and F917 (Figs 17 and 20). Layer 9016 contained one fragment of residual medieval pottery. Part of a second brick wall (F915) was also identified in this area, parallel to F914, and the gap between them was infilled with loose ash, charcoal and silt (9026, Fig. 17) containing pottery dating to the late 18th century. A brick wall (F908, Fig. 17) abutting the eastern edge of F911 (internal to the hall) is also likely to represent a later cellar wall; it was abutted by rubble 9013, which contained pottery dating to the mid-19th century.

Brickwork abutting the internal faces of the main east–west sandstone walls (F922 and F927) may have

been contemporary with the original structure, as they appeared to be incorporated within the build. Evidence for later additions and rebuilding, however, was identified immediately to the north of F927, in the form of later surfaces and walls (F925 and F926, Fig. 19).

The opening between F927 and F922 was filled with deposits similar to the upper fill of the moat (8008, not illustrated). This context (8008) is likely to date from the first half of the 18th century, and was one of two contexts that contained white salt-glazed stoneware (see Rátkai below). Overlying these deposits, and sealing the Phase 3 ditch F803 was a floor surface comprising flat red quarry tiles (F926) that extended from inside the wall to outside, overlying the upper moat deposits. Abutting F922 at right angles was a length of brick cellar wall (F925). The external edge of F922 displayed evidence of black staining of the stone, beneath a thick layer of plaster, suggesting that the moat had been filled (with coke/ charcoal etc) to this level before being re-excavated and the sandstone wall being utilised as a later cellar wall.

The Western Annexe

Other additions and alterations to the west of the building frontage included a brick wall (F901), which abutted F900. Two smaller brick walls (F902 and F903) were aligned at right angles to F901 at its southern extent. Wall F903 respected the edge of brick surface F904 and brick wall F905. Between F901 and the former pottery building foundations to the west, that occupied the site until 2002, was a foundation of orange sand and mortar with many brick fragments (9006).

Immediately to the west of F911 was a large pit (F906/ 9029 Fig. 17). This was roughly sub-circular and cut the medieval ploughsoil (5001/ 9015). The fill (9029) comprised lenses of loose rubble, ash, slag and metallic residues. Both this pit and wall F911 were truncated by a ceramic drain, which in turn was sealed by the stone and re-used brick surface F907/ 9028 (Fig. 17). Layer 9028

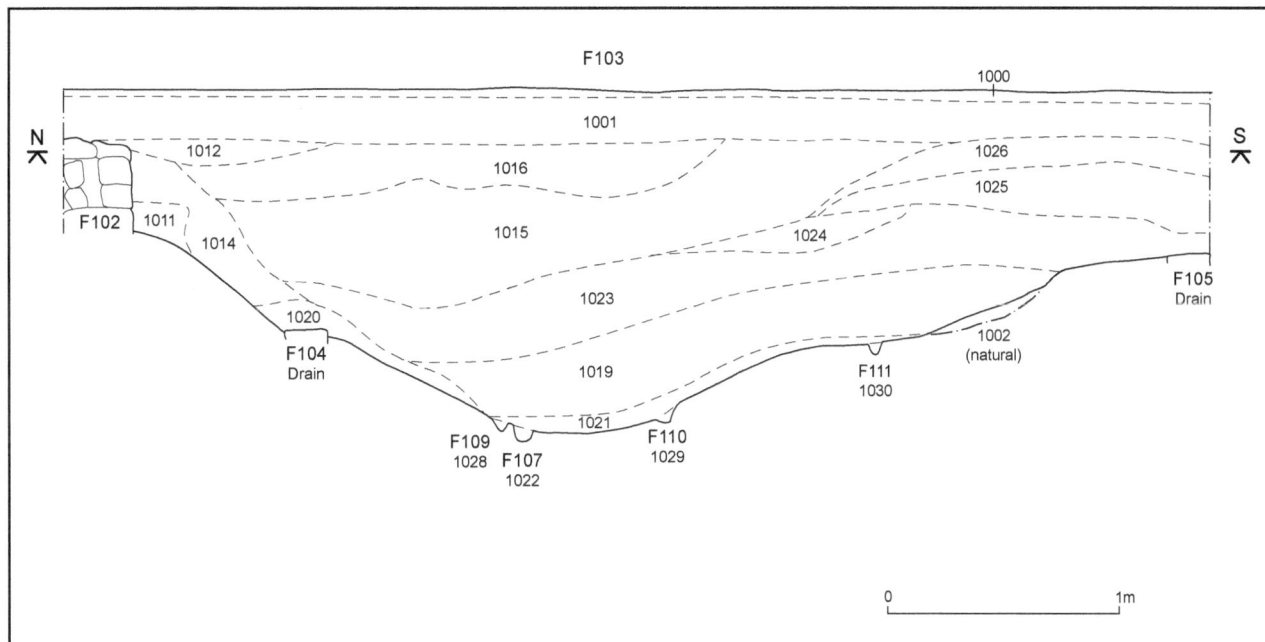

FIGURE 21 WEST-FACING SECTION THROUGH THE MOAT SOUTH OF OLD HALL STREET

possibly represented an earlier surface, and was used as a levelling layer for the later surface, extending beyond the surviving extent of F907 to the south (Fig. 17).

Within the west-facing section of the excavation area were the remains of a heat-affected rectangular brick structure (F514/ 5024 not illustrated). This feature was truncated by a second brick structure (F513, 5023, 5024, Fig. 17), which also partially truncated the main sandstone wall (F524). The fill of F514 contained one fragment of medieval pottery.

Within the interior of the annexe, cutting the red clay layer (5005), was a rectangular pit (F522, Fig. 17). This pit was approximately 2.1m long, 1.1m wide and 0.4m deep with steep sides and a flat base. The fill (5025) contained large quantities of building rubble, mortar, tile, brick and sandstone.

Two small linear features (F502, 5007, not illustrated and F523, 5026, not illustrated) also cut the red clay layer (5005). F502 contained one fragment of medieval pottery which may have been residual, and one fragment of tile. These features in turn were sealed by a thin layer of red sand (5002, not illustrated), which overlay 5005 in the centre of the site. Two shallow disturbances were also identified (F508, 5017, not illustrated and F511, 5020, not illustrated). A fragment of medieval pottery was recovered from F511, again, likely to be residual.

At the southern end of the excavation area, several discrete features also likely to date to the late post-medieval period were identified (not illustrated). These were characterised by a series of irregular pits, which were predominantly filled with coke and ash fragments and building rubble (including F509), and by a shallow ditch (F512). The

pottery recovered from F509 and F512 dated to the second half of the 18th century.

The Moat

The upper fills of the moat (F526) were truncated by a series of cellars (Figs 16 and 19). A rough sandstone wall (F528) was constructed on an east–west alignment immediately to the north of the main sandstone wall F524. This wall (F528) was cut into the upper moat fill (5037 and 5038, not illustrated), and utilised the buttress of wall F524 to the east. Abutting the north face of this wall was a brick wall (F553) that formed the southern extent of the cellars. It is likely that the sandstone wall F528 represents a support wall for the brick cellar, and is possible that sandstone blocks from the original hall buildings were reused during its construction. Another brick cellar wall (F531) was orientated east–west with a sandstone foundation course. Clay tobacco pipe fragments from a range of dates were recovered from the moat.

South of Old Hall Street

Within the evaluation south of Old Hall Street the middle and upper fills of the moat were significantly different from those encountered in the northern arm. Whereas the middle and upper fills to the north comprised significant amounts of charcoal, coke and metal residue, the deposits identified within the southern arm of the moat comprised mainly re-deposited natural and topsoil-like silt layers (1011, 1012, 1015, 1016, 1019, 1020, 1021, 1023, 1024, and 1025, Fig. 21). A similar infilling was encountered at the south end of the western arm of the moat during a watching brief in 2007. Here, the fill (1004) also contained sandstone blocks, which may represent fragments of the inner curtain wall pushed into the moat during the in-fill and levelling events.

It is known from cartographic evidence that as the usage of the hall changed from residential to industrial, so extensions were added to the back (east) of the hall. The archaeological evidence encountered during the evaluation suggests that this section of the moat may have been deliberately backfilled, perhaps in order to reclaim the land at the back of the hall for this purpose.

Metal items including a broken star-shaped iron cog and a circular metal container, and a collection of thin iron off-cuts were recovered from the moat in this area (from 1019 and 1020 respectively, Fig. 21) suggesting that the use of the area for industry had commenced prior to the moat being deliberately in-filled.

PHASE 5: LATE 19TH AND 20TH CENTURY

The brick foundations of the former pottery workshop (F515–F520, not illustrated) belonging to the Adult Education College, which was demolished prior to the excavation, represented more recent activity. A drain (F503, 5008, not illustrated) was identified, which, based on its alignment, is likely to be associated with this phase of construction, although the pottery recovered from it was dated to the second half of the 18th century. Modern overburden (5006, Fig. 18) comprising demolition rubble, brick and tile sealed the site, and was removed by machine. Similar demolition deposits were present to the south of Old Hall Street (1001, Fig. 21). The remains of three possible air raid shelters were identified during the archaeological works, one adjacent to the excavation, one to the south of evaluation Trench 6, and one to the east of the present building, identified during the construction of a new electricity sub-station.

CHAPTER 6: THE FINDS

THE POTTERY *Stephanie Rátkai*

The Medieval Pottery

A small number of medieval sherds were found mainly in the main excavation and from the eastern section of the main building during the main watching brief. To date there has been very little pottery of this period recovered from Wolverhampton. Twelve sherds were found at the Beatties site in 1999 (Rátkai 1999) and a further four sherds from the Harrison Early Learning Centre (Rátkai 2002a). The fabrics of the four sherds from the latter site were described but the pottery from the former was quantified by broad ware type, eg, whiteware, sandy cooking pot, etc. However, since 1999 medieval pottery assemblages have been excavated in Lichfield, (Rátkai 2004b, forthcoming) Brewood (Rátkai 2004a) and Birmingham (Rátkai 2009), thus giving scope to put the Great Hall medieval pottery into some sort of context. The medieval pottery was therefore divided into fabric types, using x20 magnification, and is described and catalogued below. The pottery was quantified by sherd count and sherd weight.

Cooking Pot 1 (cp1) Date: 13th–14th Century

Brown fabric with mid-grey core. Abundant rounded quartz *c* 0.5mm.

Hand-formed, hard. The fabric is pretty similar to Lichfield fabric cpj2 and Birmingham fabric cpj1.

5007, F502, Cooking pot body sherd, external soot.

Cooking Pot 2 (cp2) Date: 13th–14th Century

Mid-grey-brown with brownish external surface. Moderate to abundant rounded quartz up to 0.25mm, sparse organics, rare fine granular sandstone, small sparse flecks of mica visible on the surfaces. Hand-formed, hard. The fabric is similar to Brewood fabric cpj1 but closer to Lichfield fabric cpj7 and Birmingham fabric cpj6. The micaceous nature of the fabric may link it more closely to Birmingham since both the oxidised and reduced wares produced in the medieval period at Deritend, in the historic core of Birmingham were micaceous.

5000 Cooking pot body sherd, interior blackened.

Cooking Pot 3 (cp3) Date: ?12th/ 13th Century

Poorly sorted clay body with rounded and sub-rounded quartz up to 1mm but mainly 0.5mm or less, sparse mudstone 0.5–1mm, sparse mica more noticeable on surfaces than in matrix, sparse sandstone made up of loosely cemented grains, sparse organics and unidentified rounded dark fine grained rock, probably volcanic in origin. The source for

this fabric may well be boulder clays. Hard, hand-formed. The fabric is sandier than but similar to Brewood fabric cpj3 and may equate to Lichfield fabric cpj4a. However, the closest match was with Birmingham fabrics cpj12 and cpj13, both of which contain mudstone within the matrix.

5001, Body sherd, pale mid-grey, thin oxidised brown skin on external surface, slightly abraded interior sooted exterior.

5015, Body sherd brown to orange-brown fabric. Heavy external soot.

Cooking Pot 4 (cp4) Date 12th–13th Century

A black fabric with moderate angular quartz 0.25—0.5mm, sparse brown iron-oxide, sparse burnt out organics. There is no obvious parallel for this fabric, which may be local.

8001, Cooking pot body sherd.

Medieval Glazed Ware 1 (medgw1) Date 13th–14th Century

Sparse sub-angular quartz, generally less than 0.25mm, sparse organics.

Thin-walled, ?hand-formed, hard. The nearest parallel to this fabric was from Lawn Farm, Stoke-on-Trent (Rátkai 2006) but this is not to say that the fabric is not of more local manufacture.

1002, Jug sherd with trace of thin yellowish olive glaze on exterior. Reduced grey apart from very thin pale grey margin, interior surface orange, exterior surface where unglazed, pale grey. Some exterior sooting. Sherd very abraded.

Red-Painted Whiteware Date mid-13th–14th Century

White fabric, moderate ill-sorted sub-rounded quartz 0.27–0.75mm, sparse iron oxide, sparse white sub-rounded ?agillaceous inclusions up to 2mm. Red-painted whitewares are a common feature of south Staffordshire assemblages (cf Rátkai 2004b)

8001, Large slashed strap handle, band of red slip along the length of the handle. (Fig. 22: 01).

Iron-Poor Ware 1 (ipw1) Date: 13th–15th Century

Pale orange-cream fabric. Sparse quartz *c* 0.25mm, sparse rounded fe oxide, rare red sandstone. Hard, wheel-thrown. The fabric was similar to Lichfield fabric irp1 and close to Birmingham fabric ip01.

5000, Unglazed body sherd.

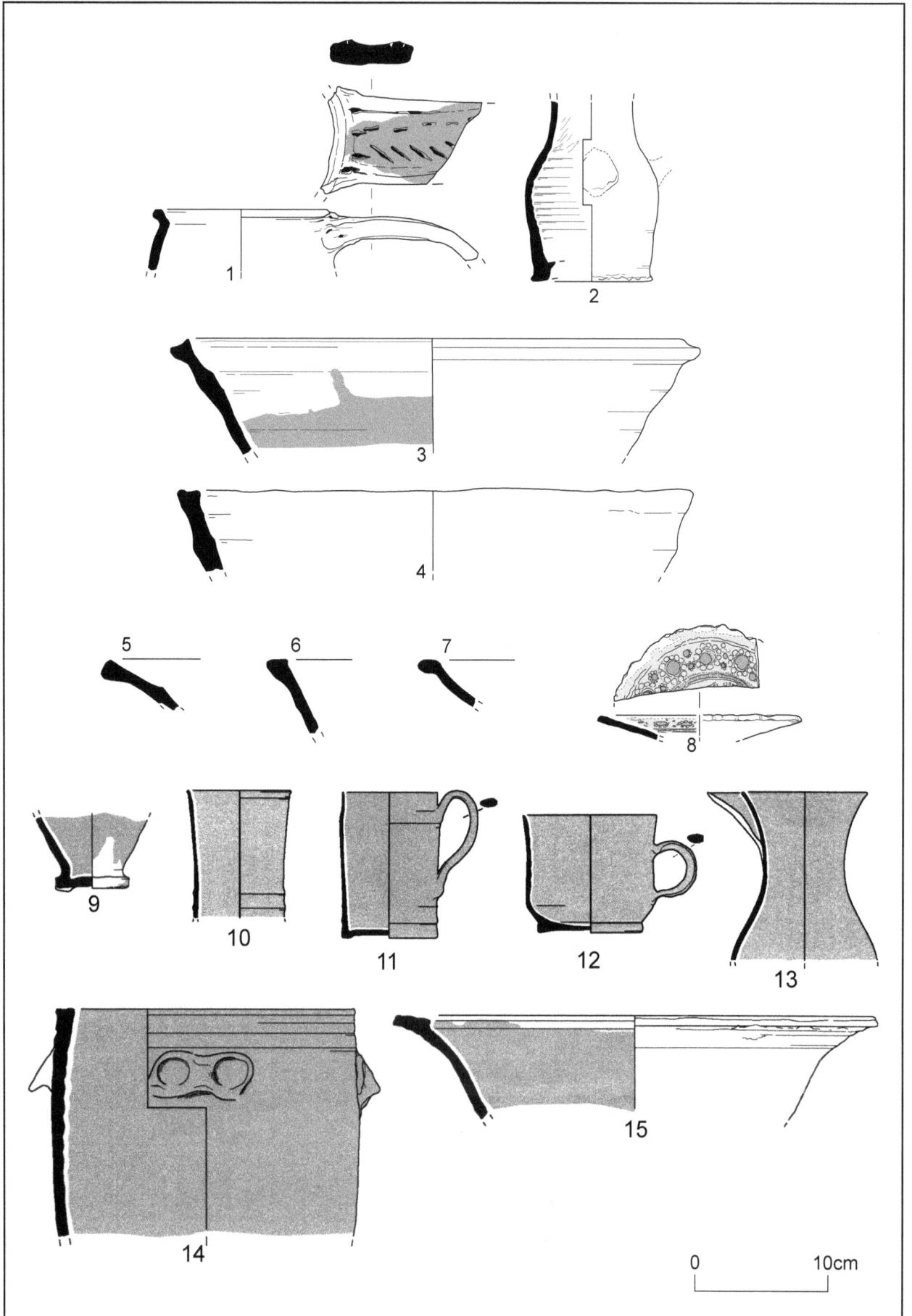

FIGURE 22 POTTERY 1–15

5001, Two unglazed body sherds.

5001, Body sherd with splashes of thin olive-tan glaze, possible trace of a handle scar.

5001, Bowl base sherd, internal splashes and spots of olive glaze.

5001, Jug body sherd, patchy external olive glaze, possible trace of stabbed or roller stamp decoration.

5015, Jug sherd, external olive glaze with darker mottles, incised horizontal line.

F514, Unglazed body sherd, surfaces orange.

8005, Body sherd from cylindrical jug, with tan glaze and thin applied red clay strip running obliquely across the vessel.

Iron-Poor Ware 2 (ipw2) Date: 13th–14th/ ?15th Century

Moderate sub-rounded quartz c 0.25mm, moderate rounded fe oxide 0.25–3mm. Wheel-thrown, hard. The fabric was unparalleled at Brewood, Lichfield and Birmingham. The fabric did appear, however, to be the same as fabric Bd1 from Shrewsbury (Rátkai 2004c). The date of this fabric is uncertain but a 13th–14th-century floruit was suggested at Shrewsbury.

5001, Jug rim sherd interior surface completely abraded. Buff fabric, yellowish surfaces, partial light grey core. One small glaze spot on external rim.

Iron-Poor Ware 3 (ipw3) Date: 13th–15th Century

Moderate rounded quartz c 0.25mm, sparse organics, sparse rounded fe oxide c 0.25mm. Hackly fracture, wheel-thrown, hard-fired. This sherd could not be paralleled but is likely to be of fairly local manufacture.

5001, Bowl base sherd, internal tan glaze external glaze spots, heavy external soot, burnt. Buff fabric.

Buff Gritty Ware (bgw) Date: 15th–16th Century?

Moderate – abundant ill-sorted quartz c 0.5–1mm, sparse, hard, sub-angular, whitish or pale grey, opaque inclusions, 0.5–1mm, sparse rounded black fe oxide up to 1mm. Wheel-thrown, hard-fired.

1004, Body sherd from jug, jar or cistern. Rough 'pimply' interior surface, somewhat smoother on exterior where ?wiped. Splash of thin purplish-olive glaze on exterior.

Late Oxidised Ware 1 (lox1) Date: 15th–16th Century

Orange fabric, slightly paler toned surfaces. Sparse organics, sparse sub-rounded quartz c 0.25mm, sparse rounded fe oxide. Inclusions poorly sorted/ unevenly distributed through the clay body. Wheel-thrown, hard-fired. The fabric can be paralleled at Lichfield fabric rw1 and is also close to Birmingham fabric lox01.

1002, Body sherd from bowl or cooking pot with rim similar to Ford 1995 'Late Medieval Orange Ware', Fig. 18, 146. Light external soot.

5005, Three small abraded body sherds.

5020, F511 Body sherd from bowl trace of thin internal patchy olive glaze, internal abrasion. Smoothed knife-trimmed external surface.

8002, Bowl rim sherd with internal bead. External patchy opaque olive glaze.

8002, Body sherd from jug, jar or cistern, two small brown spots of glaze on exterior.

8005, Base-body sherd from bowl, internal opaque yellowish-white glaze, external soot, trace of external knife trimming.

8005, Base-body sherd from bowl, internal thin tan glaze opaque in patches.

Late Oxidised Ware 2 (lox2) Date: 15th–16th Century

Fabric oxidised throughout, light brown to mid-orange in colour. Sparse rounded quartz <0.25mm, reasonably well sorted, sparse rounded fe oxide <0.25mm.

Wheel-thrown, soft (can be scratched with finger nail). The fabric was the same as Brewood fabric lmt4, close to Lichfield fabric lmt2 and similar to Birmingham fabric lox05.

1007, F100 Body sherd from ?bowl with traces of thin internal glaze.

8005, Body sherd from small jug, partial thin olive-opaque white glaze.

8006, F801, Body sherd from cylindrical jug, glossy olive-tan glaze, thick walled.

8006, F801 Body sherd from jug, glossy olive glaze. Applied white clay strip, with trace of stamp or roller stamp decoration, most of the strip has broken away from the wall of the pot.

9016, Two joining body sherds from a jug, jar or cistern, some internal glaze speckles.

Late Oxidised Ware 3 (lox3) Date : 15th–16th Century

Fabric oxidised from orange to red-brown in colour. Sparse rounded quartz, mainly less than 0.25mm, sparse organics, rare rounded fe oxide, possibly haematite. Wheel-thrown, hard-fired. This fabric, probably made at Wednesbury, was found at Brewood, fabric lmt/rw3, Lichfield, fabric rw2, and Birmingham, fabric lox02.

5009, F504, Body sherd, knife-trimmed exterior, internal splashes of tan glaze. Bowl or jar sherd. Red-brown fabric, partial grey core.

8005, Bowl body-base sherd, internal glossy olive glaze, some thin patchy glaze on exterior, probably the same

Fabric/ware	8001	8002	8005	8006	8008	8010	9013	9016	9019	9026	9028	9029	u/s	Total
Medieval (cpj4)	1													1
Medieval (ipgw1)			1											1
Medieval (Red-painted whiteware)	1													1
Late medieval (low1)		2	2											4
Late medieval (low2)				2				2					1	5
Late medieval (low2?)			1											1
Late medieval (low3)			2			1								3
Proto-Midlands Purple ware		4												4
Cistercian ware	2													2
Cistercian ware/blackware			3											3
Frechen stoneware			1											1
Blackware	1		19								1		1	22
Yellow ware	1													1
Coarseware			48							2	1		1	52
Brown salt-glazed stoneware			2										1	3
Mottled ware			5						7				1	13
Slip-coated ware			1								1		1	3
Tin-glazed earthenware			1											1
Westerwald stoneware			1											1
White salt-glazed stoneware			1		1									2
Porcelain										4				4
Creamware	1						1			3				5
wall plaster			1											1
Blue transfer-printed ware							1							1
Total	**7**	**6**	**89**	**2**	**1**	**1**	**2**	**2**	**7**	**9**	**3**	**3**	**3**	**135**

TABLE 1 POTTERY FROM THE EAST SECTION OF THE MAIN BUILDING

vessel as that from 8010 (below).

8005, A smaller, thinner walled sherd very similar to the above and possibly part of the same bowl.

8010, Bowl body-base sherd, internal glossy olive glaze two external glaze spots/splashes.

Proto-Midlands Purple Ware

Dense, smooth, brown fabric with grey surfaces. Sparse quartz grains <0.25mm, sparse iron oxide, sparse rounded off white inclusions. Possibly a differently fired version of Late oxidised ware 2.

8002, Base-body sherd with handle scar from a small jug, probably intended as a drinking jug (Fig. 22: 02).

Most of the medieval pottery could be paralleled by pottery from within a 24km radius of Wolverhampton. The near absence of whitewares is perhaps a little surprising, although whiteware sherds were found at the Beatties site. However, whitewares were not a significant feature of the Birmingham assemblages and were also in the minority at Dudley Castle (pers. inspection by author) and Brewood.

In contrast they were dominant at Lichfield. This suggests that Wolverhampton lies at the western or southwestern edge of the distribution area for whitewares. The pottery also suggests that in the medieval period economic links were fairly close-knit and centred primarily on an area bordered to the north by Watling Street, with the strongest links to Birmingham to the southeast.

The sources of the cooking pots and iron-poor wares are as yet unknown but presumably lie somewhere within the Black Country. Again it is not known whether pottery was produced at a number of small-scale operations or at a small number of rather bigger production centres. Certainly by the late medieval and early post-medieval period Wednesbury was a 'potting village' of some importance with its products widely distributed through south Staffordshire and north Warwickshire.

A higher proportion of medieval pottery was found in the eastern section of the main building which differed somewhat from that recovered from the main excavation (see Table 1). Layers 8002, 8010 and 9016 were dated to the 15th or 16th centuries by the pottery. 9016 is unlikely to be of this date as it is the infill between the walls on the frontage and abuts the 19th-century brick facing on the inside of these walls. Fill 8006 of pit F801 was probably of the same date although one of the two jug sherds from the fill was decorated with an applied stamped white clay strip. This form of decoration would be unusual on a 15th-century or later vessel, although both the vessel form, as far as it could be determined, and the glazing are more typical of the later medieval period. Either it is anomalous or fabric low2 was being made in the 14th century.

The dating of the medieval pottery suggests some occupation in the area from the 13th–15th or 16th centuries, the latest pottery being the late oxidised wares (lox1, lox2 and lox3) and proto-Midlands Purple ware (proto-mp) which date to the 15th–16th centuries. Some of the earlier medieval pottery is likely to have been from manuring scatters associated with ploughsoil, which were sealed before the construction of the hall in the 16th century. Although the medieval wares made up only a small component of the pottery from evaluation trenches 4, 5 and 6, and the main excavation, medieval pottery from the watching brief at the eastern section of the main building produced a much higher quantity of medieval, particularly late medieval/ early post-medieval, pottery which formed just over 19% of the group. In addition the sherds were not abraded and were large enough to suggest that they were associated with domestic occupation of the house. The problem with this pottery is the difficulty of dating it accurately enough to establish whether it belongs with the early years of the Levesons' Elizabethan house of the 1560s or reflects the putative earlier hall, Leland's 'auntients house of the Lusons', in this area of the moated platform. Overall there seems to be insufficient earlier medieval pottery to support this hypothesis, although it might suggest that the earliest part of the Elizabethan house lay more towards the centre of the northern edge of the platform and expanded westwards. The absence of late medieval and early post-medieval pottery in the lowest fills of the moat indicate that it had been kept scrupulously clean until 18th-century material was dumped there, most probably in the early years of the 19th century (see below).

The Post-Medieval Pottery

The post-medieval pottery was assigned to ware group and quantified by sherd count, sherd weight, minimum rim and base count. Most of the vessels were also quantified by rim percentage (*eves*) but this was not practicable for some of the creamwares and white salt-glazed stonewares which had elliptical or rectangular rims or where scalloped or royal edge rim sherds were small. All joining sherds were recorded as one sherd so the final sherd count in the report is significantly less than in the primary assessment report catalogue. A small number of cross-joins were noted but these were not significant other than highlighting the strong possibility that the moat fills were single dumps of material.

The main focus of the post-medieval pottery report, set out in the research design, were the fills from moat sections F100 (Trench 6) and F526 (main excavation). Pottery from the eastern area of the main building is also discussed as it is rather different in character from that found in the moat fills. All the remaining stratified post-medieval pottery, from both excavation and evaluation, was recorded, but is not discussed in detail. The unstratified pottery was scanned but not recorded.

In the eastern section of the main building, a group of contexts appeared to belong to the first half of the 18th century. These were 9029, the fill of F906, and 8008, 9028 and 9019. The latter consisted of mottled ware sherds comprising a chamber pot, a straight-sided bowl and a cup. There was a possible cross-join between this context and 9029. Context 8008 was one of only two contexts, the other being 8005, which contained white salt-glazed stoneware.

Layer 8005 contained the largest amount of pottery, which consisted for the main part of coarseware bowls. The fabric of the vessels was similar to coarseware fabric 1 (see below) but with elongated and irregularly-shaped voids within the matrix. Residue from within these voids reacted with hydrochloric acid, indicating the presence of calcareous material. Similar calcareous inclusions were noted in many of the coarseware fabrics from Dudley Castle (Rátkai 1987). The forms of these bowls were different from those recovered from the moat fills and appear to be of an earlier date. Illustrated vessel Fig.22.6 (and two other unillustrated examples) are similar to vessels found at Dudley Castle in Civil War destruction deposits (Rátkai 1987 fig. 6, 25–6). The other forms (Fig. 22 03–05, 07) were not closely paralleled. Roughly half the glazed sherds had a tan, red-brown or treacly brown glaze rather than the dark brown or black gazes found on the majority of the coarseware sherds from the moat fills. A smaller number of coarseware sherds, *c* 15% of the total, had a buff fabric but with a similar range of inclusions to coarseware fabric 1.

There was residual medieval pottery and 16th-century Cistercian or blackware cup sherds and Frechen stoneware sherd. The remaining pottery could be assigned to the later 17th to early/ mid-18th centuries and comprised blackware mugs, brown salt-glazed stoneware flange rim bowl and mug, three mottled ware mugs and a straight-sided bowl, a small sherd from a slip-coated ware bowl and a small, sprigged Westerwald stoneware mug sherd. A small fragment of a white-glazed wall tile also came from this context but is probably intrusive.

Layer 8001, which overlay 8002 contained a rather mixed group of pottery. Medieval wares were present, including a red-painted whiteware handle, unlikely to be later than the 14th century. Sherds of the 16th and 17th centuries were represented by Cistercian ware, blackware and yellow ware. A cream ware sherd in this layer is probably intrusive and 8001 should perhaps be seen as dating to the 17th century.

The two latest contexts, 9026 the fill of F915 and 9013, were dated to the late 18th century and ?mid-19th century

Plate 1

Plate 2

Plate 3

Plate 4

Plate 5

PLATE 1 SLIP-COATED WARE CYLINDRICAL MUG
PLATE 2 SLIP-COATED WARE VESSEL, POSSIBLY A CHAMBER POT
PLATE 3 MOTTLED WARE HANDLED BOWL
PLATE 4 SLIP-COATED WARE HANDLED BOWL
PLATE 5 WESTERWALD STONEWARE CHAMBER POT

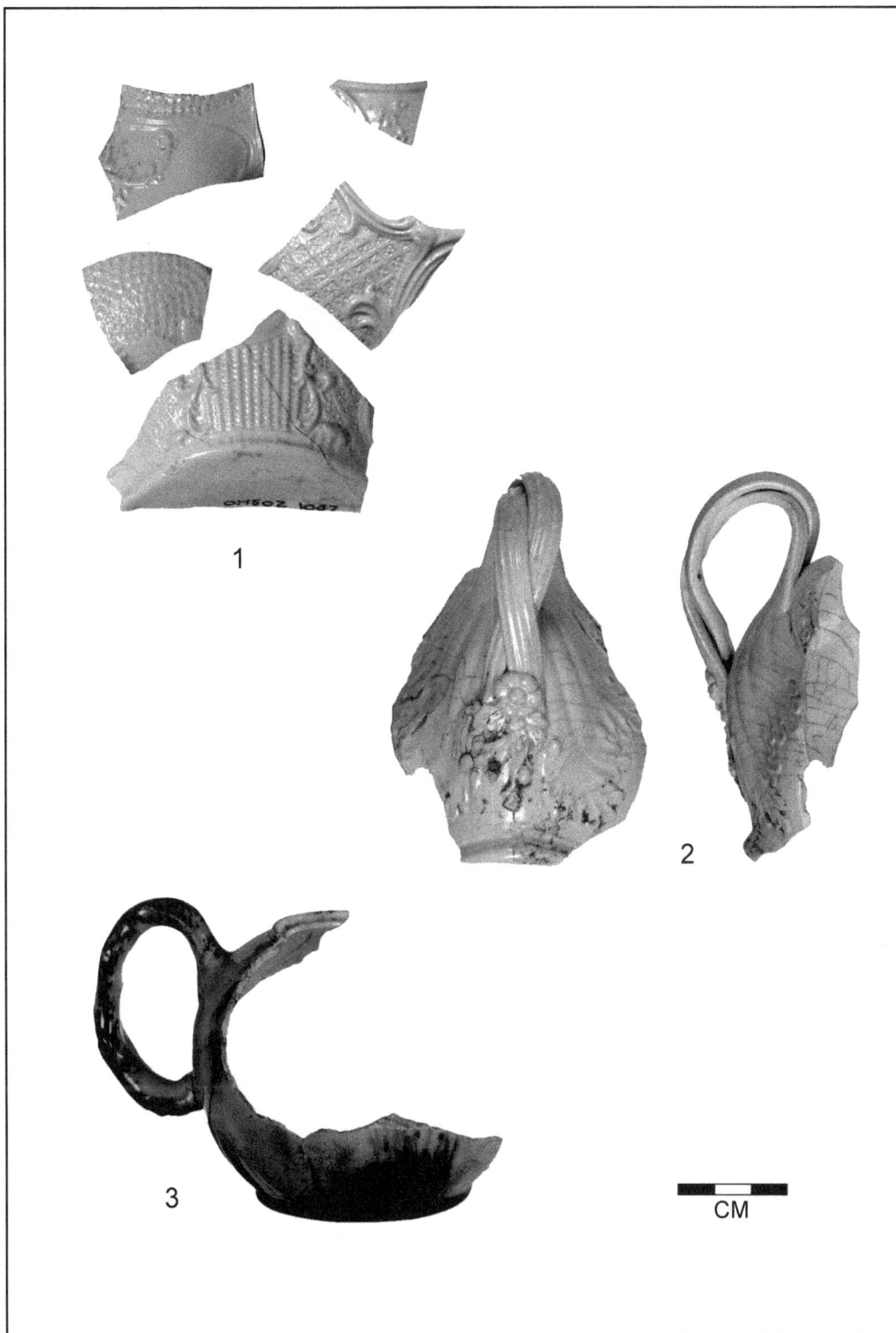

PLATE 6 CREAMWARE WITH UNDER-GLAZE COLOUR

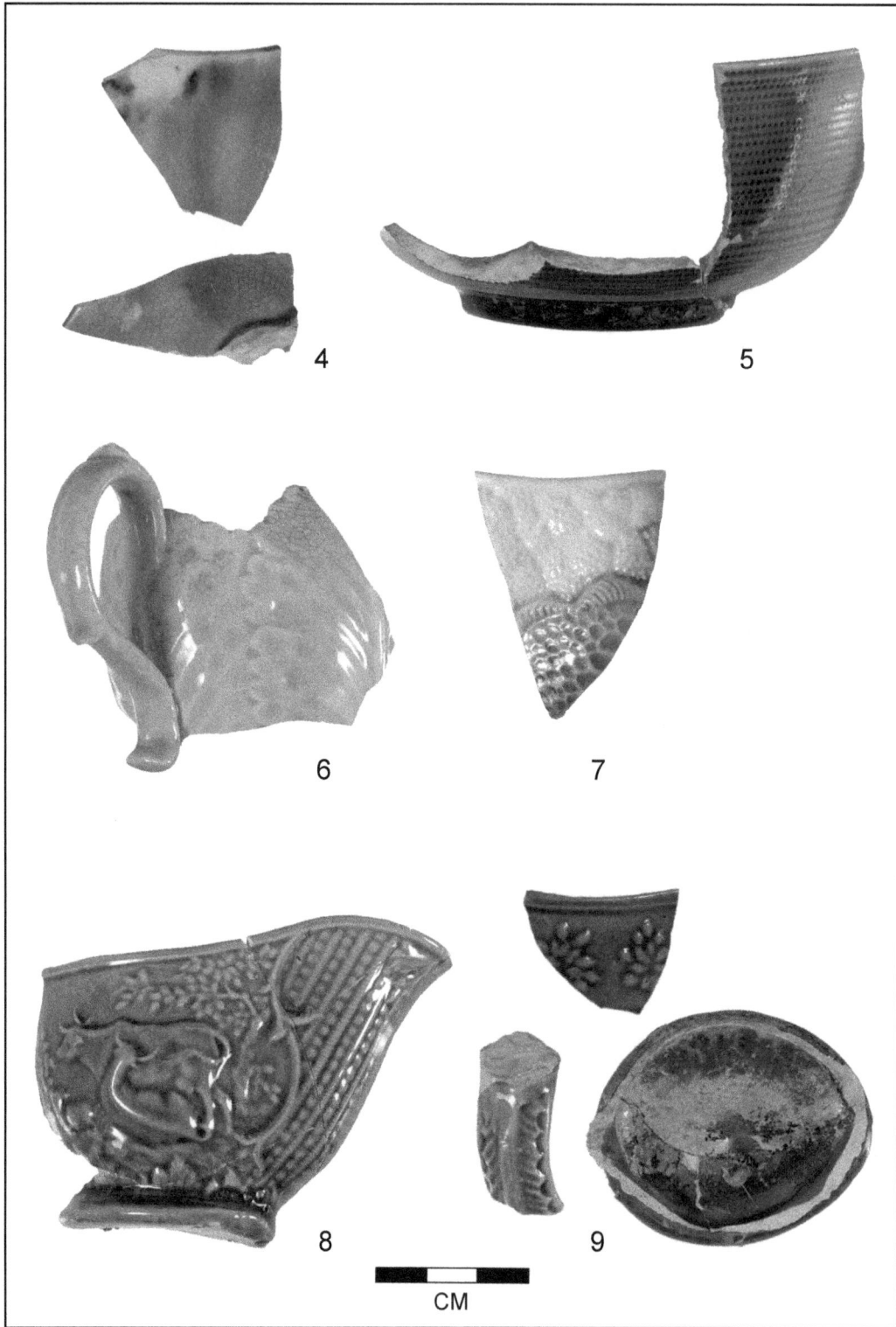

PLATE 7 CREAMWARE WITH UNDER-GLAZE COLOUR

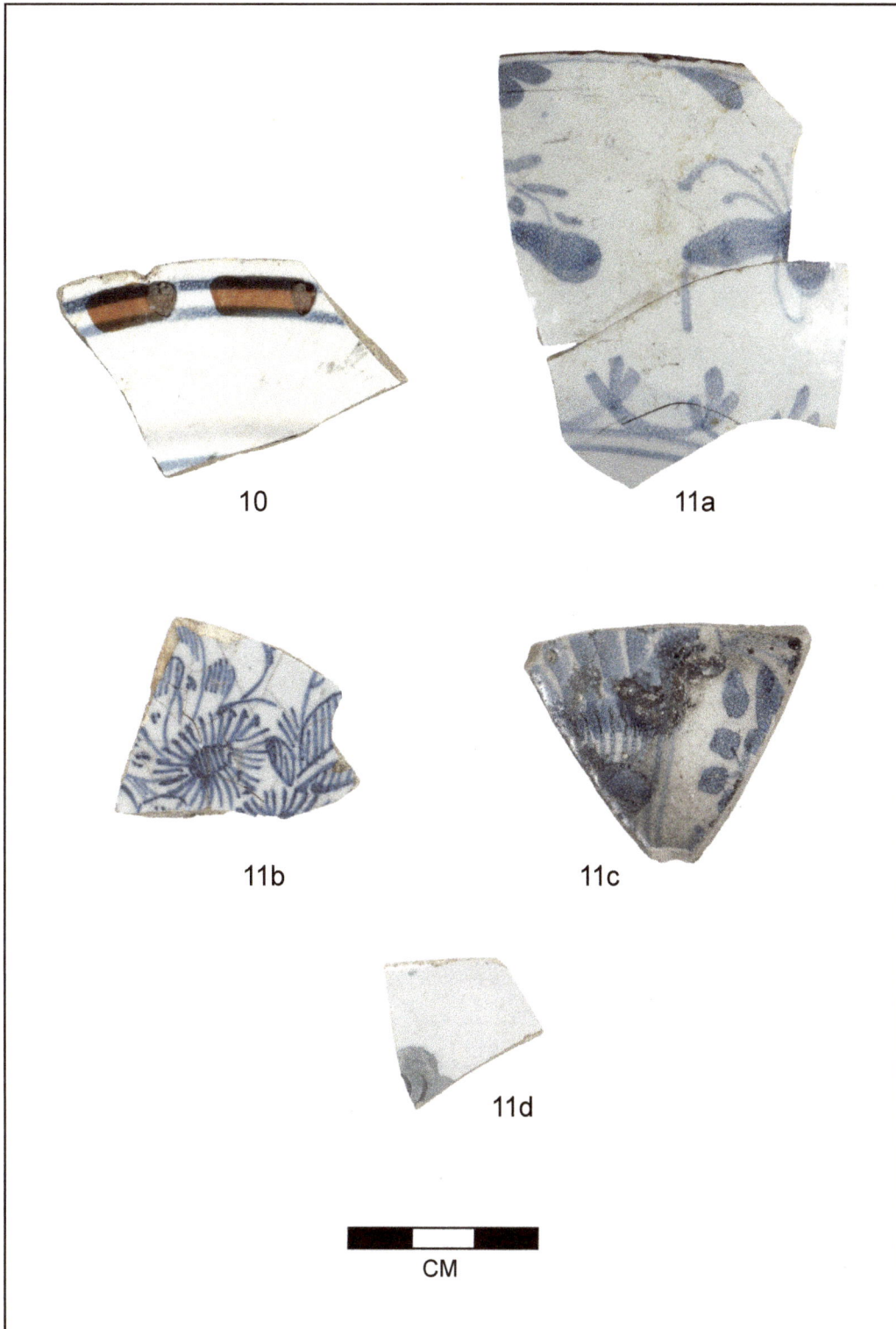

10

11a

11b

11c

11d

CM

PLATE 8 TIN-GLAZED EARTHENWARE HEMISPHERICAL BOWLS

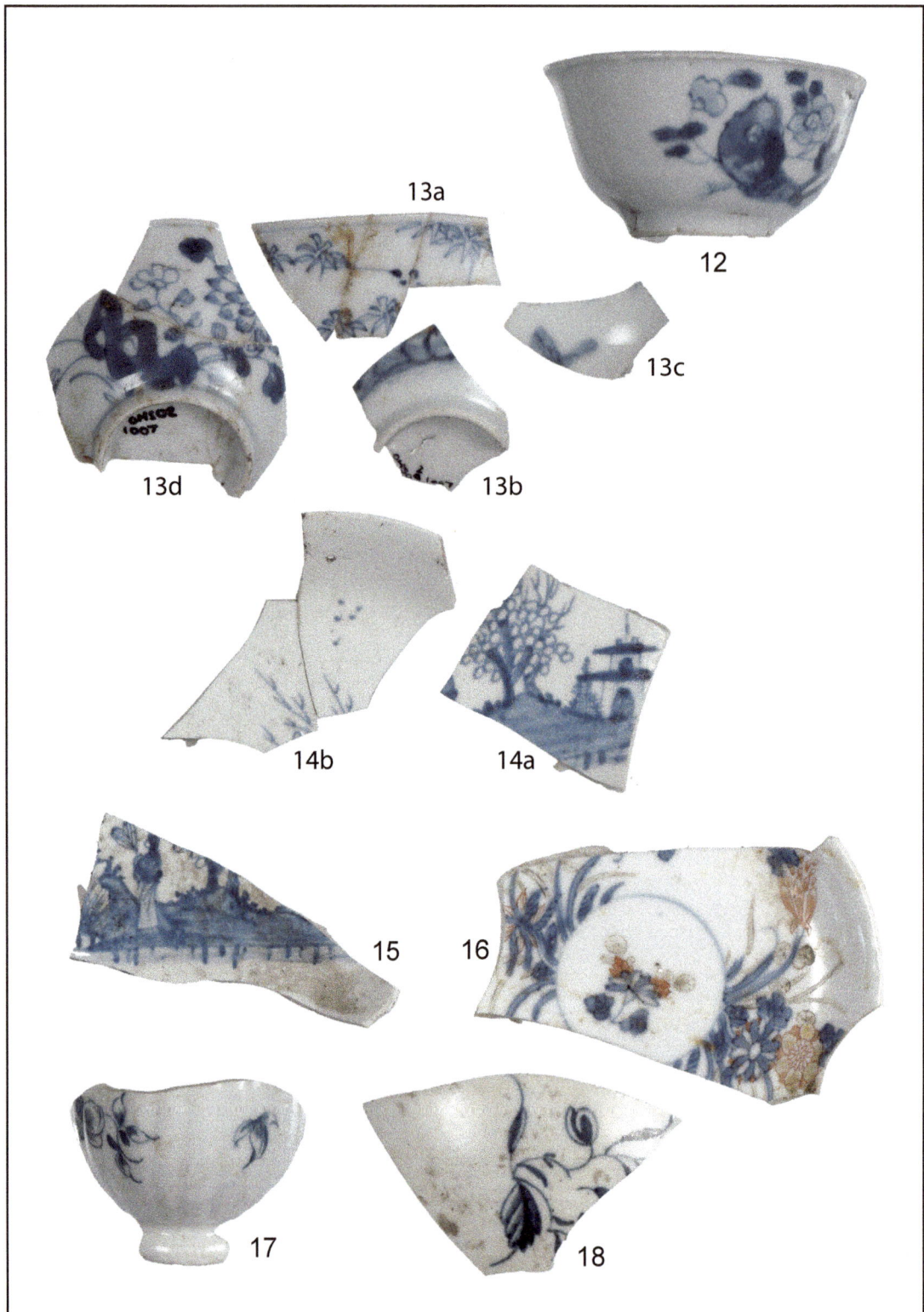

PLATE 9 PORCELAIN TEA BOWL (13), SAUCERS (14, 15, 16), POSSIBLE CUSTARD CUP OR SUGAR CASTER (17), AND BOWL (18)

19

20

CM

21

Plate 10 Pearlware tea bowls

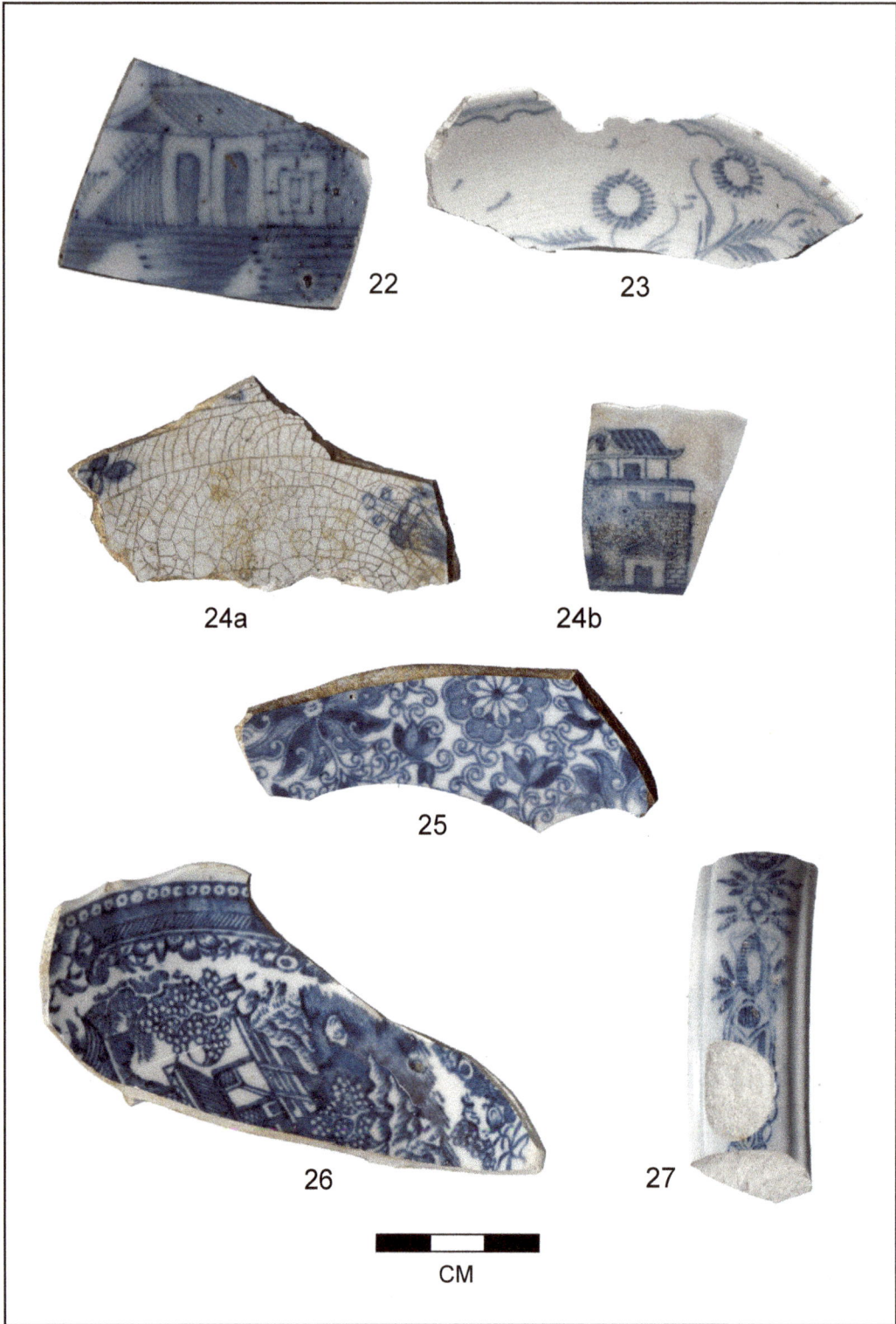

PLATE 11 PEARLWARE SAUCERS (22–6) AND JUG HANDLE (27)

respectively. The former contained two hemispherical creamware bowls, a creamware ?tea bowl and a (possibly Chinese) porcelain bowl with blue painted decoration. Although a small group, these wares are very similar to those found in the moat fills and may be more or less contemporary. An unglazed but slipped shallow bowl or dish, of uncertain function, was also found in 9026. Context 9013 was dated by a blue transfer-printed sherd with part of the 'Asiatic Pheasant' design.

Three probable wasters were recovered from the eastern section of the main building; a blackware mug sherd from 8005 and corrugated blackware mug sherd from 8001. An unstratified embossed slipware platter sherd (Fig. 22: 08) was extremely crudely made, incompletely glazed and slightly distorted. Its dubious quality may indicate nothing more than a 'second', although given the good quality of most of the other ceramics recovered from site, this seems rather strange. The reason for the presence of wasters on the moat platform is perhaps best explained as 'packing residue' from the bulk transportation of pottery onto the site. Pottery is known to have been bought in bulk by aristocratic and higher class households directly from the kiln site (cf Moorhouse 1983, 127) which may have resulted in occasional pieces of kiln waste or kiln furniture being incorporated into the pottery consigned for transport.

The pottery from the eastern section of the main building contained virtually no dining or tea wares. Mottled wares were rather better represented than in the moat fills, at the expense of slip-coated wares of which there are only three sherds. The general impression is that the pottery from this area of the site is earlier than that from the moat fills although it is just possible that the difference represents a functional bias rather than a chronological one.

The post-medieval coarse pottery from the moat fills, eg, slip-coated ware, blackware, mottled ware, is discussed generally (below), in terms of form, function and quantity and most vessel forms illustrated. The white salt-glazed stoneware, creamware, porcelain and pearlware have been catalogued but are unillustrated. However, several of these vessels have been photographed (Plates 1–11).

Yellow Ware

Only four sherds of yellow ware were found in the moat fills. Two sherds were from indeterminate hollow wares and were found in 1003 and 5037. The sherd from 1003 had an iron rich fabric and under-glaze white slip. It was glazed internally and was also heavily abraded on the interior. The sherd may have been from a jar or pipkin. The third vessel, a mug, represented by two sherds, came from 5037. These sherds could date from the 17th or early 18th centuries but all are clearly residual in the upper fills of the moat.

Blackware

The base of a bottle or possibly a mug (Fig. 22: 09) was found in 5016. It was quite crudely made and a 17th-century date is likely. Cylindrical mugs with forms similar

to slip-coated ware mugs (Fig. 25: 48) were found in 1002, 1003 and 1007. A second cylindrical mug was found in a late blackware fabric, sometimes know as 'shining black' in 1007 (Fig. 22: 10). A 'half pint' mug also in 'shining black' was found in 1019 (Fig. 22: 11). A cup (Fig. 22: 12) and a cup or mug base were found in 1003, and an indeterminate mug sherd in 1007. The cup and mug forms suggest a date in the 18th century. A possible chamber pot (not illustrated) came from 1007 and a handle possibly from a chamber pot was found in 1010. There was a single example of a jug from 5029 which could have dated to the second half of the 17th or 18th centuries. A jar rim was also found in 5029. The remaining blackware sherds were less easy to assign to form. Base sherds probably from handled bowls similar to (Fig. 24: 33) came from fills 1007 and 5029, and 1003 and 1007 both contained sherds from a straight-sided hollow ware form. A horizontal 'lug' handle, probably from a large pan, a later 18th- and 19th-century form, was found in 1007. The earliest fill of F100 (1011) contained a jug or jar body sherd with a 'dribbly' black glaze on the interior and partial glaze on the interior. The vessel's purple-red fabric and the glazing are consistent with a 17th-century date. Otherwise, indeterminate hollow ware blackware body sherds were found in 1003, 1004, 1007 and 5029.

In addition to the 'shining black' mugs (above), there were two other shining black vessels; a jug (Fig. 22: 13), from 5032 and a teapot spout and base from 1007. These vessels are likely to date from the late 18th century.

Coarseware

Four fabric variations of the basic post-medieval black- or dark brown-glazed coarseware fabric were noted. Coarseware fabric 1 had a light orange fabric often with lighter streaks within the matrix with frequent inclusions of iron ore and sparse quartz and rounded off-white inclusions. Coaseware fabric 2 had a pink fabric but with similar inclusions to Coarseware fabric 1. Coarseware fabric 3 had a hard-fired weak red fabric with sparse quartz, moderate iron ore and rare red sandstone. Streaks of white clay were sometimes visible in the matrix. Coarseware fabric 4 was buff in colour and had a sandier cleaner fabric than the foregoing, although, under x 20 magnification, thin whisps of red and white clay were visible in the matrix. Apart from the variations in colour the coarseware fabrics were broadly similar and it is quite possible that these variations are the result of differences in mixing the light-firing and darker-firing clays. Coarseware 1 was the most frequent fabric. Coarseware 2 was found mainly in F100 whilst coarseware fabrics 3 and 4 were most common in F526.

A further fabric (cwmp) was a cross between coarseware and Midlands Purple ware and was found only in F526. The fabric was clean and hard fired. The fabric colour varied between weak red and brown. Glaze tended to be black and rather 'metallic' in appearance. All the sherds were from jars. Sherds from at least one vessel (Fig. 22: 14) were found scattered throughout fills 5029, 5031, 5032 and 5033.

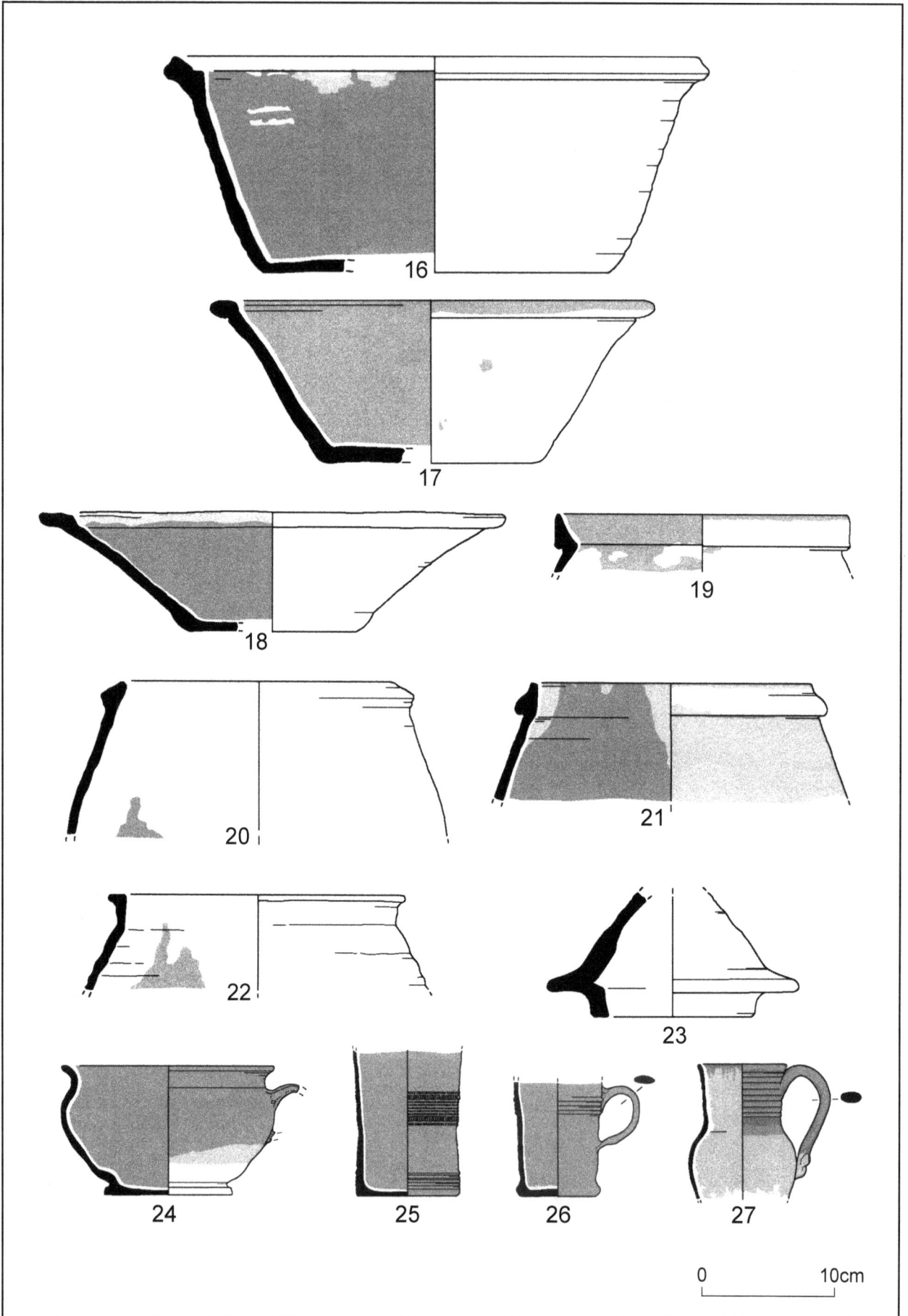

FIGURE 23 POTTERY 16–27

Two sherds, one each from fills 1002 and 1003 of F100, were classed as indeterminate coarseware/ blackware (fabric cwblw). The sherd from 1003 was from a large hollow ware (Not illustrated).

The greater number of coarseware vessels were bowls or pancheons (33 rim sherds, 20 base sherds) (Fig. 22: 15; Fig. 23: 16, 17, 18). The bowls had a black or dark brown interior glaze and generally an under-glaze red, brown or purplish slip. Splashes and streaks of glaze, tan on the unslipped surface, were sometimes visible on the exterior surface. Kiln scars on two of the vessels suggest that the large bowls had been fired in an upright position, stacked one inside another with clay 'bobs' placed between the rims. A small number of vessels had wear on the outer edge of the base where the base had rubbed against a hard surface whilst in use. This is consistent with their use for mixing ingredients and for bread making. Both mixing and kneading would have caused friction between the bowl base and the surface on which it was standing.

Jars were also represented (five rim sherds, twelve base sherds (Fig. 23: 19, 20, 21, 22), which all came from F526. There were three rim sherds (diameters, 360mm, 400mm and 490mm) and two bases, from large deep vessels, sometimes known as 'pans', (eg, Fig. 22: 14, see above) one of which had traces of a horizontal lug handle.

The only other form represented was a lid from an ?industrial vessel or an item of garden furniture, which came from 1007 (Fig. 23: 23). This had a thick matt black deposit on the interior and remnants of the same type of deposit on the exterior. The deposit, which was pre-depositional, had a faint waxy smell. The form of the vessel could be consistent with a 'forcing pot' but such an explanation does not account for the black deposit.

The utilitarian vessels were much more common in F526 where they formed roughly half of the assemblage by rim count.

Mottled Ware

All but one of the mottled ware sherds had a buff fabric. The exception was a handled bowl (Fig. 23: 24, Plate 3) from 5031 which had a red fabric and under-glaze white slip. Two further examples of this vessel form but with buff fabric were found in 1007 and 5031. A fairly small range of vessel forms were present. The most common form was the cylindrical mug with reeded bands at the base and/ or rim. Two body sherds from this type of vessel were found in 1003. Two cylindrical mug bases and one rim were found in 1007 and a cylindrical mug with a band of rouletting was found in 1008 (Fig. 23: 25). The latter seems to be imitating some of the brown-salt-glazed stoneware forms (eg, Fig. 26: 62, 63). The form of another small cylindrical mug (Fig. 23: 26) from 1007 is very similar to blackware mug forms. A mug from 1008 (Fig. 23: 27) has been included in the mottled wares, although it is something of a hybrid. This type of mug is sometimes known as a 'treacle-top' mug (pers. comm. Sarah Jennings). The mug has a clear lead glaze, giving a yellow colour over the buff

body, on the interior and lower exterior half of the vessel. The upper exterior half of the vessel has been coated with manganese (which has 'bled' slightly into the interior rim of the vessel) giving the typical brown speckled glaze associated with mottled ware. Under x 20 magnification the cream fabric contained flecks of iron oxide not visible to the naked eye. These flecks were also visible, again only under x 20 magnification, under the yellow glazed portions of the vessel, indicating that the mug had not been slipped prior to glazing.

The two-colour effect produced on this vessel is very interesting since it indicates something about manufacturing technique. From Dr Plot's account (Plot 1686, 123):

> " ....the motley colour is produced by blending lead with the manganese...."

It would appear that the glaze contained both lead and manganese but in the case of the mug from 1008 this cannot have been so. The form and glazed effect of this vessel is identical to a stoneware mug also from 1008 (Fig. 26: 70). The stoneware mug has an iron wash over the upper half of the body, producing the same two colour effect seen in the mottled ware mug. It looks therefore as if the methods used in making the stoneware mug have been transferred to the manufacture of mottled ware.

Three further mottled sherds were recovered from 1003. One was the base from a bowl or cup and the other two body sherds were from indeterminate large hollow wares, one particularly thick-walled.

Slip-Decorated Wares

All the slipwares had a buff fabric and the sherds were from moulded platters. Several different slipware decorative techniques were present. A light-on-dark slip trailed platter with pie-crust edge was found in 1007. A second pie-crust edge platter but with combed slip decoration (Fig. 24: 28) came from the same context together with two feathered slip ware platters. Three body sherds from feathered slipware platters were also found in 1003 and 1006. A pie-crust rim platter from 5032 was decorated with 'marbled' slips in yellow, tan and dark brown (Fig. 24: 29). These slipwares could date to the late 17th century but could equally as well have been made in the first half of the 18th century. The paucity of slipware and the absence of slipware cups and mugs suggest a deposition date later than c 1750.

Slip-Coated Ware

By far the greater number of slip-coated ware sherds came from hollow wares. There was a complete profile from a sloping-sided, handled bowl (Fig. 24: 30, Plate 4) from 5031 and several examples of handled bowls with a rounded profile, with rim diameters ranging from 130–210mm. The sloping-sided bowl (Fig. 24: 30) had a dished rim suggesting that the vessel may have been intended to take a lid.

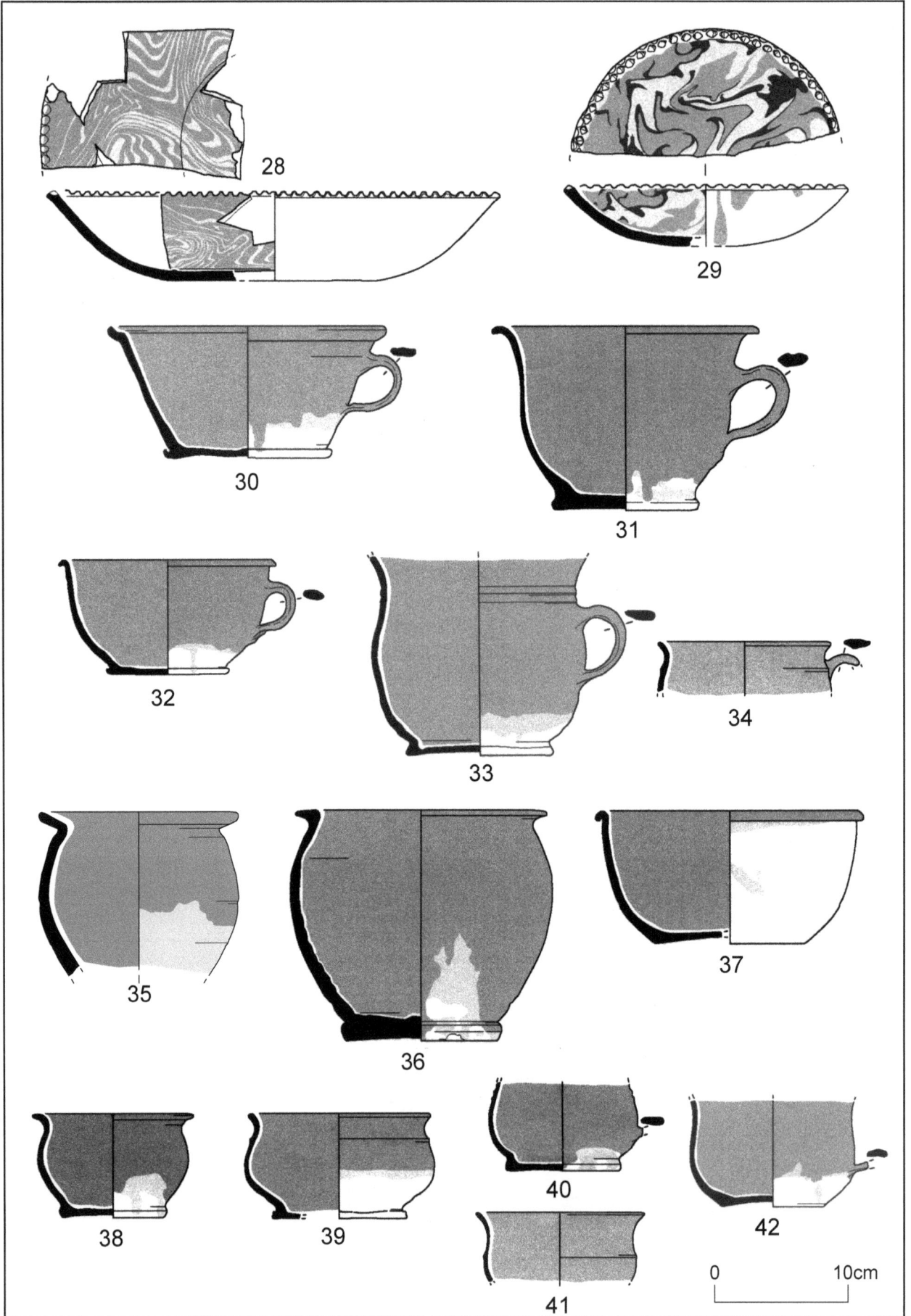

FIGURE 24 POTTERY 28–42

Some of the larger diameter vessels could have been chamber pots. Two of these vessels were represented by complete profiles; one from 1008 (Fig. 24: 31) and one from 5031 (Fig. 24: 32, Plate 2). A third vessel from 1007 had an almost complete profile (Fig. 24: 33) and a fourth was represented by the upper part of the vessel (Fig. 24: 34). Another similar vessel from 1007 was represented by a rim sherd. Eight base sherds, with diameters mostly in the 100–120m range, all from 1007, looked to have come from similar vessels to Fig. 24: 33. A further five base sherds from indeterminate bowl forms were found in 1007 and one in 1009. Three bowls with plain everted rims, a red fabric and under-glaze slip coat came from 1008, and one from 5033 (Fig. 24: 35). The complete profile of a bowl with a rounded profile was found in 1009 (Fig. 24: 36). A bowl of indeterminate form was represented by a rim sherd from 5031. A hook-rim bowl was found in 1008 (Fig. 24: 37). Two further rim sherds from 1008 (diameter 190mm) and 5031 (diameter 180mm) could have been from chamber pots.

A number of smaller vessels with rounded profiles were from small bowls or cups. Three examples of this form were found in 1008 (eg, Fig. 24: 38–39) and three more examples (eg, Fig. 24: 40) in 1003. Another vessel of this type came from 5031 (Fig. 24: 41). A cup body sherd with handle scar and a cup or porringer base were also found in 1003. A second small handled bowl came from 1009 (Fig. 24: 42).

In addition to the hollow wares with a rounded profile there were several straight-sided (Fig. 25: 43, 44, 45) or sloping-sided vessels, usually with handles. Four of the straight-sided vessels were found in 1008 and two in 1007. A number of undiagnostic straight-sided hollow ware base, body and rim sherds were found in 1008, 5029, 5031 and 5032 each representing one vessel. A minimum of three such vessels was represented in 1007 by two base, one rim and three body sherds.

Mugs were less well represented. Three examples (eg, Fig. 25: 46) came from 1007, one from 5032 (Fig. 25: 47). Two cylindrical mugs (eg, Fig. 25: 48, Plate 1) were found in 5031.

Four jar rims (eg, Fig. 25: 49, 50, 51, 52) – one a shouldered jar (Fig. 25: 52), a large jar or 'pan' (Fig 25: 53) and one jar base came from 1007 and a possible jug body sherd came from the same context. Context 1007 was the only context to contain rim sherds from flange-rim bowls or dishes (eg, Fig. 25: 54, 55, 56), which represented a minimum of six vessels.

Tin-Glazed Earthenware

Tin-glazed earthenware was not particularly well represented in the moat fills and what sherds there were, were generally small. Two hemispherical bowls (diameter 150mm), one with external blue painted decoration and a brown band along the rim and the other with exterior grey-green painted decoration were found in 1007 (Plate 8: 10–11). A flange-rim bowl (diameter 200mm) with two painted blue bands and orange blobs and a burnt base sherd, possibly from a bowl, were found in the same context, together with a possible plate base with internal blue painted decoration and an undecorated body sherd of indeterminate form. The burnt base of a foot-ring bowl was found in 5031. A complete lid (Fig. 25: 57) was found in 5037. The lid was very heavily abraded on the exterior and most of the glaze had come away from the surface. The interior retained its glaze. The date range of all of the tin-glazed earthenware would seem to lie in the period 1725–75.

Miscellaneous Refined Body Wares

A small agate ware dish (Fig. 25: 58) decorated with white slip bands, one rouletted, on the rim was found in 1007 and dates to the late 18th century. A teapot lid with a red-brown glaze and a band of combed slip came from the same context. A third sherd from a bead-rim bowl with a red brown glaze and cream slip horizontal bands was found in 1007.

A sherd from 1008 had a white earthenware fabric with a cream coloured glazed exterior and a bright, yellow interior. The sherd appears to be intrusive and of late 19th or 20th-century date.

Stonewares

Westerwald Stoneware

Three chamber pots were represented (Fig. 25: 59, Fig. 26: 60, 61, Plate 5). The illustrated vessels, from 1007, 1008 and 1009 were decorated with applied lion and rosette motifs outlined in cobalt blue. The surface of (Fig. 26: 61), found in 1007, had light vertical ribbing.

Brown Salt-Glazed Stoneware

Most of the brown salt-glazed stoneware came from 1007. It comprised a cylindrical mug with a band of rouletting (Fig. 26: 62), a cylindrical mug with a reeded base, a mug handle, two flange rim dishes (eg, Fig. 26: 64), a dish with a scalloped rim (Fig. 25: 65), a campanulate cup or bowl (Fig. 26: 66, diameter 150mm), the lower half of which was rouletted, and a possible cup sherd. A second rouletted cylindrical mug was found in 1008 (Fig. 26: 63). A hemispherical bowl with a plain rim (diameter 250mm) and reeded decoration (Fig. 26: 67) was found in 5031 and a smaller version of the same form (diameter 180mm) was found in 5032 (Fig. 26: 68). A rounded bowl or dish with a flange rim was found in 5032, together with a flange rim (diameter 340mm) possibly from the same vessel. The above vessels, with the exception of the campanulate form (Fig. 26: 66), had a glossy, good quality glaze.

One of the upper fills of moat F100. Context 1000 contained a substantial amount of a stoneware bottle (Fig. 26: 69). The upper half of the vessel had a thin rather patchy salt glaze. There was some evidence of burning around the bottle rim.

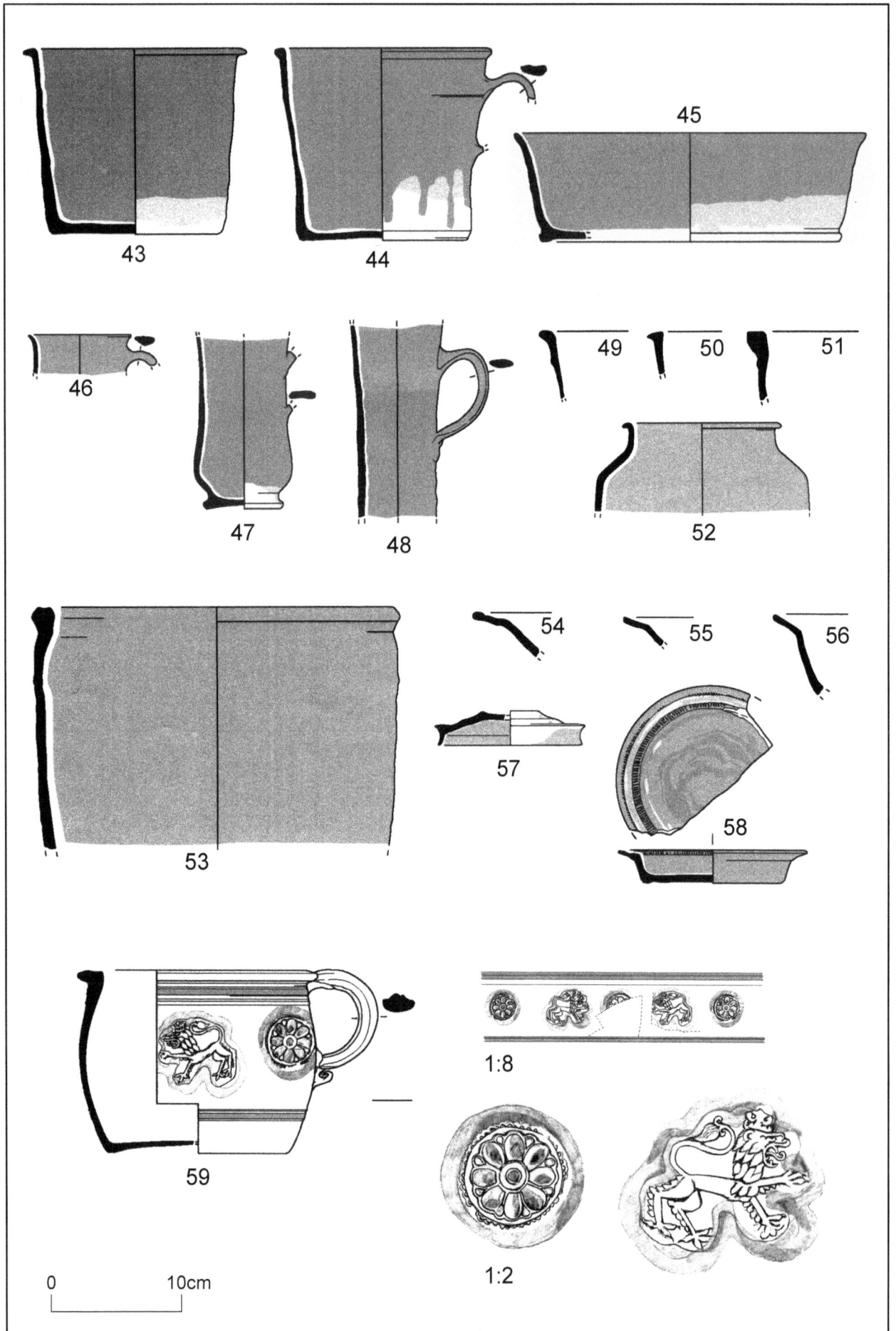

FIGURE 25 POTTERY 43–59

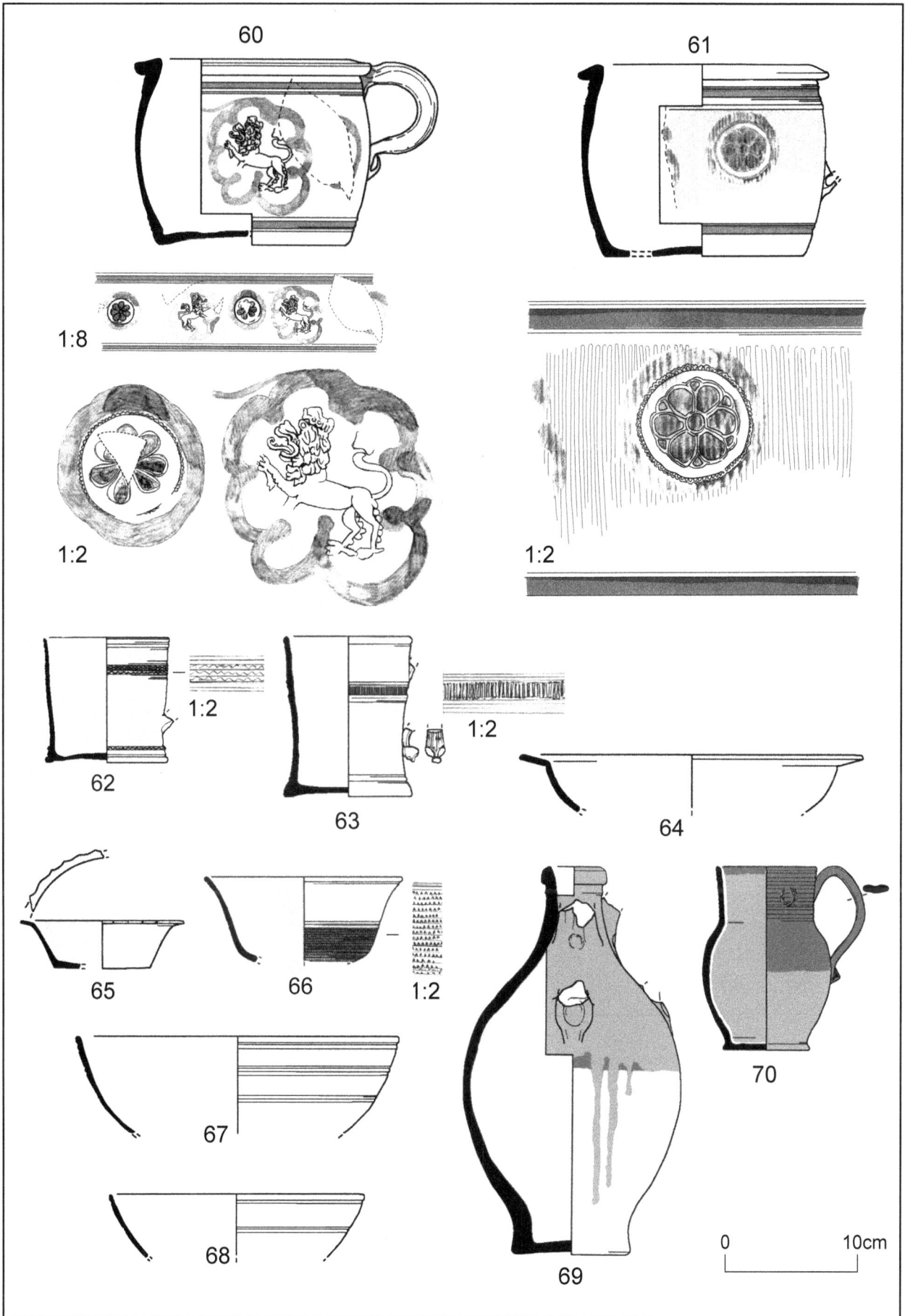

FIGURE 26 POTTERY 60–70

Light-Bodied Stoneware

A single mug (Fig. 26: 70) was found in 1008. The upper half of the mug had an iron wash so that the upper half of the vessel was brown and the lower half of the vessel cream. The form and the decorative effect is exactly the same as a mottled-type ware mug from 1008 (Fig. 23: 27).

White Salt-Glazed Stoneware

Hemispherical Bowl with Plain Rim

1007, Eight separate vessels were represented by rim sherds from this form, their diameters falling between 140–160mm probably suggesting an original intended diameter for the bowls of 6ins (152mm).

5029, One bowl with a 180mm diameter was represented.

Hemispherical Bowl with Hook-Rim

1007, Two vessels were represented. The hook rim bowls had a larger diameter at 210mm (c 8ins) and 250mm (10ins) than the plain rim variety.

Sloping–sided bowl with hook rim

1007, There were two examples of this form. Only one diameter could be measured which was 250mm.

Chamber Pot

1007, Three chamber pots (diameters 180–190mm) were represented with a hollow-rolled bead or hooked rim.

5032, A hook-rim hollow ware (diameter 180mm) was probably from a chamber pot.

5033, One chamber pot was represented by a base sherd. This base and the hook rim sherd from 5032 above may have been from the same vessel.

Jug

1007, Two jugs were represented one by a rim sherd (100mm diameter) and the other by a base-wall sherd. The lower part of the handle remained, including the terminal. The terminal form was the same as a milk jug illustrated by Jennings (1981, fig. 102: 1629).

1008, Large plain jug sherd (rim diameter 150mm).

Jug/ Sauceboat

1007, Two small jugs or sauceboats were recovered, one with dot, diaper and basketwork design, the other with a foliate and 'pecked' ?strawberry design (Plate 6.1).

Mug

1007, A number of cylindrical hollow wares, probably mugs, were found (cf Barker 1984, fig. 7: 55–57). These were represented by two base sherds (diameters 45mm and 120mm), a handle and two rim sherds (diameters 140m and 90mm). The 140m base was a cross-join with a more

substantial base sherd from 1008. The 90mm base mug had a raised turned band above the base.

1008, Three body sherds probably from a mug were recorded in this context.

Miscellaneous Hollow Wares

1007, A bead rim hollow ware (diameter 220mm) could have been from a bowl or a fourth chamber pot. A base sherd may have come from a bowl. A further 35 hollow ware sherds which could not be assigned to form were found in this context.

1007, small sherd with a raised horizontal rib from a large hollow ware.

1008, An everted rim sherd, probably from a bowl similar to Barker (1987, fig. 74: 19–20) was present and a body sherd from a rounded hollow ware, possibly a hemispherical bowl.

Dish with Flange Rim

1007, There was one example of this form (diameter 250mm) where the rim had a slightly raised 'bead' on the edge of the rim.

1008, A second example of this form was represented by a base-wall sherd which had a small piece of the rim-wall junction remaining. A second dish (or soup plate) had a dot diaper and basket design rim.

Plate

1007, A minimum of eleven plates were represented by rim sherds. Four base sherds each with a tiny piece of the rim-wall junction could be from a further four plates or part of the eleven. The dot, diaper and basket design was most frequently found with six or seven (see below) examples. Where it was possible to estimate the rim diameter the plates looked to be 9 or 10ins (229 or 254mm). Three further rims were decorated; one with seed pattern, one with basket work and the third had a feather-edge. The edged rim sherd appeared to come from an 8in (203mm) plate. A possible 10in (254mm) plate had a rim decorated with a 'rope work' design.

There were two plates with plain flange rims (diameters 235mm and 240mm) and two shallow plates or shallow dishes with a scalloped flange rim (diameters 180mm and 230mm). This form was exactly the same as found in brown salt-glazed stoneware (Fig. 26: 65) (diameters 180mm and 230mm).

1008, One plate was represented with dot, diaper and basket design, which was probably part of one of the plates from 1007.

5029, A maximum of three plates were represented by two rim sherds and a base sherd. One of the rims had dot, diaper and basket decoration and the other had 'rope' edge similar to the 10in plate from 1007

Serving Plate or Dish

1007, There were two large oval plates with basketwork and trellis deign on the rim (cf Barker 1984, fig. 9: 70–3). There was a further rim sherd, a cross-join, from one of these plates from 1008. There was also a large plate possibly oval with dot, diaper and basket design on the rim. A fourth serving dish had a plain octagonal flange rim (cf Barker 1984, fig. 10: 79).

1008, A rim sherd from an oval dish with basket work and trellis design and almost certainly part of one of the plates from 1007 and an oval dish with a plain flange rim were found.

5031, A large oval plate with seed design was found in this context.

A further ten flatware base sherds were recovered from 1007 and two probable flatware body sherds.

Formal dining wares were well represented in 1007 with both serving plates and possible sauceboats being present in addition to the plates and soup plates. However, more everyday table wares, eg, bowls and mugs were also well represented. Nearly all the white salt-glazed stoneware came from F100 and particularly fill 1007. The small number of white salt-glazed stoneware sherds from 1008, the cross joins between 1007 and 1008 suggests that the white salt-glazed stonewares formed one dump of material.

Porcelain

1007, Tea bowl, external blue painted ?bamboo, interior border of ?diaper pattern, Chinese 1760s–80s (Plate 9: 13).

1007, Tea bowl, external blue painted decoration, blue mark on base interior Chinese 1760s–80s (Plate 9: 13).

1007, Tea bowl external blue painted decoration Chinese 1760s–1780s (Plate 9: 13).

1007, Tea bowl interior narrow blue band Chinese 1760s–80s (Plate 9: 13).

1007, Tea bowl exterior blue painted floral decoration, interior border, narrow blue band above base and mark on base. Chinese 1760s–80s (Plate 9: 13).

1007, Saucer, Imari style decoration, blue and red painted design with gilding, dated to 1770–80s (Plate 9: 16).

1007, Saucer interior blue painted decoration, same design as saucer from (1008), Chinese 1770s–80s (Plate 9: 14).

1007, Saucer interior blue decoration. There is a small neat hole drilled into the sherd for a riveted repair, Chinese 1770s–80s (Plate 9: 14).

1007, Fluted hollow ware, possibly a custard cup or sugar caster (pers. comm. David Barker), external blue painted decoration, dated to the 1770s–80s (Plate 9: 17).

1008, Saucer internal blue painted decoration of a Chinese figure in a ?garden, Chinese 1770s–80s (Plate 9: 15).

1009, Tea-bowl, external blue painted decoration, small flower painted on interior base, Chinese c 1725–50 (Plate 9: 12).

5031, Bowl with blue painted decoration on interior and exterior, English, possibly Liverpool, 1770s–80s (Plate 9: 18).

It is interesting that the porcelain tea wares were found mainly in the lower fills of the moat and occur in the greatest quantity where pearlware was absent or less well represented.

Creamware

Hemispherical bowl with plain rim

1008, One rim sherd (diameter 125mm).

Chamber Pot

1008, Small rim fragment (200mm diameter).

Jug

1007, A plain handle fragment in a very pale creamware, possibly dating to c 1800.

1008, Double twisted handle possibly from a milk jug.

1008, Hollow ware sherd with broad shallow turned horizontal bands, possibly from a jug or mug.

Jug or Sauceboat

5031, Small jug or sauceboat with moulded decoration and a double-twist handle, dating to the mid-1760s to early 1770s (Plate 6: 2).

Miscellaneous Hollow Wares

5032, Two undiagnostic sherds.

Plate

1007, Three plates were represented by two rim sherds and a base sherd.

1008, Six plates, three with a royal edge, two with plain flange rims and one with a moulded scroll and pendant ?vine motif.

1011, One body sherd.

5029, Two royal edge plates.

5031, One royal edge plate.

5032, ?Soup plate with royal edge and plate with feather edge.

Serving Plate or Dish

1007, Part of a rim from a rectangular dish with rope work

decoration on rim. The colour of the sherd is a yellow-cream suggesting a date in the 1760s or early 1770s.

1008, Oval serving plate with plain flange rim.

5029, One or two oval dishes represented by a royal edge rim and a base sherd.

5031, One oval plate with royal edge rim.

Miscellaneous Flatwares

1008, Five base sherds from plates or dishes.

5031, Three vessels represented by four base sherds.

Creamware with Under-Glaze Colour

A number of sherds with oxide colour beneath the glaze were found. These mainly came from 1007 and were entirely absent from section F526.

1007, Small teapot in 'tortoiseshell ware'. Lid seated rim, crabstock handle, some burning around the base of the vessel. Late 1750s–1760s (Plate 6: 3).

1008, One tiny tortoiseshell ware sherd possibly part of the above.

1007, Chamfered rim sherd, (60mm diameter), from ?lidded jug, pale green external colour, 'tortoiseshell ware' late 1750s–60s (Plate 7: 4).

1007, Rim-body sherd from a small ?jug, pale green external colour similar to above and trace of moulded decoration or handle scar late 1750s–60s.

1007, Small jug or sauceboat rim in 'cauliflower ware' and small body sherd (1005) probably from the same vessel dating to the 1760s to early 1770s (Plate 7: 7).

1007, Base-handle sherd from small jug, yellow ochre colour, moulded leaf decoration, possibly 'cauliflower ware' (pers. comm. David Barker) dating to 1760s (Plate 7: 6).

1007, Flange-rim bowl with foot-ring base, possibly a slops bowl. Under-glaze yellow and green colour, 'melon ware' rouletted, dating to 1760s. Rim diameter 150mm, base diameter 70mm (Plate 7: 5).

1007 and 1008, Sauceboat with moulded decoration of cattle and foliage, known as 'landskip' in the 18th century (pers. comm. David Barker), bright green colour, dating to the 1760s to early 1770s (Plate 7: 8).

1007, Complete base from sauceboat identical to the above (Plate 7: 9).

1007, 'Landskip' handle sherd and body sherd, probably from one of the above sauceboats (Plate 7: 9).

1008, 'Landskip' rim sherd, rim sherd, bright green colour, probably from one of the above sauceboats.

Pearlware

1007, Saucer with fuzzy, indistinct blue painted chinoiserie decoration on the interior 1780–1810 (Plate 11: 22).

1007, Tea bowl rim-body sherd with blue printed decoration 1800–10 (Plate 10: 19).

1008, Tea bowl blue printed chinoiserie decoration, faults in the application of the transfer print c 1800–1810 (Plate 10: 20).

1008, Tea bowl blue printed chinoiserie decoration, badly applied transfer print, which was clearly too large for the tea bowl c 1800–10 (Plate 10: 21).

1008, Saucer, blue painted decoration on the interior base 1780–1810 (Plate 11: 23).

1008, Saucer, blue printed chinoiserie decoration. 1790–1810 (Plate 11: 24).

1008, Saucer orientalising blue floral printed decoration c 1810–20 (Plate 11: 25).

1008, Fluted bowl with scalloped or wavy rim, printed blue chinoiserie decoration c 1800 (Plate 11: 24).

1009, Tea bowl base, traces of blue painted decoration on interior and exterior 1780–1810.

5032, Saucer, blue printed decoration, wavy or scalloped edge c 1800–10 (Plate 11: 26).

5037, Jug handle, blue printed decoration, 1820s–30s (Plate 11: 27).

Pearlware was only found within the fills of the moat and mainly within the fills of section F100.

Flowerpot

Two flowerpot rims were found in 1007 and 1008 and a complete base in 1007. All were from small diameter pots. The base sherd had a central perforation and also three regularly spaced circular perforations about 7mm above the base. Similarly perforated flowerpots, although of a much larger size were found as wasters at Floodgate Street Birmingham, in a late 18th-century context (Rátkai 2002b).

Industrial Vessels

Two crucible fragments were found in 1007 and a further seven fragments in 1003. There were four rim sherds in 1003. One from a thick-walled vessel with a rim with an internal bevel and may be late medieval or early post-medieval in date. Two plain rim sherds, possibly from the same vessel, were from a thin-walled upright form, with a diameter of c 160mm. This form could also be late medieval or early post-medieval in date. The fourth rim sherd, also thin-walled, had a triangular, pulled pouring lip and could be of 15th- or 16th-century date. The sherd may possibly be from the same vessel or vessels represented by the upright rims. On the internal surface of the pouring lip was a green copper or copper alloy residue. The thin walled crucibles were all in the same fabric which appeared to be a coarsely sandy buff bodied ware, quite similar to the buff gritty ware sherd from 1004. The bevelled rim sherd was in a harder, smoother, denser fabric, although one was probably originally buff in colour.

The crucible sherds bear no relation to the 18th-century crucibles found at Park Street Birmingham (Nicholas 2003) and it seems safe to assume that they are certainly no later than the 17th century. The pulled lip is described as dating to the 15th century and later by Bayley (1992, 5). Although no base sherds survive from the crucibles it

seems most likely that the crucibles from the Great Hall were of the straight-sided flat bottomed type introduced in the 14th century (*ibid*, fig. 5). The likely date range for these crucible fragments would therefore seem to lie in the 15th to 17th centuries. Perhaps their use was associated with the construction of the hall in the 16th century.

Discussion

The fill of moat section F100 contains pottery which for the most part seems unlikely to date before *c* 1725. A single buff gritty ware sherd and a glazed jug sherd both from 1002, a late fill of the moat, date to the medieval period. Sherds from the 15th or 16th century were found in 1007

	Quantification by sherd count			Quantification by min. rim count			Quantification by min. base count		
Fabric/Ware	**F100**	**F526**	*All Moat*	**F100**	**F526**	*All Moat*	**F100**	**F526**	**All Moat**
Medieval	0.65%	0.00%	*0.48%*	0.00%	0.00%	*0.00%*	0.00%	0.00%	*0.00%*
Blackware	4.95%	4.38%	*4.80%*	2.65%	3.57%	*2.90%*	5.04%	2.94%	*4.62%*
Brown salt-glazed stoneware	2.80%	3.13%	*2.88%*	5.30%	5.36%	*5.31%*	4.32%	0.00%	*3.47%*
Creamware	9.89%	15.00%	*11.20%*	13.91%	14.29%	*14.01%*	7.91%	23.53%	*10.98%*
Coarseware	15.27%	48.75%	*23.84%*	11.92%	42.86%	*20.29%*	16.55%	35.29%	*20.23%*
Coarseware/ blackware	0.43%	0.00%	*0.32%*	0.00%	0.00%	*0.00%*	1.44%	0.00%	*1.16%*
Coarseware/ Midlands Purple ware	0.00%	5.63%	*1.44%*	0.00%	3.57%	*0.97%*	0.00%	5.88%	*1.16%*
Industrial slipware	0.22%	0.00%	*0.16%*	0.66%	0.00%	*0.48%*	0.00%	0.00%	*0.00%*
Mottled ware	3.01%	1.25%	*2.56%*	1.32%	1.79%	*1.45%*	4.32%	2.94%	*4.05%*
Pearlware	1.94%	1.25%	*1.76%*	3.31%	1.79%	*2.90%*	2.16%	2.94%	*2.31%*
Porcelain	2.37%	0.63%	*1.92%*	2.65%	0.00%	*1.93%*	5.04%	0.00%	*4.05%*
Refined body wares	0.22%	0.00%	*0.16%*	0.66%	0.00%	*0.48%*	0.00%	0.00%	*0.00%*
Agate ware	0.22%	0.00%	*0.16%*	0.66%	0.00%	*0.48%*	0.72%	0.00%	*0.58%*
Slip-coated ware	23.87%	8.75%	*20.00%*	19.21%	7.14%	*15.94%*	24.46%	17.65%	*23.12%*
Slipware (combed)	1.29%	0.00%	*0.96%*	0.66%	0.00%	*0.48%*	0.72%	0.00%	*0.58%*
Slipware (feathered)	1.29%	0.00%	*0.96%*	0.66%	0.00%	*0.48%*	0.00%	0.00%	*0.00%*
Slipware (three-colour)	0.00%	0.63%	*0.16%*	0.00%	1.79%	*0.48%*	0.00%	0.00%	*0.00%*
Slipware (trailed)	0.22%	0.00%	*0.16%*	0.66%	0.00%	*0.48%*	0.00%	0.00%	*0.00%*
Stoneware	0.22%	0.00%	*0.16%*	0.66%	0.00%	*0.48%*	0.72%	0.00%	*0.58%*
Tin-glazed earthenware	1.29%	1.25%	*1.28%*	1.99%	1.79%	*1.93%*	0.72%	2.94%	*1.16%*
Westerwald stoneware	1.08%	0.63%	*0.96%*	1.32%	1.79%	*1.45%*	1.44%	0.00%	*1.16%*
White salt-glazed stoneware	25.60%	6.88%	*20.80%*	27.15%	12.50%	*23.19%*	23.74%	5.88%	*20.23%*
Yellow ware	0.22%	1.88%	*0.64%*	0.00%	1.79%	*0.48%*	0.00%	0.00%	*0.00%*
Miscellaneous	0.22%	0.00%	*0.16%*	0.00%	0.00%	*0.00%*	0.00%	0.00%	*0.00%*
Flowerpot	0.65%	0.00%	*0.48%*	1.32%	0.00%	*0.97%*	0.72%	0.00%	*0.58%*
Crucible	2.15%	0.00%	*1.60%*	3.31%	0.00%	*2.42%*	0.00%	0.00%	*0.00%*
Total	100.00%	100.00%	*100.00%*	100.00%	100.00%	*100.00%*	100.00%	100.00%	*100.00%*

TABLE 2 QUANTIFICATION OF POTTERY FROM F100 AND F526

and 1002. A yellow ware sherd from 1003, another late fill, may date to the 17th century. Feathered, combed and trailed slipware sherds from the fills could conceivably date to the late 17th century but these wares were current through to the mid-18th century. Overall, therefore, there is nothing to suggest that there was a gradual accumulation or a dump of material before the 18th century. This suggests that the moat was kept clean throughout the 16th and 17th centuries. How this ties in with the moat being at some stage a garden feature and with the possibility of an earlier hall on the site is difficult to say. Fills 1019 and 1021 of feature F103 (the section cut through the southern side of the moat during evaluation) and 1012 an evaluation layer sealing wall F102 seem to be 18th century in date, although they contained little pottery. The evaluation pottery did not contain any formal dining wares or tea wares but there was an almost complete 'shining black' mug (Fig. 22: 11) from 1019. Only feature F105 in Trench 5 appears to have a mid- to late 17th-century fill composed of three sherds comprising a blackware jug, a coarseware (fabric cwmp) jar and an indeterminate yellow ware hollow ware. The paucity of pottery dating to the 16th and 17th centuries from the moat fills and the western section of the main building provides little help in understanding the early history of the site.

The dominant wares in the moat fills in Trench 6 and the main excavation were white salt-glazed stoneware, slip-coated ware, coarseware and creamware (see Tables 2, 3 and 4). The latest ware was pearlware which dated to c 1790–1810 with the exception of a saucer from 1008 which dated to c 1810–1820 and may therefore be intrusive. As pearlware was present in fills 1007, 1008 and 1009 it seems reasonable to assume that the fills represent one contemporaneous dump.

The fills of F100 are dominated by formal dining wares and tea wares (see Table 5). A greater number of the tea wares are Chinese porcelain which date to before the Commutation Act of 1784 when tea drinking was an expensive, ritualised, high-status activity. The extremely small size of the tortoiseshell ware teapot reinforces the expensive nature of tea in the middle years of the 18th century, before the act drastically reduced taxes on tea and hence made it more accessible to the public at large. The dining wares also bear out the apparent high status of the assemblage. In addition to several white salt-glazed and creamware plates, there were serving dishes and sauceboats all of which suggest formal dining on a reasonably grand scale. The creamware dining wares date from the 1750s through to the 1770s and although the white salt-glazed stonewares could be as early as the 1720s they were made into the fourth quarter of the 18th century and may have been in contemporary use with the creamwares at the Great Hall.

The remaining pottery from F100 fell into several groups. At one step down from the formal dining wares, were wares which could be classed as 'ordinary' table wares such as dishes, bowls, mugs, platters and jugs, ie, vessels for the consumption or serving of food in an informal setting.

Some vessel types such as the tin-glazed earthenwares are difficult to categorise and have been classed as table/dining wares. Clearly an attempt at categorising the function of vessels is an imperfect science since some wares which began life as high status may become 'demoted' as fashions change and may end their life amongst the servants.

Away from the consumption of food and drink the next category of wares has been termed utilitarian or kitchen wares. The utilitarian wares consist of bowls, pancheons, pans and large storage jars. The primary use of these vessels is the preparation and storage of food but it is possible that they served other uses apart from culinary. A small sub-category has been termed kitchen wares. These comprise blackware and mottled ware hollow wares of uncertain function. Also included in this category as kitchen/table wares are brown salt-glazed stoneware flange rim dishes and bowls and slip-coated ware jars, bowls and handled bowls.

Moat section F100 also contained several chamber pots, classed as sanitary wares, three in Westerwald stoneware but with other examples in white salt-glazed stoneware and creamware. There were also two possible chamber pots in black ware and slip-coated ware. The final two function categories, only found in F100, were garden furniture and industrial vessels.

The fills of moat section F526 had a rather different make-up from those of F100 (see Table 2). Although the same four wares, creamware, coarseware, white salt-glazed stoneware and slip-coated ware were dominant, their relative proportions were not the same. Coarseware was by far the most frequent, with smaller amounts of white salt-glazed stoneware and slip-coated ware. The latest pottery within the fills was pearlware dating to 1800–10 and to the 1820s–30s. The balance of probabilities is that the material within this area of the moat was dumped at more or less the same time as that found in F100. Again there was little pottery which need pre-date c 1725, the exceptions being two yellow ware vessels from 5037 and possibly a three colour moulded slipware platter from 5031 although this could be as late as the mid-18th century.

The fills of features F503, F509, F512 and F530 seemed to date to the second half of the 18th century. Feature F536 contained a single combed slipware sherd dating to the late 17th or early 18th centuries. Context 5047 contained only coarseware sherds including two jars (eg, Fig. 23: 22) which were very similar to jars found in Civil War deposits at Dudley Castle (Rátkai 1987). Two further features F540 and F541 each contained a coarseware sherd of indeterminate date. Thus a similar picture emerges, as seen above, of very little evidence for earlier post-medieval activity on the site in the western section of the building and most fills, although the small group of pottery from the eastern section does appear to have a greater proportion of earlier material.

The amount of medieval pottery was greatest in the eastern section of the main building, followed by that from Trench

Fabric/ware	dining ware	dining ware serving	garden	industrial	kitchen storage	kitchen ware	kitchen/table ware	sanitary	sanitary?	table ware	table ware ?serving	table ware drv	table ware jug	table/dining ware	teaware	teaware teapot	utilitarian	utilitarian bowl	utilitarian hw	utilitarian jar	utilitarian jug	utilitarian large bowl	utilitarian pan	unknown	Total
Medieval																								3	3
Blackware							10	3				7	4			2				3			1		30
Brown salt-glazed stoneware							9			2		6									1				18
Creamware	59	7						1																	67
Coarseware				2								1					17	19	36			63	11		149
Coarseware/blackware																	1						1		2
Coarseware/Midlands purple ware																	2		6				1		9
Industrial slipware							1																		1
Mottled ware							7					9													16
Pearlware	2														9										11
Porcelain	2														10										12
Refined body ware																1									1
Agate ware										1															1
Slip-coated ware					7		99		2	6		11													125
Slipware (combed)											6														6
Slipware (feathered)											6														6
Slipware (three-colour)											1														1
Slipware (trailed)											1														1
Stoneware									1																1
Tin-glazed earthenware					2									6											8
Creamware (tortoiseshell)	3																								3
Westerwald stoneware								6																	6
White salt-glazed stoneware	66	6					3	5		3		7		40											130
Yellow ware						2						2													4
Miscellaneous																								1	1
Flowerpot			3																						3
Crucible				10																					10
Total	132	13	3	12	9	2	129	15	3	12	14	43	4	46	19	3	20	19	42	3	1	63	14	4	625

TABLE 3 VESSEL FUNCTION BY SHERD COUNT (F100 AND F526)

Fabric/ware	dining ware	dining ware serving	garden	industrial	kitchen storage	kitchen/table ware	sanitary	sanitary?	table ware	table ware ?serving	table ware drv	table ware jug	table/dining ware	teaware	teaware teapot	utilitarian	utilitarian bowl	utilitarian hw	utilitarian jar	utilitarian jug	utilitarian large bowl	utilitarian pan	Total
Blackware							1				3	1							1				6
Brown salt-glazed stoneware						5			2		3									1			11
Creamware	23	4					1																28
Creamware (tortoiseshell ware)	1																						1
Coarseware				1												1	8	3			25	4	42
Coarseware/Midlands purple ware																		2					2
Industrial slipware						1																	1
Mottled ware						1					2												3
Pearlware	1													5									6
Porcelain														4									4
Refined body ware									1														1
Agate ware															1								1
Slip-coated ware					5	19		2	6		1												33
Slipware (combed)										1													1
Slipware (feathered)										1													1
Slipware (three-colour)										1													1
Slipware (trailed)										1													1
Stoneware											1												1
Tin-glazed earthenware					1								3										4
Westerwald stoneware							3																3
White salt-glazed stoneware	31	5					4	1	2		2		3										48
Yellow ware											1												1
Flowerpot			2																				2
Crucible				5																			5
Total	56	9	2	6	6	26	9	3	11	4	13	1	6	9	1	1	8	5	1	1	25	4	207

TABLE 4 VESSEL FUNCTION BY MINIMUM RIM COUNT (F100 AND F526)

Function	By minimum rim count			By minimum base count		
	F100	F526	Total	F100	F526	Total
utilitarian	1		1	3		3
utilitarian bowl	5	3	8	4	4	8
utilitarian hw		5	5	7	5	12
utilitarian jar		1	1			
utilitarian jug	1		1	1		1
utilitarian large bowl	10	15	25	7	5	12
utilitarian pan	1	3	4	3		3
kitchen storage	5	1	6	1		1
kitchen ware						
kitchen/table ware	19	7	26	34	6	40
table ware	11		11	2		2
table ware ?serving	3	1	4	1		1
table ware drv	12	1	13	19	2	21
table ware jug		1	1			
table/dining ware	4	2	6	1	1	2
dining ware	47	8	55	40	6	46
dining ware		1	1		1	1
dining ware serving	6	3	9	3	3	6
teaware	9	1	10	10	1	11
sanitary	8	1	9	2		2
sanitary?	1	2	3			
garden	2		2	1		1
industrial	6		6			
Total	**151**	**56**	**207**	**139**	**34**	**173**

TABLE 5 COMPARISON OF VESSEL FUNCTION BETWEEN MOAT SECTIONS F100 AND F526

6. The fill of F514, despite being a later feature, contained only medieval pottery as did F502 and layers 5001 and 5015. Layer 5005 and features F504 and F511 contained pottery of 15th- or 16th-century date and F538 of 16th-century date. It seems most likely that this small amount of pottery was associated with the 16th-century hall.

The functional composition of the pottery from moat section F526 was dominated by utilitarian wares with vessels for food consumption much less well represented (see Table 5). However, amongst the latter class were formal dining wares, represented primarily in creamware, although there was one oval serving dish in white salt-glazed stoneware.

The differences between the two moat fills presumably reflect the areas of the Great Hall from which the pottery derived. One might therefore expect the kitchen to have been the source for the pottery from F100 where not only kitchen and utilitarian wares would have been found but also formal dining wares stored. Further to the west in the main excavation area other activities such as brewing, preserving, laundering and dairying may have been found, with a concomitant increase in large coarse earthenware forms. However, the presence of some formal dining wares in this area somewhat confuses the picture. It is possible that these wares have been disturbed and redeposited with the utilitarian wares but this is certainly not provable.

The pottery from F100 indicates high status occupation in the 18th century. The high incidence of white salt-glazed stoneware is similar to the assemblage from St Mary's Grove, Stafford (Kershaw 1987), although there were no creamwares or pearlwares. Kershaw (ibid) describes the St Mary's Grove assemblage as coming from a prosperous, middle to high status household, and its deposition c 1775 may represent a house-clearance. Clearly the tea wares and creamware from F100 indicate a rather later deposition date, probably in the early years of the 19th century. The pottery from F526 is most closely paralleled by material from a pit group to the east of Sir Martin Noel's Almshouses, Mill Street, Stafford (Barker and Holland 1986), although in the latter deposit there was a much greater amount of pearlware. The suggested deposition date for this pit group is c 1800–1810. Thus it seems clear that both groups of pottery within the Great Hall Moat were deposited in the early 19th century but contained a considerable amount of material which was 30–50 years earlier than this.

There are also close similarities between the pottery recovered from two 'industrial' tanks at Park Street, Birmingham (Barker and Rátkai 2009) and the Great

Hall moat fills. In the Park Street tanks, creamware was the dominant refined ware followed by white salt-glazed stoneware. Dining and tea wares were well represented although items such as sauceboats were not represented. The deposition of the tank fills occurred towards the end of the 18th century or possibly early 19th century and may well have been a clearance marking the downgrading of the area.

The Turton family were prosperous ironmongers who lived at the hall from at least 1702. Joseph Turton's (d. 1709) grandson (d. 1764) and great grandson (d. 1806) were respectively a doctor and Physician in Ordinary to the King and the Prince of Wales and would have been ideal candidates for ownership of the formal dining wares. The evidence is equivocal, however, for there is some evidence that the Turton family moved out of the hall shortly after 1735 (Shaw above). If the Turtons moved out of the hall at about this date it is too early for most of the formal dining wares apart, possibly, from the white salt-glazed stonewares, to have belonged to them. Unfortunately this period of the history of the hall and its premises is far from clear, if not contradictory, from the surviving documentation. The exact date of the establishment of a japannery (Shaw above) is uncertain and accordingly the question of who owned the formal dining wares and tea wares cannot be answered at the moment. The pottery speaks of high status occupancy and, if the Turtons were long since gone, it would be necessary to posit the existence of a second unknown and unrecorded wealthy family living there or to suggest that the owners of the japanning factory were of sufficient status to have owned the wares (they are likely to have lived on the premises also).

The first undeniable record of japanners at the Old Hall is dated to 1783 (Shaw above). This and documentary references to the ruinous state of hall towards the end of the 18th century would suggest that further accumulation of fine dining wares must have ceased by the 1780s. Unfortunately, this is too early for the various pearlware vessels, which are unlikely to predate 1790. The pearlwares in moat section F100 seem to date the deposition of the earlier dining and tea wares (see above), all of which together appear to be a clearance dump, the pottery having presumably been left by 'pre-japanning' residents on their departure. At what point could such a clearance be feasible?

In the early 19th century, the Ryton brothers, who were japanners by trade, took possession of the hall, which they used for both *residential* and business purposes. Whether some of the pearlware tea wares, some of rather inferior quality, actually belonged to the Rytons is difficult to say. There was certainly virtually no other pottery consistent with their occupation of the building. It seems likely that the Rytons cleared the hall either on taking up residence or possibly on the death of Obadiah Ryton in 1810, which may have resulted in some reorganisation of the hall. Both events could account for the clearance, of pottery in moat section F100, at least. As the moat was partially open in

1839 but appears to have been filled in by *c* 1842, in theory, there was enough time for their debris to accumulate, and, as japanners, one might have expected a pottery group of somewhat less grand aspect to represent their occupation of the hall. This evidence is not present, which suggests that for the most part the pottery found within the moat is unconnected with the Rytons.

The author would like to thank David Barker for his helpful comments on the later 18th-century ceramics.

BOTTLES AND OTHER GLASSWARE *Robert Bracken*

A total of 499 fragments from wine bottles, 8 fragments from other bottles, 3 fragments from a drinking vessel, 18 fragments of window glass, and 22 fragments from a large spherical vessel were recovered. The weight of the assemblage was 32.75 kg. The assemblage was quantified by count and weight and was examined macroscopically for the purposes of this report. There was a low to medium degree of fragmentation with several near complete items being noted among the assemblage.

Wine Bottles

The earliest wine bottles recovered from the site were of 17th-century date, and came from a sondage through the moat that was carried out during the excavation (5029). Three partial base and body fragments of mid-green shaft-and-globe wine bottles were recovered from this sondage. The distinctly bulbous bodies, shallow depth and small diameter of the kick-up dates these bottles to 1630–70 (Dumbrell 1983, 29). Other 17th-century bottles recovered from the site included a neck fragment from a green onion wine bottle (1007), with the cork still *in situ*. The distinctly short neck, broad shoulder and the position of the string ring around the rim of the bottle dates this piece to 1660–70 (*ibid* 29). A base fragment of a light green onion bottle (1007) was also of late 17th-century date, with the depth and crude design of the kick-up dating it to between 1680 and 1729 (Morgan 1976, 30).

The most complete example from the entire assemblage (only a fragment from the shoulder and body is missing) is a 17th-century olive green shaft-and-globe wine bottle (Plate 12). The angular shoulder, the shape of the neck, which is slightly shorter than earlier examples, and the position of the collar date this bottle to 1660–70. A very similar example, and of similar date, is a sealed bottle of the Crown Tavern in Oxford (Dumbrell 1983, 54, fig. 23).

Early 18th-century wine bottles are represented by two near complete base fragments (5032) and a mid-green neck fragment (1003) from green onion wine bottles. The wide bases and shallow kick-ups date these fragments to 1700–1710 (Dumbrell 1983 30). These fragments are the only onion wine bottles recovered from the site. The only other early 18th-century glass recovered was a dark green base fragment (1007) of a wine bottle, which was recovered from the moat during the 2002 evaluation. This bottle, which had straighter sides than that of the earlier

PLATE 12 NEAR COMPLETE WINE BOTTLE

shaft-and-globe and onion wine bottles, was identified as an example of a squat cylinder bottle dating to 1720–40 (Cosbert 2001).

Six fragments (1008) of a mid-18th-century green glass squat cylinder wine bottle were also recovered from the moat. The very deep kick-up dates this bottle to 1740–50 (Dumbrell 1983, 30). A mid-green base fragment (1007) of a squat cylindrical wine bottle, is of similar appearance, and probably of similar date but is too fragmentary to date precisely. Amongst the other mid-18th-century bottles was a complete neck and a partial shoulder fragment of a light green cylindrical wine bottle (1005). The attitude of the shoulder, parallel neck and position of the string-ring dates this bottle to 1740–60. A mid-18th-century base fragment of a green upright squat cylindrical wine bottle was also recovered from context 1008. The cone-shaped kick-up dates this bottle to 1750–60 (Morgan 1976, 25). A base fragment from a mid-green squat or cylindrical wine bottle was tentatively dated to between 1740–50 after comparison with more complete examples (Dumbrell 1983, 31), whilst a neck and lip fragment of a dark green wine bottle (5032) was dated to between 1750 and 1780. This fragment has a long, straight neck and an applied lip, which has been tooled smooth and is situated quite close to the top of the neck (Morgan 1976, 5).

A neck of a light brown cylindrical wine bottle (1007) was also recovered; the long neck and ample string ring suggests that this bottle dates to 1750–80 (Morgan, 1976, 29).

Several large, concave, and quite thick fragments of 'sea green' glass, including a base and neck fragment of the same vessel, were recovered during the 2002 excavation (5031, 5033). A number of the fragments were conjoining, and sufficient reconstruction was possible to allow identification of the vessel as a demijohn. A demijohn is a large glass vessel, holding between five and eight gallons (c 23–36 litres), used for transport or storage of wines and spirits in the 18th and early 19th century. The vessels were often covered with a protective layer of raffia, osier or wicker to help cushion them in transit. The demijohn was first used on a large scale in the 18th century, and remained in use until the early 19th century. Each vessel was free blown and hand finished. The vessel recovered from the site had a large bulbous protrusion, which had been applied after the vessel was blown, on the bottom of the base sherd. The function of this protrusion is unclear, but it is possible that it was designed to be used as a handle to steady the vessel when its contents were being poured. The position of the string-ring on the neck of this vessel suggests that this vessel may date from the mid-18th century.

The most interesting mid-18th-century bottle was a base from an octagonal olive-green wine bottle (1008), dating to 1740–60 (Dumbrell 1983, 87). This fragment is an example of mid-18th-century experimentation in English glass production. Shortly after production of the first true cylindrical bottles began, these distinctive and appealing octagonal bottles began to be produced. A gather of glass was blown into a one-piece mould, which tapered slightly at one end to permit removal upon cooling, giving the characteristic taper at the base of the bottle. The pontil rod was attached to the base of the bottle and the neck and the lip finished in the usual way. This process was known as dip-moulding, and represented a dramatic technological step for glass-makers, enabling bottles to be produced in a predetermined size or shape.

Forty-four fragments were dated to the later part of the 18th century. Two shoulder fragments of green cylindrical wine bottles (1007) can be tentatively dated to between 1750 and 1790 (Dumbrell 1983, 31), whilst a partial base fragment (1007) and a shoulder fragment from a cylindrical bottle (5032) could both be dated with reasonable certainty to between 1750–1800.

Some of the later 18th-century fragments were closely dated to 1760–70. This close dating was partly due to the fact that many bottles of this date were manufactured in dark green glass, which was darker than that used for many of the other bottles in the assemblage (Dumbrell 1983, 30). Two of these bases, however, (1007, 1008) were from light brown glass wine bottles, which showed the same physical characteristics as the green glass bottles. The pieces, which were all base fragments from upright cylindrical wine bottles (1007 x 3, 1008 x 2, 5032 x 3,

9019 x 1) had deep and acute kick-ups and slightly sagged bases - both characteristic of bottles of this date (Dumbrell 1983, 31). Two further dark green wine bottle fragments were recovered from an un-stratified area of the site, a neck fragment with a lip/collar dating to 1770–1780 and a near complete base fragment with a full and deep kick up of the same date (Morgan 1976, 25).

Another set of closely datable late 18th-century bottles were dated to 1770–80. Most of these fragments were recovered during the 2002 excavation. This included a complete neck, a complete base and three body fragments from brown glass cylindrical wine bottles (5032), as well as six base fragments from dark green cylinder bottle bases (5039), a partial base from a light green cylindrical wine bottle (5032) and a body fragment from a mid-green cylindrical wine bottle (5029). An unstratified base and neck were also recovered. This neck fragment, in common with the complete neck from context 5032, was dated by the position of the lip and collar on the neck (Morgan 1976, 25). The bases displayed the same sagged base and deep kick-up as the slightly earlier bottles discussed in the previous paragraph, but the kick-up was much wider, leading to the 1770–80 dating of this group (ibid; Dumbrell 1983, 31).

Other closely datable later 18th-century fragments included a complete neck and upper shoulder, and a partial neck and shoulder. The complete neck and upper shoulder was from an amber-coloured cylindrical wine bottle (5032). This vessel had very square shoulders, and was manufactured from good quality glass. The position of the string ring dates this fragment to 1770–80 (Dumbrell 1983, 31). The partial neck and shoulder (1008) came from a light green cylindrical wine bottle. The longish neck, the appearance of the rim, and the general fine quality of the glass dates this fragment to 1790–1800 (Dumbrell 1983, 31).

A further ten fragments could be broadly dated to the late 18th century. Four dark green body fragments from a cylindrical wine bottle (5032) were dated to 1760–1800 (Dumbrell 1983, 31), and a shoulder and body fragment from a light brown cylindrical wine bottle was dated to 1770–1800 due to the attitude of the shoulder in relation to

the body (ibid, 31). Another base and body fragment from a light green cylindrical wine bottle (5032) had a slightly sagged base and a high, wide kick-up with no pontil scar. This fragment was dated to 1780–1800 (Morgan 1976, 25), as was a complete neck and partial shoulder fragment of a light green cylindrical wine bottle (5032). This fragment was dated by its long neck and the shape of the lip (ibid, 24). The neck from a green cylindrical bottle (9019) was dated by its length and the position of the string ring to 1780–90. Three olive green base fragments from context 5031 were also identified as being of the same date, due to the shape and height of the kick-ups (ibid, 24).

The most complete mid-18th-century bottle was also the only sealed wine bottle to be recovered from the site (5031). This was a brown glass mallet type wine bottle (Dumbrell 1983, 82 plate 24), which has a seal situated just below the bottle shoulder. The practice of placing a glass seal on the body of a bottle became more common from the mid-17th century onwards, and although the earliest seals were made for wealthy private individuals, vintners soon also adopted the practice, both for the prestige of having an identifiable bottle, and to stop rivals from re-using their bottles. The seal on this bottle has the initials WH stamped in a roundel on the shoulder of the vessel and above the initials stands a left facing cockerel with a small star on each side. An inn by the name of the Cock Inn stood less than half a mile away in nearby Berry Street and records held in Wolverhampton's archives state that a William Hollyer was innkeeper of the Cock Inn in the later 18th century (Wolv ALS D-JSR/ 44/ 60). It seems possible that this bottle could have been one of William Hollyer's bottles, and could have been discarded in the moat after it was broken.

Only five pieces of 19th-century wine bottle glass could definitely be identified. Possibly the earliest of these was the base of a very upright green glass wine bottle (9019). This was identified by its base and shallow kick-up as dating to 1800–10 (Dumbrell 1983, 32). Another piece of early 19th-century date was a near-complete brown glass cylindrical bottle base (5039). The depth and width of the kick-up and the overall quality of the glass dates this fragment to 1810–20 (Dumbrell 1983, 32).

Context	Number of Fragments	Type of Fragment	Colour of Glass	Comments
5018	1	base	dark green	Too fragmentary to date
5029	8	body	mid green	Too fragmentary to date, one fragment has heat/ fire damage
5031	5	body	dark green	Too fragmentary to date
5032	3	body	1 x dark green, 1 x brown	Too fragmentary to date
5033	3	body	dark green	Too fragmentary to date
5039	7	6 x body, 1 x base	4 x mid green, 3 x brown	Too fragmentary to date
North end of Building	1	Body	dark green	Too fragmentary to date
U/S	87	27 x base, 60 x body	63 x dark green, 24 x brown	Too fragmentary to date

TABLE 6 UNDATABLE GLASS FRAGMENTS

The sondage through the moat (5029) produced two near-complete base fragments from light green cylindrical wine bottles. The moulded seams on these bottles, combined with the absence of a pontil scar date these two fragments to the early 19th century.

Later 19th-century wine bottle glass was represented by a complete base of a light green cylindrical wine bottle. The combination of a shallow, wide, evenly contoured kick-up, with no pontil scar, together with the evenly shaped base dates this bottle to 1820–90 (Morgan 1976, 25). This bottle appears to have been moulded rather than free blown.

Undateable Wine Bottle Glass

Some other wine bottle fragments were either too small and fragmentary or damaged to be conclusively dated, although the quality of these fragments and their location on the site suggest that they are likely to be of the same date as the more complete examples described above. The distribution of these fragments is shown in Table 6.

Other Bottle Glass

Twenty-seven fragments of other glass bottles were also recovered from the site. The most complete of these vessels was a phial (1008), which was intact, despite having been deposited in the moat. A near complete phial (1007) and three fragments from a third vessel were also recovered from the moat, and the similarity between all three vessels suggests that they are of the same date. Phials were in common use from the late 18th century through to the early 20th century and would have contained a variety of oils and liniments. The general crudeness and evidence of pontil scars on these examples would suggest a late 18th-century date of manufacture.

Beer bottles were represented by eleven body fragments (9019) from dark green vessels. These fragments are probably of late 19th- to early 20th-century date, as is a body fragment from a brown beer bottle (1011). The good quality glass from which this vessel is made suggests a late 19th- to early 20th-century date of manufacture.

One fragment of Opaline or Milk, straight sided bottle glass (5013) was recovered. Opaline bottles are opaque and were produced to contain medicines. These bottles were in common use throughout the late 19th and early 20th century.

A body fragment of a clear glass mineral water bottle was also recovered (5021). This vessel is part of a Codd or Hamilton type bottle of late 19th- to early 20th-century manufacture. The fragment is embossed with the words PATENT LIVERPOOL.

A rim fragment from another clear glass bottle (1007) is too fragmentary for the form to be accurately identified; the quality of glass however suggests a late 19th- to early 20th-century date of manufacture.

Drinking Glasses

Three fragments of an ornate clear drinking glass recovered from 5032, consisting of part bowl, stem and foot. The bowl is a 'bucket' shape with an applied twisted rope encircling its base, the knop, which is part of the stem, is a segmented hollow ball overlying a protruding collar which runs down to the conical foot. This glass bears strong similarities with other 'rummer' type glasses. The name 'rummer' perhaps derives from German *roemer*, but its association with rum, the drink of the Navy, seems more plausible. Towards the end of the 18th century and into the 19th century a hot toddy of rum, water, spices and sugar would be drunk from these glasses. The drinking glass recovered is, therefore, contemporary with much of the bottle assemblage recovered from the same context.

Two small, thin and concave fragments from a clear drinking glass were also recovered (1007). The fragments are too incomplete to suggest a date for the vessel. Four other undateable drinking glass fragments were also recovered. One was a very small, concave fragment of light purple glass (5000) and the other fragments were slightly concave spherical fragments of clear glass (U/S).

Etched Window Glass

Three conjoining fragments of a corner of a clear window pane were recovered from the moat (5032). These fragments were etched with a verse. The verse reads:

> *'the struggle for Knowledge*
> *hath a pleasure in it, like that*
> *of wrestling with a fine Woman'*

This verse, attributed to the Marquess of Halifax, is from a bibliography of erotica written by Henry Spencer Ashbee, a Victorian pornographer who wrote under the pseudonym of Pisanus Fraxi (Ashbee 1969). Ashbee was a silk mercer, and also exported machinery to Europe; he gave the outward appearance of a respectable businessman, but he also had a secret passion for pornography, and he was responsible for compiling a monumental systematic bibliography of erotica, the first three volumes of which appeared in 1887 (Gibson 2002).

The style of the lettering used for the verse is similar to that used in the later 19th and early 20th century, and it appears to have been etched into the glass as a piece of graffiti.

Other Window Glass

A total of 18 clear window glass fragments were recovered from the site, (9017 x 5, 5008 x 2, 5032 x 3, 5031 x 2, 5029 x 2, 1007 x 2). Two fragments of late 20th-century grid-wired safety glass were also recovered from the mixed layer over F524. All fragments, with the exception of the two fragments from F524, are of a fair quality, suggesting a date of manufacture, late 19th to mid-20th century. The three fragments from context 5032 are etched with graffiti, as noted above.

Other Glass

Other glass recovered from the site consisted of five, slightly concave, clear glass fragments from a large round vessel (5032). The small size of the fragments means that the exact use or age of the vessel could not be determined.

A modern blue glass marble was also recovered (8009), as was a small fragment of glass slag, which was recovered from an unstratified context.

Discussion

The Old Hall Street assemblage shows the development of bottle forms from the late 17th century through to the late 19th century. Glass bottles were originally hand blown and were relatively expensive. Wealthy households would have had their own bottles, which they sent to wine merchants for refilling. These bottles often had the owner's stamp on the body, a practice that was soon copied by vintners and even individual taverns, as seen in the only stamped bottle recovered from the assemblage. Later advances in technology made glass much easier and cheaper to produce, and it became a more disposable commodity.

The glass assemblage was dominated by wine bottles, and seems to have been deposited on the site over a period of about 200 years. The earliest glass recovered from the site is of 17th-century date; this material was recovered from moat fills (1007, 5029), which also contained pottery of the same date (Rátkai, above). Together, the pottery and glass seem to represent the first use of the moat for the dumping of refuse; it having previously been kept clean.

Unlike the glass assemblages from other sites in the region, such as Park Street and Edgbaston Street, Birmingham (Orton and Rátkai, 2009), the assemblage from the earlier phases of the site seem to contain only wine bottle glass, which was presumably discarded by the household. A dump that was accessible to all at this time should have produced a much wider range of vessel types, including medicine and food or sauce bottles, as is the case with the Park Street and Edgbaston Street assemblages, whereas this assemblage is much more like the bottle assemblages from the Oxford taverns, discussed at length by Leeds (1949) and is exclusively made up of wine bottles, and a few drinking vessel fragments.

The change of use of the Great Hall from a residential to a commercial property in the mid-18th century (Shaw, above) does not seem to be accompanied by a great change in the types of glass recovered from the site. Wine bottles still dominate the assemblage after the first known commercial use of the Great Hall in 1745, and continue to do so after the site was given over to japanning in the 1770s, although the quantities of wine bottles recovered from the site decline after this date, with only 44 fragments of later 18th-century wine bottle glass, and five fragments of 19th-century wine bottle glass being recovered. The change of use of the site to a japanning factory also sees the first other types of glass appearing on the site, including phials, beer bottles, a mineral water bottle, and a fragment of medicine bottle, all of which could have been discarded by the employees of the japanning factory. These small quantities of other glass would suggest that the site, and the moat, were still not generally accessible to the public during this period, as, if they had been, a larger assemblage of more general glass refuse would have been expected.

THE WOOD *Steven J Allen*

Three wooden artefacts were examined by the Wet Wood Laboratory. The artefacts concerned consist of a small peg or locking wedge, a handle and a bowling ball.

All species identifications follow Schweingruber (1982) or Wet Wood laboratory reference samples (Table 7).

All three artefacts are of interest. The 'peg' is similar to wedges used to lock a dovetail tenon into a chase mortice (Plate 13). The notch is probably an eroded peghole broken when the joint of which it formed part was taken apart. As such it indicates the presence, here or nearby, of a substantial timber-framed structure.

Identification	Comment	Species identification
F100 1007	Peg or locking wedge. Cut from tangentially faced heartwood. Tapers along length with notch or truncated peg hole on one edge towards thicker end. Surfaces very abraded and localised fe mineral staining/light concretion. 207 l, 46 w, 17 th.	*Quercus spp.*
F100 1008	Bowling ball. Turned from tangential slice of heartwood. Not a true sphere, being slightly flat around the circumference. Spindle marks present on one face. All surfaces smoothly rounded. Occasional surface damage. 101 l, 106 dia	*Guiacum officinale*
F526 5031	Handle for socketed tool. Spindle turned from radially faced heartwood to form elongated teardrop shape. Thinner end has shallow step around it indicating former presence of terminal. Single narrow incised line around circumference at thickest part of handle. Much surface damage and heavy Fe mineral staining 132 l, 36 dia..	*Alnus spp.*

Alnus spp.-   Alder. Sub species not determinable

Quercus spp.- Oak.   Sub species not determinable

Guiacum officinale- Lignum Vitae

TABLE 7 WOODEN ARTEFACTS

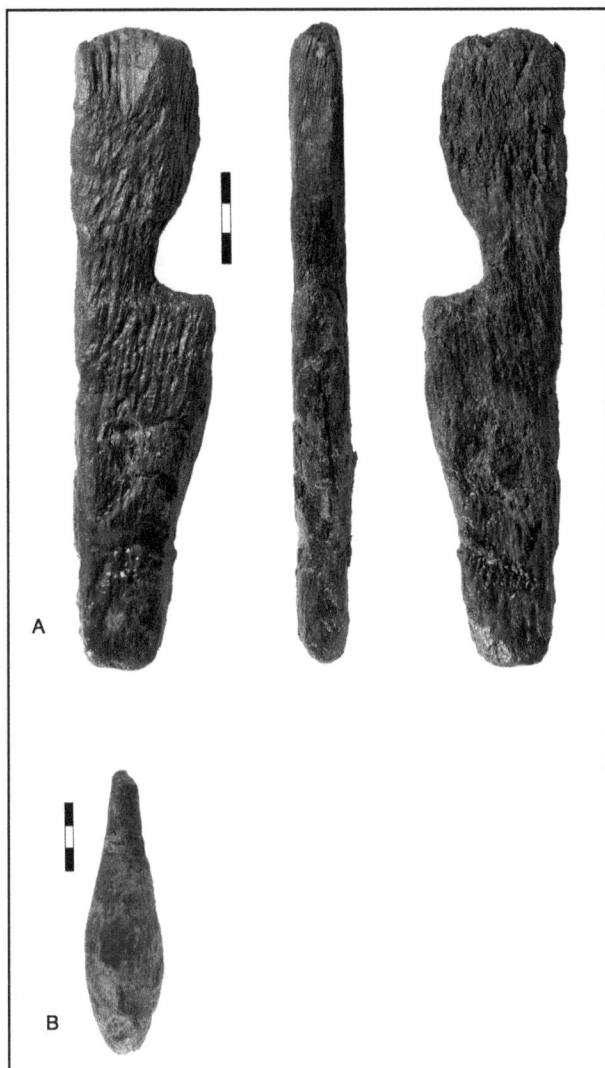

PLATE 13 THE WOODEN PEG

CM

PLATE 14 THE BOWLING BALL

The handle is shaped to fit into a socket and is reminiscent of a chisel or similar. It is thus distinct from the type of handle used for a tanged tool such as an awl. Sadly the surface condition means that no traces of any use wear can be identified. None the less, these items normally only survive as broken mineral preserved organics (MPO's) in metal sockets.

The bowling ball is a very rare survival (Plate 14). Wooden balls of late medieval to early modern date are known from Exeter (Allan and Morris 1984, 309) and York (Morris 2000, 25) among others but none appear to be of the same quality as the example here. Cut from a tropical hardwood, its raw material would have been imported, if not actually made abroad and it would have been an important possession. The lack of damage suggests accidental loss rather than deliberate disposal and should indicate the nearby presence of a bowling green.

THE LEATHER *Quita Mould*

The leather was examined as excavated; it had not been conserved; the wet leather had been washed. Shoe sizing has been calculated according to the modern English shoe-size scale with the sole measurement rounded up to the nearest size as necessary, continental sizing is provided in brackets. Leather species were identified by hair follicle pattern using low powered magnification. Where the grain surface of the leather was heavily worn identification was not always possible. Shoe soles and repairs are assumed to be of cattle hide unless stated otherwise. The seam and stitch conventions used in the illustrations are after Goubitz (1984, 188–90, fig. 1).

A small amount of leather was found in the moat (F526) and unstratified, comprising principally shoes apparently thrown away as domestic rubbish. A sole from a welted

G

F

Insole

Upper
linings

G

G

F

G

Sole, middle and heel.

G

Half sole

G

G

G

G

Quarters with edge / flesh back and side
seams, flesh outward. Seperate strap.

G

Ramp with butted edge / flesh side
seams - flesh outward decorative
stitching across the toe.

Welt

Reconstruction
(not to scale)

G	grain
F	flesh
●	hobnail
～	whip stitching
∘∘∘	grain/flesh stitching
∧∧∧	edge/flesh stitching
⠿	tunnel stitching

0   10cm

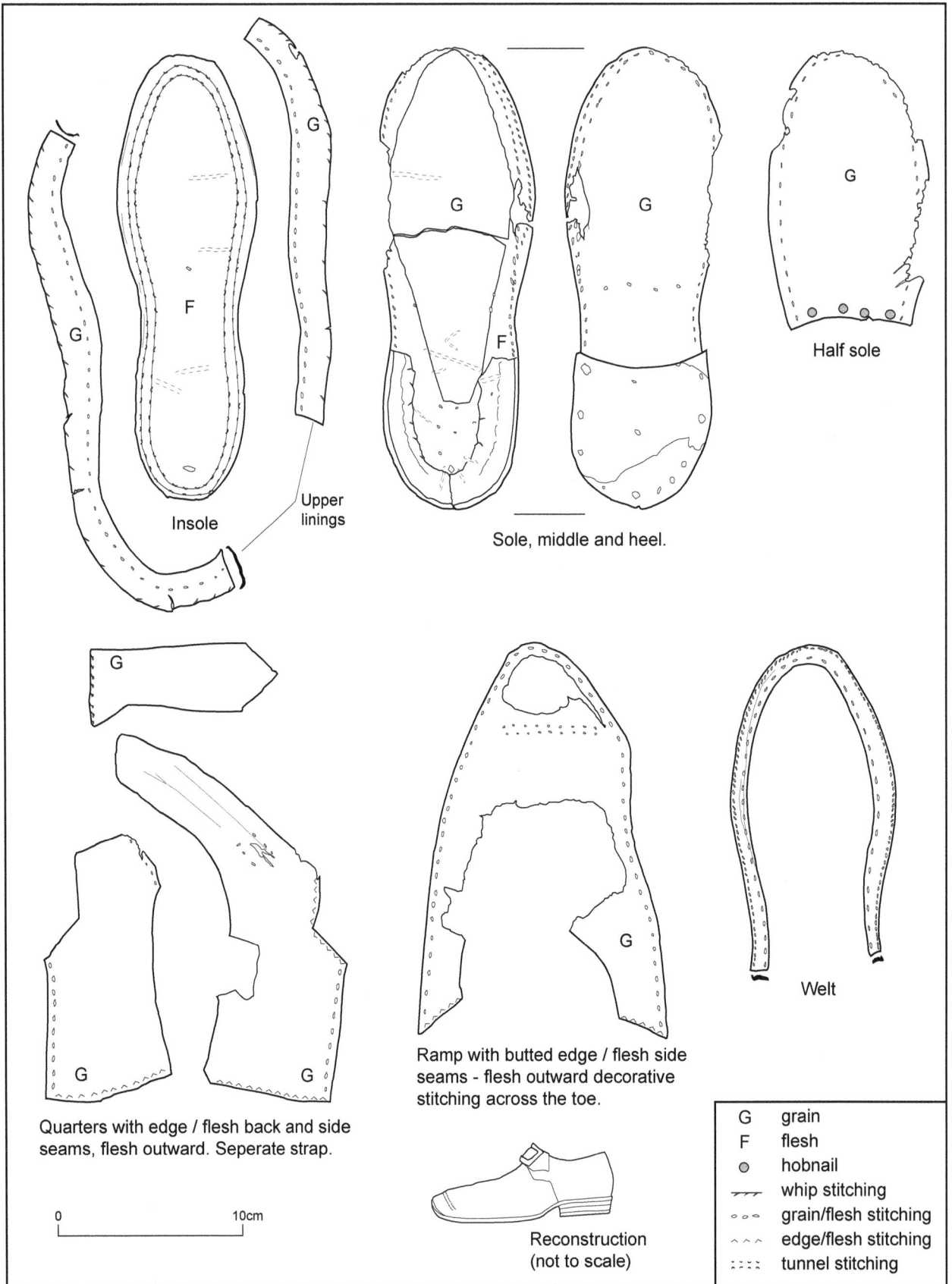

FIGURE 27 LEATHER SHOE

shoe of adult size was found in the primary fill (5033) of the moat (F526) and can be dated no earlier than the 18th century. A near complete 18th-century buckled shoe (Fig. 27) of a style popular in the 1770s was found in the upper fill (5032) of the moat (F526). It was a working shoe of a size to fit an adolescent or woman, adult size 3 (35): the style suggests it was worn by a boy. Other shoe parts, including the remains of a second working shoe to fit a man, adult size 7 (41), were found in the upper fill (1008) of the moat (F100) in Trench 6. A bottom unit of a woman's shoe, adult size 1 (33), of similar date, and a fragment from the vamp of a brogue dating to the Victorian period or later were found unstratified. The leather recovered agrees with the ceramic evidence that the moat was kept clean until the 18th century (Rátkai above).

Catalogue

OHW 02 F526/ 5032 condition: wet, clean drawn (Fig. 27)

Bag 1: Near complete welted shoe of 18th-century date, made straight but worn on the left foot. Bottom unit with oval/ round toe, medium tread, wide waist and seat. Insole with raised rib seam, middle packing with bracing thread present at the lower waist and sole with grain/ flesh seam. Clump sole repair with grain/ flesh stitching around the edge and hobnails across the waist. Large, low D-shaped heel of two lifts and a top piece with hobnails around the edge, height 15mm. Welt around the forepart 10mm wide. Vamp with large hole worn through the toe, and the throat area torn off. Dog-leg side seam present with edge/ flesh seam. Line of paired stitching present across the toe possibly marking the former position of a toe cap. Two-part quarters 66mm high with dog-leg side seams extending into a wide strap to buckle over the instep. The strap on the left side is integral, that on the right is a separate strap seamed to the front edge of the quarters. Bovine leather 2mm thick flesh outward.

Insole length 230mm, width tread 75mm, waist 53mm, seat 57mm Adult size 3(35).

Bag 2: Sub-rectangular piece of leather broken down one side with a line of three large, oval holes, 12mm long, along the other, spaced 45mm apart. Bovine leather 7mm thick. 182x64mm.

OHW 02 F526/ 5033 condition: wet, clean

Welted shoe sole. Half sole (forepart) with oval/ short pointed toe, made straight. Grain/flesh seam within a stitching channel and grain/ flesh seam across the waist. Bovine leather 2mm thick. Length 140mm, width 83mm. Adult size.

OHW 02 U/S condition: dry, soil adhering

Bottom unit if welted shoe of 18th-century date. Complete insole made straight, worn on the left foot with blunt oval toe, medium tread, wide waist and seat. Raised rib seam on the flesh side. Black coloured cattle hide. Insole length 218mm, width tread 75mm, waist 56mm, seat 55mm.

Adult size 1 (33). Part of a matching sole, lower tread and waist area, moulded down the heel breast with edge/ flesh seam to join to the top piece of the separate heel (now missing). Grain/ flesh seam within a stitching channel. 46 x 34 x 3mm.

Fragment of shoe upper from a brogue of 19th- to 20th-century date with a short V-shaped butted edge/ flesh seam, c 28mm long, and decorated edge. Edge is serrated with decorative punched circular cut-outs between two lines of fine grain/ flesh stitching. Brown polished surface preserved in places. Bovine leather 2mm thick. 95 x 67mm.

OHS 02 Trench 6 F100/ 1008 condition: wet, clean

Welted shoe of 18th- to early 19th-century date. Bottom unit made straight, probably worn on the right foot. Insole with short, pointed toe, medium tread, waist and wide seat. Raised rib seam around the edge. Middle packing. Half sole and separate seat seamed across the waist, both with grain/ flesh seam and hobnails around the edge. Impression from a large D-shaped heel (now missing) also with stitching and hobnails. Welt 10mm wide. Upper linings and toe area of vamp. The left side and the throat area of the vamp are missing, torn away. The toe is worn through; stitching is present from a toe cap; also a double line (raised rib) of decorative stitching runs upward obliquely from the lasting margin. Grain surface appears polished in places. Leather ?bovine 2mm thick.

Insole length 264mm, width tread 80mm, waist 48mm, seat 57mm Adult size 7 (41)

Forepart of insole or middle from a man's shoe, with skived sides and impression from bracing thread. Might come from middle packing of the shoe above, but uncertain. 147 x 82mm.

Heel areas from a bottom unit component, probably middle, with grain/ flesh stitching at the edge, from a woman's shoe.

Two wooden stave fragments, one broken into two pieces 147 x 38 x 5mm; 112 x 33 x 4mm

THE STONE *Rob Ixer and Erica Macey-Bracken. Architectural identifications Malcolm Hislop and Michael Lobb*

A total of 28 pieces of stone were recovered from the site. Most of these stones are medium to coarse-grained slightly pebbly ardulacious sandstones, apart from the worked pieces of tracery, which are fine-grained freestones. Three pieces of probable burnt shale, a piece of chalk and a piece of mortar were also recovered during the watching brief. Almost all of the rocks, including most of the tracery pieces, are local Permo-Triassic sandstones, possibly from the upper Coal Measures. The only exception to this was one of the larger worked pieces, which was a southern English import.

Four of the pieces recovered had definitely been worked.

PLATE 15 THE WORKED STONE (GOTHIC TRACERY)

A piece of multi-angular masonry of unknown function or period was recovered from the excavation (F522, 5025). This piece was pale brown fine-grained micaceous sandstone, quite indurated and homogeneous. One end of the item was broken, and traces of burning could be seen at this end. The 2002 excavation of the site also produced a fragment of 14th- to 15th-century window tracery, the shoulder of one side of a cusped arch containing a glazing groove (F552, 5072 Plate 15). This item was made from fine-grained homogeneous pale-yellow indurated sandstone with mason's keying-in marks on the back. There were no signs of bedding, and the item was finer-grained than the other piece of worked stone from the excavation, described above.

The 2003 watching brief at the site produced a possible plinth, sill or jamb (9013). This piece of stone, homogenous and fine-grained, was a pale-coloured calcareous sandstone or sandy limestone. As with the window tracery above, the stone showed no sign of bedding, and is probably a southern English import. An unstratified piece of stone from the watching brief was a possible cornice or string course. The piece had ogee and quarter circle moulding, and was later medieval or early post-medieval in date. A circular hole, approximately 15mm in diameter, on the reverse side of the piece may have been a fixing hole.

The watching brief also produced a roughly-worked, pale brown fine-grained indurated micaceous sandstone, which was homogeneous (S1). This item had anthropogenic grooves on a smooth surface, and may be an unfinished piece.

The rest of the material from the site was unworked, although five pieces of stone from the watching brief had mortar adhering to one surface (8002, S2, S7, S8 and S9). One of these pieces (8002) was a medium-grained carbonate-cemented yellow-brown indurated homogeneous sandstone with limonite staining. Traces of mortar were visible on one side of this piece. The piece from sample S2 had a layer of mortar with traces of charcoal in. This piece was an irregular piece of yellow-brown indurated carbonate-cemented micaceous sandstone. Pale quartz pebbles 2mm in diameter were also associated with this piece. Another piece of medium-grained indurated carbonate cemented sandstone (S7), brown-grey in colour, also had mortar adhering. This piece also showed signs of burning. The sample S8 was also a browny-grey carbonate-cemented indurated sandstone, although finer-grained than the piece from S7. This piece had a highly irregular top and a flat bottom surface, with mortar attached to both of these. Sample S9, a small, unworked fragment of very fine-grained reddish-brown carbonate-cemented sandstone also had mortar attached.

The remainder of the material in the assemblage was unworked, but a variety of local Permo-Triassic sandstones were represented, as shown in Table 8.

Site	Context	Description
2003 excavation	8008	3 pieces of possible burnt shale.
2003 watching brief	S3	Indurated, fine-grained pale-brown carbonate-cemented sandstone.
2003 watching brief	S4	2 small fragments of unworked yellow-brown coarse-grained carbonate-cemented arkosic sandstone with small pebbles.
2003 watching brief	S4	Small fragment of banded red-brown drab friable carbonate-cemented sandstone. Unworked.
2003 watching brief	S4a	Fragment of medium-grained indurated pale-brown carbonate-cemented sandstone. Unworked.
2003 watching brief	S5	Dark brown friable medium-grained arkosic sandstone.
2003 watching brief	S5	Pale-coloured, indurated slightly micaceous carbonate-cemented sandstone with smooth curved outer surface.
2003 watching brief	S6	Two buff-coloured, carbonate-rich carbonate-cemented sandstone.
2003 watching brief	S10	Small fragment of lightly carbonate-cemented worked fine-grained sandstone. Slightly friable, yellow-brown, micaceous and homogeneous.
2003 watching brief	S10 (Fragments from easternmost N/S wall)	Fine-grained marly sandstone, red and drab, patchy, quite indurated.
2003 watching brief	S10	Unworked fragment of poorly-bedded coarse-grained yellow-brown sandstone with 1cm quartz pebbles. Same as 2 small fragments from S4, above.
2003 watching brief	S11	Carbonate-cemented sandstone
2003 watching brief	S11	Piece of mortar
2003 watching brief	Outside brick wall	Red-brown, medium-grained Permo-Triassic sandstone. Not carbonate-cemented.
2003 watching brief	Outside brick wall	Fine-grained carbonate-cemented sandstone. Unworked.
2003 watching brief	Outside brick wall	Piece of chalk. Unworked.

TABLE 8 UNWORKED STONES

MISCELLANEOUS FINDS *Erica Macey-Bracken*

Clay Pipe

A total of 43 clay tobacco pipe fragments were recovered from the site. The majority of these fragments were from pipe stems (see Table 9) but 11 bowls or partial bowls were also recovered. The earliest piece was a probable 17th-century bowl with a stamp showing three vertical lines on the heel. This was recovered from the moat during the 2002 evaluation (1003). A bowl of early 18th-century date (Ayto 1999, 8) was also recovered from the same layer.

The moat also produced three bowls and two bowl fragments of mid-19th-century date. These were large bowls with very thin walls, which dated to 1840–60 (Ayto 1999, 7). Two of these bowls (1006, U/S) were plain, as were the two bowl fragments (1007) but the third (1008) was decorated with a fluted pattern on the front of the bowl, and an arch with interlocking V shapes on each side of the bowl. A bowl which appeared to be of the Dutch style that was copied by some English pipe makers in the late 19th and early 20th century (*ibid*, 7) was also recovered from the moat (1007).

Two bowls represented late 19th-century pipes from the 2002 excavation (5000, 5038). Both of these bowls were decorated, one (5000) with an eagle claw, which was moulded around the base of the bowl, and the other (5038) with a faint pattern of what appeared to be foliage, although this pattern was very worn, making definite identification difficult.

Iron, Lead and Other Metals

Iron and other metal finds were recovered from the 2002 excavation and from the site at Old Hall Street south. The assemblage was highly corroded, and some items were difficult to identify due to the amount of corrosion products adhering to them.

Eleven pieces of iron were recovered from the 2002 excavation. This included three nails (5031, 5053, U/S), the threaded end of a bolt (U/S), and two circular iron rods (5029 x 1, 5031 x 1) of uncertain function. Four pieces of narrow iron gas pipe were also recovered (5032 x 2, U/S x 2). Three of these pieces may possibly be from the same pipe, as they were all 19mm thick, and of similar appearance. The other pipe section (U/S) was slightly

Context	Bowls	Stems
Evaluation		
1003	3	4
1004	-	1
1005	-	1
1006	1	-
1007	3	5
1008	1	3
U/S	-	2
Excavation		
5000	1	-
5009	-	2
5017	-	1
5032	-	1
5038	1	-
5039	-	4
U/S	1	1
Watching Brief		
8001	-	1
8005	-	1
9017	-	1
9029	-	1
U/S	-	2

TABLE 9 CLAY PIPE STEMS AND BOWLS

narrower, at 16mm, but may well have also been a gas pipe.

Possibly the most interesting item was the possible broken-off end of a dagger blade (5053), 223mm long and 36mm wide, and tapered to a precise point. Despite being heavily corroded, the resemblance to a dagger point is unmistakeable.

Two lead strips, which were also recovered from the 2002 excavation (5037, U/S), were 6mm wide and 3mm thick, had a narrow gully running down each edge, and were identified as window leading.

The site at Old Hall Street south also produced a small quantity of metal items, including a broken star-shaped iron cog (1019), and a collection of 27 iron offcuts (1020). These offcuts are all very thin, with most being only 1mm thick, and had obviously been discarded after some manufacturing process. Their location within the site may suggest they were off-cuts from the tin-plating industry. The base of a circular metal container was also recovered from the same context as the cog. This item, 95mm in diameter, was filled with a hardened white putty-like substance. The container had broken off between 16 and 25mm from the base, and was likely to have been discarded for this reason.

Shell

Forty-one oyster shells or partial oyster shells were recovered from the 2002 excavations (36 shells), the 2003

watching brief (4 shells) and Old Hall Street south (1 shell). None of the shells showed evidence of having been worked, and are most likely to be food waste; having been discarded after the contents of the shell had been removed.

Crucibles

Fifteen crucible fragments were recovered from the moat during the 2002 evaluation (1007), and a further three fragments were recovered from the 2002 excavation (5031). Other crucible fragments were noted in the pottery assemblage, and are discussed in detail in the pottery report (Rátkai, above). In common with the sherds discussed in the pottery report, eleven of the sherds from the evaluation conform to the flat-based 'flower pot' form with everted walls, which dates from the 15th century onwards (Bayley 1992, 5). At least two, if not three, vessels of this type are represented in the assemblage recovered from the moat (1007). The vessels were made in a hard-fired blue-grey-purple fabric, 13mm thick, and the external surfaces were coated with metallic residue.

Four sherds from vessels with thicker walls of around 25mm were also recovered from context 1007; three of these sherds appeared to be from the same vessel, which had a very hard-fired blue-grey fabric and was coated with metallic residue on the exterior surface. Two further fragments in this fabric were recovered during the 2002 excavation (5031), suggesting that at least two of these vessels were dumped in the moat.

The final fragment from context 1007 was a base fragment made from a light brown, coarse, sandy fabric. In contrast to the other fragments from this context, no external residues were visible. Another base sherd in the same fabric, again with no visible residue on the external surfaces, was recovered during the 2002 excavation (5031).

Tile

The tile assemblage consisted of 128 fragments of ceramic tile, weighing 25,905g and six fragments of stone tile. The material displayed a high incidence of fragmentation, with only one complete example being recovered (8007), although individual fragments were largely unabraded. The assemblage was quantified by count and weight and was examined macroscopically for the purposes of fabric identification. The tile fabrics were of good quality, evenly fired and well-levigated. This suggested they were almost certainly associated with the Great Hall.

The tile was spread evenly across the site, with no significant concentrations of quantity or fabric. The tile was recovered from contexts dating to all phases of the site, most of the assemblage was recovered from contexts containing pottery dating from the 17th to early 19th centuries (Rátkai, above), or from features interpreted as post-medieval. This suggests that the tile was part of deposition over time and was associated with piecemeal replacement of the roof and not associated with a single destructive episode such as the demolition of the Great Hall.

Site	Context	Fabric 1	Fabric 2	Fabric 3	Fabric 4	Fabric 5	Fabric 6
Evaluation	1002	2	1	-	-	-	-
	1004	-	1	-	-	-	-
	1007	7	3	-	-	-	-
	1009	-	1	-	-	-	-
	1012	2	-	-	-	-	-
	1025	3	-	2	-	-	-
	U/S	1	1	-	-	-	-
Excavation	5007	1	-	-	-	-	-
	5008	1	-	-	-	-	-
	5009	1	2	-	-	-	-
	5010	1	1	-	-	-	-
	5016	6	-	4	-	-	-
	5020	-	-	-	3	-	-
	5029	-	2	-	-	-	-
	5031	7	3	-	-	-	-
	5032	1	1	-	-	-	-
	5033	1	1	-	-	-	-
	5054	2	-	-	-	-	-
	5062	1	-	-	-	-	-
	5069	-	-	-	-	-	1
	F514	-	-	-	-	1	-
	F522	1	1	2	-	-	-
	Layer over F524	-	2	1	-	-	-
	U/S	1	2	-	-	-	-
Evaluation (south of Old Hall Street)	1019	2	6	2	-	-	1
	1020	1	-	-	-	-	-
Watching brief	8000 / 8001	1					
	8002	1	-	-	-	-	-
	8005	8	-	-	-	-	-
	8006	4	2	-	-	-	-
	8007	1	-	-	-	-	-
	9017	4	-	-	-	-	-
	F906	-	1	-	-	-	-
	U/S	4	4	-	-	-	-

TABLE 10 QUANTITY OF TILE FRAGMENTS BY CONTEXT AND FABRIC

Six different fabrics were identified in the assemblage, with two particular fabrics dominating the assemblage, as can be seen in Table 10.

Fabric Descriptions

Fabric 1: Hard-fired, dense, coarse orange sandy fabric with occasional large sub-rounded pebble inclusions.

Fabric 2: Very hard-fired dark red sandy fabric with occasional small sub-angular stone inclusions.

Fabric 3: Very coarse pale orange fabric with smooth sandy surfaces.

Fabric 4: Dark orange-red fabric with smooth orange-brown surfaces.

Fabric 5: Dark orange-red fabric with smooth orange-brown surfaces.

Fabric 6: Very dense, hard fired dark grey-blue fabric. Similar in appearance to an engineering brick fabric.

Fabric 7: Well-levigated mid-grey fabric with a yellow-green glazed surface.

Discussion

The predominance of Fabrics 1 and 2 suggest that most of the tile was manufactured from the same clay, probably at the same time, with the other fabrics coming from tiles that were manufactured later in order to carry out repairs to the Great Hall. Little diagnostic evidence was present in the assemblage, and although it could be assumed that most of the tile dates from the construction of the hall, lack of diagnostic features mean that the tile could date from any time between the construction of the Great Hall and the 1850s (Steve Litherland, pers. comm.).

One fragment of tile (5069) was very different to the rest. This was a fragment of hand-made blue-black tile, which had been very heavily fired. This fragment had had ventilation holes made by pressing a ½in (13mm) dowel into the tile before it was fired, and then three smaller holes that pierced the back of the tile were made at the base of this hole. Subsequently, some of the vent holes had been filled with lime mortar. The function of this tile is unclear; its thickness of ¾in (19mm) makes it too thin to be a floor tile, although it is possible that it may have been used for ventilation, perhaps during the Hall's latter incarnation as a factory. As with the remainder of the assemblage, however, the fragment is difficult to date, and may have come from any time between the Elizabethan period and the mid-1850s.

Brick *Erica Macey-Bracken, with comments by Steve Litherland*

Eighteen brick fragments were sampled from the site. These fragments were from hand-made red bricks, and were deposited during one or more phases of demolition on the site. The assemblage was quantified by count and weight, and examined macroscopically for the purposes of identification.

A single complete brick (8005) constituted a waster, was curved and displayed evidence that it had warped during the firing process. The brick had a narrow strip impression on both ends of one face, and may have been pressed against something whilst wet. The brick measured 2 x 4 x 9ins (51 x 102 x 229mm), making it a similar size to the other bricks recovered from the site.

The largest brick fragment was recovered from the lower moat deposits dated to the mid- to late 18th century (F526, 5031). This was a piece of hand-made red brick, originally measuring 2¼ x 4⅜ x c 9ins (57 x 111 x 229mm), in a coarse dark red fabric. The fragment had been quite heavily fired, and large stone inclusions were visible in the fabric. The brick had been made in a mould that had been coated with sand. The size of the brick is consistent with deposition in the 18th century but could date to an earlier period of construction.

The remainder of the assemblage (1007 x 8, 1010 x 2, 5005 x 3, 5031 x 1) consisted of small fragments of hand-made brick and were largely undiagnostic possibly dating from the late 16th to the early 19th centuries. Some of the partial brick fragments recovered from the site had also been heavily fired. Two distinct fabrics were noticed; a fine orange fabric and a coarse, irregularly-fired dark red fabric like that of the brick described above. This may suggest a mixture of lower quality bricks and more refined facing bricks, as would have been used in the construction of the hall.

CHAPTER 7: THE ENVIRONMENTAL EVIDENCE

THE WATERLOGGED PLANT REMAINS *Wendy Smith*

Table 11 presents the results for all three samples and Table 12 provides a breakdown of the possible habitats the taxa may represent. Wild plants typical of waste ground and water/ waterside vegetation dominate all three assemblages. A small quantity of stones or seeds of fruit (eg, fig, plum/ greengage/ bullace/ damson and wild/ dwarf cherry) that are most likely cultivated (with the possible exception of wild/ dwarf cherry) were also recovered. Because the results from all three samples are so similar, they will be discussed below as a whole.

Discussion

The waterlogged assemblage from Wolverhampton Great Hall provides limited evidence for the deposition of settlement waste within the moat. There is some evidence for cultivated fruits, which may suggest a possible orchard or garden in the immediate vicinity. The assemblage does provide good evidence for conditions within the moat, as well as the nature of the surrounding vegetation.

Absence of Settlement Waste within the Moat

A few fragments of charcoal were observed in sorting, but charred plant remains and waterlogged macrofossils that might be indicative of human waste were absent. Fig (*Ficus carica L.*) seeds were recovered from sample 5031. These often are not digested but, instead, passed with faeces (Cappers 1996, 325), so one possible source for this deposit may be human cess; however, the absence of any other indicators for cess (eg, insect remains) means that this possibility is fairly unlikely.

Fruit Remains from the Moat

Fig (*Ficus carica L.*), plum/ greengage/ bullace/ damson (*Prunus domestica s.l.*) and wild/ dwarf cherry (*Prunus avium (L.) L./ cerasus L.*) were recovered from the northern section of the moat (samples 5031 and 5033). These most likely were intentionally planted as garden or orchard fruit trees in the vicinity of the moat, although they can occasionally naturalize, especially in sheltered locations.

The Surrounding Environment

The assemblage recovered from the moat samples provides evidence for three main types of habitat occurring in and around the moat. There are several plants specific to water/ waterside conditions. These include celery-leaved buttercup (*Ranunculus sceleratus L.*), lesser celandine (*Ranunculus ficaria s.l.*), buttercup (Ranunculus subgenus BATRACHIUM (DC.) A Gray),

downy birch (*Betula pubescens Ehrh.*), water-cress (*Rorippa nasturtium-aquaticum (L.) Hayek*), narrow-fruited water-cress (*Rorippa microphylla* (Boenn.) ex. Á. and D. Löve, hemlock (*Conium maculatum L.*), Gypsywort (*Lycopus europaeus L.*), water-starwort (*Callitriche spp.*), possible water plantain (*Alisma cf. plantago-aquatica L.*), pondweed (*Potamogeton spp.*), duckweed (*Lemna spp.*), common spike-rush type (*Eleocharis palustris (L.)* Roem. and Schult. – type) and sedge (*Carex spp.* – 2-sided and 3-sided). The recovery of water-starwort (*Callitriche spp.*), pondweed (*Potamogeton spp.*) and duckweed (*Lemna spp.*) suggests that the water was slow-flowing. The presence of Coleoptera, such as Agabus, Hydreana and Octhebius species (Smith and Tetlow 2005), as well as large quantities of water flea (Daphnia spp.) egg cases within these samples (see also Ciaraldi 2005: 21) also supports this conclusion.

A small quantity of tree seeds was also recovered, which may suggest the presence of stands of trees in or around the moat. In addition to the fruit trees discussed above, taxa identified include oak (*Quercus sp.*), downy birch (*Betula pubsescens Ehrh.*), elder (*Sambucus nigra L.*) and possible beech (cf. *Fagus sylvatica L.*). The recovery of nipplewort (*Lapsana communis L.*) and rough chervil (*Chaerophyllum temulum L.*) also provide limited evidence for woodland in the vicinity of the moat; however, these taxa can also occur in grassland or cultivated ground.

Several taxa recovered are typical of grassland or cultivated ground, and may suggest that pasture, fields and/or orchards were located near to the moat. Taxa identified include meadow/ creeping/ bulbous buttercup (*Ranunculus acris L./ repens L./ bulbosus L.*), common nettle (*Urtica dioica L.*), common chickweed (*Stellaria media s.l.*), possible shepherd's-purse (cf. *Capsella bursa-pastoris (L.) Medik.*), salad burnet (*Sanguisorba cf. minor spp. minor Scop.*), petty spurge (*Euphorbia peplus L.*), rough chervil (*Chaerophyllum temulum L.*), greater plantain (*Plantago major L.*), smooth sow-thistle (*Sonchus oleracaeus L.*), stinking chamomile (*Anthemis cotula L.*) and crown daisy (*Chrysanthemum sp.*). The Coleoptera also support this interpretation. Smith and Tetlow (2005) argue that the presence of Geotrupes, Onthophagus and Aphodius 'dung beetles', which are typically associated with the dung of grazing indicates the presence of pasture in the vicinity of the moat.

Comparison with other Moat Deposits

Frequently, toward the end of their use, such features as moats or ditches become the site of repeated dumping events for domestic/ agricultural wastes and often are overgrown with plants typical of waste and derelict places.

Feature Context Context Type Sample volume Seeds per litre Period	F103 1018 Moat (lowest fill) 500 ml 208 pre 18C	F526 5031 Moat (middle fill) 500 ml 612 18C	F526 5033 Moat (lowest fill) 500 ml 240 pre 18C	
Latin Binomial				English Common Name
Ranunculus acris L./ *repens* L./ *bulbosus* L.	3	4	1	Meadow/ creeping/ bulbous buttercup
Ranunculus sceleratus L.	21	-	4	Celery-leaved buttercup
Ranunculus ficaria s.l.	-	44	1	Lesser celandine
Papaver sp.	1	-	-	Poppy
Ficus carica L.	-	3	-	Fig
Urtica dioica L.	2	38	2	Common nettle
cf. Fagus sylvatica L.	-	-	1	Possible beech
Quercus sp.	-	1	-	Oak
Betula pubescens Ehrh.	1	-	-	Downy Birch
Chenopodium spp.	-	-	1	Goosefoot
Atriplex spp.	3	4	1	Orache
Stellaria media s.l.	2	5	7	Common chickweed
cf. CARYOPHYLACEAE indet.	-	-	-	Possible Pink Family
Persicaria hydropiper (L.) Spach	-	2	-	Water-pepper
Persicaria spp.	9	17	2	Knotweed
Polygonum cf. aviculare agg.	2	1	-	Knotgrass
Polygonum spp.	-	7	3	Knotgrass
Polygonum spp./ Rumex spp./ Carex spp.	4	20*	-	Knotgrass/ Dock/ Sedge
Rumex sp.	3	1	3	Dock
Rorippa nasturtium-aquaticum (L.) Hayek	3	1	2	Water-cress
Rorippa microphylla (Boenn.) ex Á. & D. Löve	3	38	3	Narrow-fruited water-cress
Cardamine/ Arabis sp.	-	-	2	Bitter-cress/ Rrock-cress
cf. Capsella bursa –pastoris (L.) Medik.	-	-	1	Possible shepherd's-purse
Rubus spp.	1	9	-	Bramble (blackberry)
Rubus spp./ Rosa spp. (thorn)	-	4	1	Bramble (blackberry) / rose
Potentilla spp.	1	2	-	Cinquefoil
Sanguisorba cf. minor ssp. minor Scop.	-	1	-	Salad burnet
Prunus domestica s.l.	2	-	-	Plum/ greengage/ bullace/ damson
Prunus avium (L.) L./ cerasus L.	1	-	-	Wild/ Dwarf Cherry
Epilobium sp.	1	-	1	Willowherb
Euphorbia peplus L.	2	-	-	Petty spurge
Euphorbia spp.	1	-	-	Spurge
Chaerophyllum temulum L.	-	-	1	Rough chervil
Conium maculatum L.	-	2	4	Hemlock
cf. Bupleurum sp.	-	-	5	Possible hare's-ear
Stachys spp.	4	-	1	Woundwort
Lycopus europaeus L.	3	1	1	Gypsywort
Callitriche spp.	-	5	-	Water-starwort
Plantago major L.	1	3	4	Greater plantain
cf. Plantago major L.	-	1	-	Possible greater plantain
Verbascum sp.	-	-	6	Mullein
Veronica anagallis-aquatica L.	-	-	1	Blue water-speedwell
Sambucus nigra L.	1	2	2	Elder
Carduus sp.	-	1	-	Thistle
Lapsana communis L.	1	-	1	Nipplewort

Feature Context Context Type Sample volume Seeds per litre Period	F103 1018 Moat (lowest fill) 500 ml 208 pre 18C	F526 5031 Moat (middle fill) 500 ml 612 18C	F526 5033 Moat (lowest fill) 500 ml 240 pre 18C	
Picris spp.	-	-	2	Oxtongue
Sonchus oleraceus L.	1	1	-	Smooth sow-thistle
cf. Sonchus oleraceus L.	1	-	-	Possible smooth sow-thistle
Lactuca spp.	-	2	-	Lettuce
Taraxacum spp.	1	-	2	Dandelion
cf. Artemisia sp.	-	-	1	Possible mugwort
Anthemis cotula L.	-	2	-	Stinking chamomile
Anthemis sp.	-	-	7	Chamomile
Chrysanthemum sp.	-	1	-	Crown daisy
APIACEAE indet.	1	-	2	Carrot Family
Alisma cf. plantago-aquatica L.	2	2	1	Possible water plantain
Potamogeton spp.	6	3	2	Pondweed
Lemna spp.	-	12	-	Duckweed
cf. Lemna spp.	-	-	1	Possible Duckweed
Luzula spp.	1	8	-	Wood-rush
Eleocharis palustris (L.) Roem. & Schult. - type	-	1	-	Common spike-rush type
Carex spp. – 2-sided	1	1	-	Sedge
Carex spp. – 3-sided	3	10	4	Sedge
CYPERACEAE indet.	-	-	1	Sedge Family
Poa sp.	1	-	1	Meadow-grass
POACEAE (small) indet.	8	13	5	Small-seeded wild grass
POACEAE – culm node	-	-	1	Wild grass
POACEAE – glume	-	-	1	Wild grass
Large anther	-	-	2	Large anther
Bud	1	3	3	Bud
Leaf abscission pad/ Bud scar	-	2	5	Leaf abscission pad/ Bud scar
Deciduous leaf fragments	-	1	-	Deciduous leaf fragments
Thorn	-	1	1	Thorn
Moss	++	++	+	Moss
Unidentified	-	-	5	Unidentified
TOTAL	104	306	120	

* = estimate count – material quite fragmentary

+ = 1-5 fragments and ++ = 6-12 fragments

TABLE 11 WATERLOGGED PLANT REMAINS RECOVERED FROM THE MOAT

Habitat / Latin Binomial	Water	Waterside	Wet/Damp ground	Slow-flowing rivers	Fens/Moors	Open ground (unshaded)	Grassland	Cultivated ground	Waste ground	Rough ground	Hedgerow/Scrub	Woodland clearings/ Edge	Woodland	Well drained soil	Acid soils	Calcareous/Base-rich soil	English Common Name
Ranunculus acris L./ repens L./ bulbosus L.			?				✓										Meadow/ creeping/ bulbous buttercup
Ranunculus sceleratus L.	✓	✓	✓														Celery-leaved buttercup
Ranunculus ficaria s.l.		✓	✓														Lesser celandine
Ranunculus subgenus BATRACHIUM (DC.) A. Gray	✓	?															Buttercup
Urtica dioica L.					✓			✓					✓				Common nettle
cf. Fagus sylvatica L.														✓	?	✓	Possible beech
Betula pubescens Ehrh.			✓												✓		Downy Birch
Stellaria media s.l.						✓		✓									Common chickweed
Persicaria hydropiper (L.) Spach	✓	✓	✓														Water-pepper
Polygonum cf. aviculare agg.						✓											Knotgrass
cf. Capsella bursa –pastoris (L.) Medik.						✓		✓									Possible shepherd's-purse
Rorippa nasturtium-aquaticum (L.) Hayek	✓	✓															Water-cress
Rorippa microphylla (Boenn.) ex Á. & D. Löve	✓	✓															Narrow-fruited water-cress
Sanguisorba cf. minor ssp. minor Scop.							✓									✓	Salad burnet
Prunus domestica s.l.									✓		✓						Plum/ greengage/ bullace/ damson
Prunus avium (L.) L./ cerasus L.											✓		✓				Wild/ Dwarf Cherry
Euphorbia peplus L.								✓	✓								Petty spurge
Chaerophyllum temulum L.							✓				✓	✓					Rough chervil
Conium maculatum L.		✓	✓						✓								Hemlock
Lycopus europaeus L.		✓	✓														Gypsywort
Callitriche spp.	✓																Water-starwort
Plantago major L.							✓	✓									Greater plantain
Veronica anagallis-aquatica L.		✓	✓														Blue water-speedwell
Sambucus nigra L.									✓	✓	✓		✓				Elder
Lapsana communis L.									✓	✓	✓	✓					Nipplewort
Sonchus oleraceus L.								✓	✓								Smooth sow-thistle
Anthemis cotula L.								✓	✓	✓						?	Stinking chamomile
Chrysanthemum sp.								✓	✓								Crown daisy
Alisma cf. plantago-aquatica L.	✓	✓		✓													Possible water plantain
Potamogeton spp.	✓			?													Pondweed
Lemna spp.	✓			?													Duckweed
Eleocharis palustris (L.) Roem. & Schult. - type	✓	✓	✓														Common spike-rush type
Carex spp. – 2-sided			✓														Sedge
Carex spp. – 3-sided			✓														Sedge

TABLE 12 HABITATS OF WATERLOGGED PLANT MACROFOSSILS RECOVERED FROM THE SITE

The archaeobotanical assemblage of wild plants recovered from the moat at the Great Hall is similar to those from other moat and ditch deposits, eg, Birmingham Moat 73–5, West Midlands (Greig 1980); Cowick, South Humberside (Greig 1986; Hayfield and Greig 1989); Edgbaston Street and Park Street, Birmingham (Ciaraldi 2009); Stone, Staffordshire (Moffett and Smith 1996). The results from Wolverhampton Great Hall are particularly similar to those from the 16th-century watercourse which linked the manorial moat with the parsonage moat, at the Edgbaston Street, Birmingham excavations where agricultural/ settlement waste is not obviously present. In both cases the assemblages were dominated by taxa typical of water/ waterside habitats and waste ground. Small quantities of trees/ scrub were also present in both assemblages. In both cases, the deposits are likely to be representative of the environment as the watercourse/ moat fell out of use.

THE POLLEN *James Greig*

The pollen results from the moat fill show the presence of possible hops, hay and straw as well as a local weedy vegetation around the moat, some trees, and a few aquatic plants in it. These results are compared with other moat studies.

The pollen types have been listed in taxonomic order according to Kent (1992), in Table 13.

The three pollen spectra are rather similar and can be discussed together.

Wetland and aquatic vegetation is only indicated by a few rather small records of *Ranunculus Batrachium-tp* (water crowfoot) in 5033, *Cyperaceae* (sedges, etc) possible *Potamogeton* (pondweed) and *Sparganium tp.* (spike-rush), together with the alga Pediastrum which show that the deposit was probably laid down in water. Finds of caddis and fish scales (Ciaraldi 2005) confirm the water-filled nature of the moat at the time the deposits were laid down. The Brassicaceae record probably corresponds with the macrofossil record of *Rorippa* (water-cress, W. Smith, above).

Trees are usually shown up well by pollen, and a range was present (in decreasing abundance), such as *Quercus* (oak), *Coryloid* (probably hazel), *Alnus* (alder), *Betula* (birch) and *Sambucus nigra* (elder). The finds of macrofossils of oak birch and elder (see W. Smith, above) show that these trees probably grew close to the moat. There were small records of *Fraxinus* (ash) and *cf. Acer* (possibly maple or sycamore) and a trace of *Pinus* (pine), *Ulmus* (elm) and *Tilia* (lime). The moderate amount of pollen suggests that there were trees growing around the site, and the macrofossils show that they were probably close, but it was not a settlement in a densely wooded area like Brewood (Greig 2004). Small records of *Ericales* (heathers) in 5031 and 5033 suggest that there was heathland in the area, but the records are too small to suggest heathland material brought to the site.

Grassland plants possibly include *Poaceae* (grass) pollen, which was the most abundant of all. However grasses grow in all kinds of habitats, as well as grassland. There are more specific indications from records such as *Plantago lanceolata* (ribwort plantain), *Trifolium repens* and *T. pratense* (red and white clovers) and *Centaurea nigra* (knapweed), the latter indicating tall grassland such as hay meadow. The presence of dung beetles (Smith and Tetlow, below) show that at least some of the probable grassland pollen could have been derived from dung containing the remains of either grazed pasture plants, or ones from hay, and the presence of *Sitona* corresponds to the clover on which it feeds.

Crops and weeds are indicated by much *Cerealia* (cereal) pollen, including some probable *Secale* type (rye), which could represent the remains of any of the products of cornfields such as straw or chaff. These contain much pollen (Greig 1982) and it is more likely that the pollen comes from such material rather than directly from cornfields. Remains of straw and chaff could also have been derived from the dung of animals which had been fed such material. A small *Cannabaceae* record could be from hemp or hops, and hops were found as macrofossils by Ciaraldi (2003). Hops grow freely in hedges, as well as being cultivated for brewing beer.

Weeds are shown by some rather unspecific records such as *Chenopodiaceae* and *Caryophyllaceae* (chickweeds), *Rumex* (docks), *Anthemis* type (mayweeds and corn marigold). Some more specific records were *Polygonum aviculare* (knotgrass) and *Spergula arvensis* (corn spurrey) in 5033. There are corresponding macrofossil records of a number of weeds.

There are signs of traces of sewage, but no more, in the moat fill from the finds of single ova of the intestinal parasites *Ascaris* (roundworm), found in 5031, and *Trichuris* (whipworm) found in 5033.

Correlation with other sites

Other moat fills have also shown, beside the usual flora of ditches and ponds and the weeds around them, some evidence of the plants being stored, processed, used or discarded in the occupied area close by, as at Saxon and medieval Stafford (Greig 2005), medieval Cowick, Humberside (Hayfield and Greig 1989) and post-medieval Birmingham (Greig 1980). Since moats generally preserve plant remains well, they can be valuable in providing a snapshot of what was around the occupied site, such as the crops being used, and the general state of the surroundings, even if preservation conditions are not good on the drier parts of the site. The value of the Wolverhampton moat is that it seems to be a fairly late fill, from a period with fewer comparative results. The difficulty with moat fills is often in determining the date of the deposits, and in knowing whether they reflect a time when the site was in active use, or whether the moat silted up during a phase of inactivity or abandonment, as seems to have been the case at Cowick.

spores	5031	5033	F103	
Pteridium	1	4	4	bracken
Polypodium	1	1	1	polypody
pollen				
Pinus	+	1	1	pine
Ranunculus-tp.	-	-	5	buttercup, crowfoot
R. cf. *Batrachium*-tp.	-	5	-	possible water crowfoot
Ulmus	+	1	1	elm
Cannabis-tp.	2	2	1	hop, hemp
Urtica	1	1	-	nettle
Quercus	9	1	8	oak
Betula	3	-	1	Birch
Alnus	3	1	2	alder
Corylus type	4	5	6	hazel
Chenopodiaceae	-	-	6	goosefoot
Caryophyllaceae	2	-	1	stitchwort family
Spergula	-	1	1	corn spurrey
Persicaria bistorta-tp.	1	11	8	bistort etc.
Polygonum aviculare	1	-	-	Knotgrass
Rumex-tp.	4	4	4	docks and sorrels
Tilia	-	-	1	Lime
f. *Salix*	1	-	1	possible willow
Brassicaceae	3	-	-	brassicas
Ericales	1	2	-	Heathers
Potentilla-tp.	-	1	-	tormentil, cinquefoil
Trifolium repens	1	-	-	white clover
Trifolium pratense	+	2	-	red clover
cf. *Acer*	4	-	-	maple or sycamore
piaceae	1	-	-	umbellifers
Mentha-tp.	2	-	-	mints
Plantago lanceolata	14	18	10	ribwort plantain
Fraxinus	1	-	2	ash
Rubiaceae	-	1	-	bedstraws
Sambucus nigra	3	-	-	elder
Cirsium-tp	-	2	-	thistles
Centaurea nigra	2	4	+	knapweed
Lactuceae	9	9	17	a group of composites
Aster-tp	5	4	1	daisies etc
Anthemis-tp.	3	2	-	mayweeds etc.
cf. *Potamogeton*	-	2	1	possible pondweed
Cyperaceae	1	2	3	sedges
Poaceae	102	109	140	grasses
Cerealia-tp.	10	21	16	cereals
cf. Secale	1	3	-	probable rye
Sparganium	3	8	4	spike-rush
pollen sum	198	222	242	
algae	+			
Pediastrum		-		
parasite ova	+			
Ascaris	-	-	-	
Trichuris		-	+	

TABLE 13 POLLEN AND SPORES

	Ecological coding	Synanthropic coding				Phytophage host plant (data from Koch 1989, 1992; plant nomenclature from Stace 1997)
Feature			1008	526	526	
Context			1018	5033	5031	
Weight (kg)			8	8	8	
Volume (l)			10	10	10	
COLEOPTERA						
Carabidae						
Loricera pilicornis (F.)	oa		-	-	1	
Bembidion spp.	oa		-	1	1	
Bradycellus spp.	oa		-	-	1	
Platynus ruficornis (Goeze.)	oa		2	-	-	
Haliplidae						
Haliplus spp.	oa-w		-	-	1	
Dytiscidae						
Agabus spp.	oa-w		-	-	1	
Hydraenidae						
Hydraena spp.	oa-w		1	-	1	
Limnebius spp.	oa-w		1	1	10	
Helophorus spp.	oa-w		-	1	3	
Hydrophilidae						
Cercyon melanocephalus (L.)	rt	st	-	1	1	
Cercyon sternalis Shp.	oa-w		1	1	1	
Cercyon analis (Payk.)	rf	sf	-	1	1	
Cercyon spp.			-	-	2	
Crptopleurum minutum (F.)	rf	st	1	2	-	
Laccobius spp.	oa-w		-	-	1	
Hydrobius fuscipes Leach	oa-w		-	-	2	
Cymbiodyta marginella (F.)	oa-w				1	
Clambidae						
Clambus spp.			-	-	1	
Catopidae						
Catops spp						
Staphylinidae						
Phyllodrepa floralis (Payk.)			1	-	-	
Phyllodrepa spp.			-	2	1	
Omalium rivulare (Payk.)	rt		-	-	1	
Omalium spp.	rt		-	1	1	
Lesteva longelytrata (Goeze)	oa-d		-	-	1	
Lesteva spp.			-	-	1	
Oxytelus sculptus Grav.	rt	st	-	1	-	
Oxytelus sculpturatus Grav.	rt			3	5	
Oxytelus rugosus (F.)	rt		2	2	3	
Oxytelus tetracarinatus (Block.)	rt		-	1	2	
Oxytelus nitidulus Grav.	rt		2	-		
Oxytelus spp.			-	1	1	
Aploderus caelatus (Grav.)	rt		-	-	1	
Platystethus cornutus (Grav.)	oa-d		-	-	1	
Stenus spp.			1	1	3	
Staphylinus spp.	u		-	-	1	
Philonthus spp.			1	1	3	
Quedius spp.			-	1	1	
Lathrobium spp.			1	-	-	
Gryohpnus fracticornis (Mull.)	rt	st	-	-	1	
Xantholinus linearis (Ol.)			-	1	-	
Xantholinus spp.			3	-	2	
Tachyporus spp.			-	1	2	

Tachinus rufipes (Geer.)			-	-	1	
Tachinus spp.			-	-	2	
Aleocharinae gen. & spp. Indet.			1	4	8	
Dryopidae						
Elmis aenea (Mull.)	oa-w		-	-	1	
Nitidulidae						
Brachyterus urticae (F.)	oa-p		-	-	2	*Urtica dioica* L. (common nettle)
Cucujidae						
Monotoma picipes Hbst.	rt	sf	-	-	1	
Monotoma spp.	rt	sf	1	1	2	
Cryptophagidae						
Cryptophagus setulosus Sturm.	rd-h	st	-	-	1	
Cryptophagus spp.	rd-h	st	1	1	3	
Atomaria spp.	rd-h	st	-	2	3	
Mycetophagidae						
Typhaea stercorea (L.)	rd	ss	-	-	3	
Lathridiidae						
Encimus minutus (L.)	rd-h	st	-	-	3	
Encimus spp.	rt	sf	1	2	2	
Corticaria spp.	rt	sf	1	1	9	
Endomychidae						
Mycetaea hirta (Marsh.)	rt	sf	-	-	1	
Anobiidae						
Anobium punctatum (Geer.)	l	sf	-	2	5	Decaying timber
Ptinidae						
Tipnus unicolor (Pill.Mitt.)	rd-h	sf	-	-	1	
Ptinus fur (L.)	rd-h	sf	1	-	-	
Scarabaeidae						
Geotrupes spp.	oa-rf		-	1	-	
Onthophagus spp.	oa-rf		-	-	1	
Aphodius contaminatus (Hbst.)	oa-rf		-	-	1	
Aphodius sphacelatus (Panz.) or *Aphodius prodromus* (Brahm.)	oa-rf		-	-	4	
Aphodius fossor L.	oa-rf		-	-	1	
Aphodius spp.	oa-rf		1	1	9	
Anthicidae						
Anthicus floralis (L.)	rt	st	-	1	-	
Anthicus spp.	rt		-	1	1	
Mordellidae						
?Anaspis pulicaria Costa	oa-p		-	-	1	
Anaspis spp.	oa-p		-	-	1	
Chrysomelidae						
Lema spp.	oa-p		-	-	1	
Chaetocnema concinna (Marsh.)			-	1	-	
Chaetocnema spp.			-	1	3	
Aphthona spp.			1	-	17	
Phyllotraeta spp.			1	1	13	
Scolytidae						
Leperisinus varius (F.)	l		1	-	1	Mainly *Fraxinus* spp. (ash)
Curculionidae						
Apion urticarium (Hbst.)	oa-p		-	-	2	*Urtica dioica* L. (common nettle)

Apion spp.	oa-p		1	4	2	
Polydrusus spp.	l		-	-	1	Foliage of a range of trees
Barynotus obscurus (f.)	oa-p		1	-	-	
Barynotus spp.	oa		-	-	1	
Sitona tibialis (Hbst.)	oa-p		1	-	-	*Trifolium* species (Clover)
Sitona flavescens Marsh	oa-p		1	0	2	*Trifolium* species (Clover)
Sitona humeralis Steph.	oa-p		-	3	4	*Trifolium* species (Clover)
Sitona spp	oa-p		1	2	-	
Tanysphyrus lemnae(Payk.)	oa-w		-	1	-	*Lemna* species (duckweed)
Ceutorhynchus contractus Marsh.	oa-p		-	2	1	*Brassicaceae* (cabbage family) sometimes Papaveraceae (the poppy family)
Ceutorhynchidius troglodytes (F.)	oa-p		-	-	1	On *Plantago lanceolata* L. (ribwort plantain)
Ceutorhynchus spp.	oa-p		1	-	-	
Gymnetron spp.	oa-p		1	2	6	*Plantago lanceolata* L. (ribwort plantain)

Ecological coding (Kenward and Hall 1995)
oa (& ob) - Species which will not breed in human housing.
w- aquatic species.
d- species associated with damp watersides and river banks.
rd- specie primarily associated with drier organic matter.
rf - species primarily associated with foul organic matter often dung.
rt - insects associated with decaying organic matter but not belonging to either the rd or rf groups.
l - species associated with timber.
h - members of the 'house fauna' this is a very arbitrary group based on archaeological associations (Hall and Kenward 1990).

Synanthropic codings (Kenward 1997)
sf - faculative synanthropes - common in 'natural' habitats but clearly favoured by artificial ones.
st - typically synanthropes - particularly favoured by artificial habitats but believed to be able to survive in nature in the long term.
ss - strong synanthropes - essentially dependant on human activity for survival.

TABLE 14 THE INSECT REMAINS

THE INSECT REMAINS *David Smith and Emma Tetlow*

The soil samples provided were paraffin floated using the standard method as outlined in Kenward *et al* (1980). The sample weights and volumes are shown in Table 14.

The insect remains were sorted from the paraffin flot using a low power binocular microscope and all sorted material was stored in ethanol. The Coleoptera (beetles) were identified by direct comparison to the Goraham and Girling collections of British Coleoptera. The various taxa of insects recovered are presented in Table 14. The taxonomy follows that of Lucht (1987).

Where applicable each species of Coleoptera has been assigned to one, or more, ecological groupings and these are indicated in the second column of Table 14. These groupings are derived from the preliminary classifications outlined by Kenward (1978). The classifications used here replicate those in Kenward and Hall (1995). The groupings themselves are described at the end of Table 14. The various proportions of these groups, expressed as percentages of the total Coleoptera present, are shown in Table 15 and Figure 29.

Some of the Coleoptera have also been assigned codes based upon their extent of synanthropy (dependence on human settlement). These codes are derived from those used by Kenward (1997). DNS is grateful to Kenward for supplying him with a listing of the species in each grouping. The synanthropic groupings are described at the end of Table 14 and the individual codes for the relevant species are shown in column 3 of Table 14. The proportions of these synanthropic groupings, expressed as a percentage of the total fauna, is presented in Table 16 and Figure 30.

Those beetles that are specifically associated with particular plants (phytophage) are indicated in column 7 of Table 14, and this information is primarily derived from Koch (1989, 1992).

Note: Some of the Coleoptera recovered could not be assigned to a specific ecological grouping and, therefore, the percentages presented in this table for a sample do not total 100%. The codings are explained at the bottom of Table 14.

Results

The three insect faunas recovered are all very similar. This is despite the apparent differences in sediments and the amounts of artefacts included between the lower and upper fills of the moat. This is indicated by the near uniformity of the proportions between the various ecological and synanthropic groupings (see Tables 15 and 16, Figs 28 and 29). As a result of this similarity the faunas will be discussed together.

	1018	5033	5031
total number of individuals	35	58	182
total number of species	30	39	73
oa%	40.0%	34.5%	36.8%
w%	8.6%	6.9%	12.1%
d%	0.0%	0.0%	1.1%
p%	22.9%	22.4%	12.6%
l%	2.9%	3.4%	3.8%
rd%	5.7%	5.2%	7.7%
rt%	20.0%	25.9%	17.0%
rf%	5.7%	8.6%	9.3%
h	5.7%	5.2%	6.0%

TABLE 15 THE PROPORTIONS OF THE ECOLOGICAL GROUPS FOR THE COLEOPTERA PRESENT

	1018	5033	5031
st%	5.7%	13.8%	6.6%
sf%	11.4%	12.1%	12.1%
ss%	0.0%	0.0%	1.6%

TABLE 16 THE PROPORTIONS OF THE SYNANTHROPIC FAUNA PRESENT

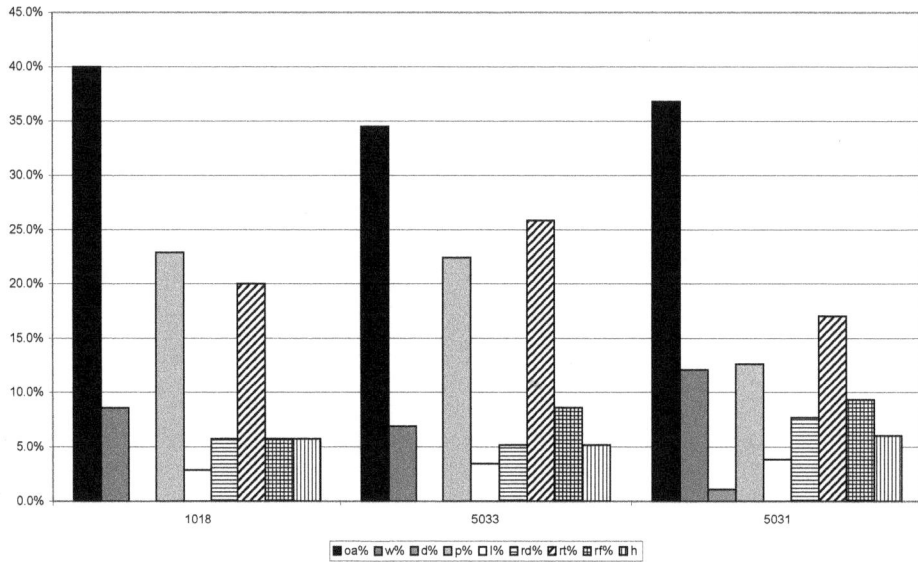

FIG. 28 THE PROPORTIONS OF THE ECOLOGICAL GROUPS FOR THE COLEOPTERA PRESENT AT OLD HALL, WOLVERHAMPTON

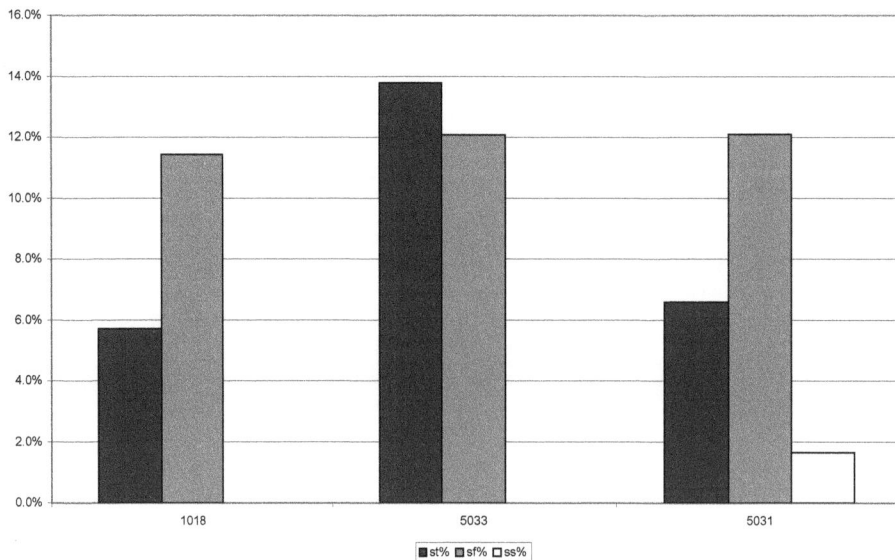

FIGURE 29 THE PROPORTIONS OF THE SYNANTHROPIC FAUNA PRESENT

In general the insect faunas recovered are typical of an open area of rough grassland or waste ground. This suggested by a number of the *phytophage* (plant feeders) recovered since their host plants are themselves typical of open ground, cultivated land and waste areas. For example, *Brachypterus urticae* and *Apion urticarium* from context 5031 indicate the presence of stands of stinging nettle (*Urtica dioica L.*, Koch 1989, 1992). This was probably at the edge of the moat itself. Similarly, local patches of clover (*Trifolium spp.*) are suggested by the *Sitona* species and ribwort plantain (*Plantago lanceolata*) by *Ceutorhynchidius troglodytes* and the *Gymnetron* species (Koch 1989, 1992).

There is almost no evidence for woodland or trees amongst the insects, suggesting the area was extensively cleared. The only species recovered that is associated with a single species of tree is the 'bark beetle' *Leperisinus* varius that lives on ash (*Fraxinus spp.*) (Koch 1992). *Polydrusus* species are associated with the foliage of trees, and do occur in some numbers. However, this can easily be from isolated scrub and trees rather than dense woodland.

There is also some evidence that cattle or other grazing animals may have been present in the area. This is suggested by occurrence of *Geotrupes*, *Onthophagus* and *Aphodius* 'dung beetles', which are associated with the dung of grazing herbivores. However, these species appear to have a wide flight potential and, as a result, it is difficult to suggest how near pasture/ grazing land may have been.

These insects appear to have been deposited into a relatively open body of water. The water beetles recovered, such as the *Agabus* species and the various *Hydreana* and *Octhebius*, are typical of bodies of slow flowing or still water (Hansen 1987; Nilsson and Holmen 1995). However, there appears to have been no waterside vegetation such as water reed in the pool given the absence of either *Donacia* or *Plateumaris* 'reed beetles'. Duckweed (*lemna spp.*),indicated by the presence of the small weevil *Tanysphyrus lemnae*, may have covered some of the surface of the moat.

The fills of the moat also contain a very limited fauna of insects that are associated with human settlement and waste. These species are included in Kenward's putative 'house fauna' (Hall and Kenward 1990; Kenward and Hall 1995, Kenward 1997) and make up the various synanthropic groupings seen in Tables 15 and 16 and Figs 28 and 29. These are often species associated with drier organic materials around settlement such as *Monotoma* species, *Cryptophagus* species, *Lathridius minutus*, *Typhaea stercorea* and the *ptinid* 'spider beetles'. However, these ecological groupings account for less than 6% of the insect fauna recovered suggesting that the contribution of rotting settlement waste to the deposits in the ditch was limited. This is also indicated by a complete lack of any remains of the common species of flies (*Diptera*) associated with human occupation. This may indicate that any settlement waste or insects that entered the moat did so by 'accident' over a longer period of time rather than deliberate deposition.

Conclusions and comparisons to other sites

Very few insect faunas have been recovered directly from deposits of a similar date to those seen at the Great Hall, Wolverhampton in the Midlands. The nearest direct comparison must be the 16th-century watercourse which linked the manorial moat with the parsonage moat, Edgbaston Street, Birmingham. Again there is evidence for open water with a limited amount of waterside vegetation and that cattle grazed nearby (Smith 2003). Similarly, at Edgbaston Street there appears to have been no deliberate deposition of settlement waste into the moat (*ibid*). The 12th-century moat at Banbury Castle also matches this pattern (Smith 1999). A similar picture was also indicated by the insect faunas recovered from 17th-century and later recuts of the abbey ditch at Peterborough despite the earlier ditches having been clogged with settlement rubbish (Smith 1996).

It would therefore seem that, certainly in the later and post-medieval periods, these moats were generally kept clear of waterside vegetation and were not used to dump rubbish. This does make some military sense but it is more probable that this is ascetic and relates to the use of moats as 'garden features'.

THE ANIMAL BONE *Emma Hancox*

Two boxes of animal bone were recovered during the evaluation and subsequent excavation (14,517g). Countable bones and/ or notable elements derived from eight contexts in Trench 6 of the evaluation and ten from the excavation.

Two contexts (5031, 5032) from the lower fills of the moat were dated to the early post-medieval period (Phase 3), and one to modern disturbance (5000, Phase 5). The rest of the faunal assemblage was dated to the late post-medieval (Phase 4).

Overall the preservation of the bone was fair to good. Most of the bones were slightly degraded with exfoliation of the outer layers. A few contexts contained fairly fragmented bones.

The faunal assemblage was recorded on the standard BU Zooarchaeological Unit recording form which follows a modified version of a system used by Davis (Davis 1992; Albarella and Davis 1994). This involves considering certain elements as countable, eg, distal femur, whilst also noting the presence of non-countables such as horncores, antlers, evidence of butchery or pathology and any unusual species. Measurable bones and teeth were noted. Only lower teeth of known position are considered measurable, bone measurements mostly follow Von den Driesch (1976). Mandibles are considered ageable when at least two teeth are present with recordable wear stages. No attempt was made to distinguish between sheep and goat at this stage, or between the galliforms (chicken/guinea fowl/

pheasant). As it is such a small assemblage all the contexts were examined in detail.

Range and Variety

Cattle, sheep/ goat, pig, horse, and chicken/ guinea fowl/ pheasant were identified along with the remains of at least two cats and a large bird species. The two cats came from the modern context (5000).

In Phase 3 the presence of five horse bones were noted, including the entire skull and upper jaw, along with four post-cranial elements. This probably represents a single animal. Only four other countable elements were noted from this phase (four sheep and two cow bones in 5031 and 5032). Evidence of butchery and gnawing was also noted in 5031.

Phase 4 contains 15 contexts from which countable bone were recovered. Sixteen cow, 15 sheep, 7 pig and 5 bird bones were recorded with a total of only ten measurable bones/teeth and two ageable mandibles. Butchery was noted in eight contexts. The presence of four pieces of worked horn (from 1007), a piece of worked antler (from 5038) and a segment cut from a cow horn is interesting. This could suggest the working of horn and antler in the vicinity. The area became used for small-scale industry in the post-medieval period with the manor house being used as a japanning factory. Therefore, it is possible that other local industries were located in the vicinity.

THE MEDIEVAL PLOUGHSOIL: SOIL MICROMORPHOLOGY, CHEMISTRY AND MAGNETIC SUSCEPTIBILITY *Richard I Macphail and John Crowther*

The examination of the monoliths showed that the ridge and furrow soils were developed over a strong brown (7.5YR5/8) sand and gravel rich subsoil (C horizon; 5057). Above, the ridge soils (5015) are composed of mottled reddish brown (5YR5/4), brown (7.5YR4/2) and light greyish brown (10YR6/2) stony sandy loam to loamy sand. The sampled sequence here is sealed by a charcoal and coal-rich dark reddish brown (5YR3/2) loamy sand (post-medieval? context 5012). In the furrow area, the 'furrow' soil is composed of brown (7.5YR4/2) loamy sand (5015) over a mixed and stony, mottled strong brown (7.5YR5/8) sand and clay (5046).

The Soil Survey of England and Wales has mapped soils around the urban area of Wolverhampton, and this survey suggests that typical stagnogley soils are present, either on Permo-Triassic and Carboniferous sandstone and siltstone or Reddish Till of a similar origin (eg, Clifton soil series; Avery, 1990; Ragg *et al*, 1983, 366). Siltstone and sandstone rock fragments are present in the thin sections (Table 17).

Chemistry

The results are presented in Table 18. All four samples are largely minerogenic and contain only small concentrations of organic matter (LOI: range, 1.36-1.80%). It seems unlikely that the medieval soils would have contained so little organic matter, and that this is the result of subsequent decomposition under reasonably well-aerated conditions. Somewhat unexpectedly, the highest LOI was recorded in the 'subsoil' beneath the ridge (sample x2b), though the range of values is very small.

The concentrations of phosphate-P are also relatively low (range, 0.456–0.810 mg g^{-1}), and provide no clear evidence of manuring. Since the highest concentration was recorded in the subsoil (sample x2b), it is possible that some phosphate has been leached out of the topsoil and has accumulated lower down the profile. This would be most likely in conditions where the topsoil has a low phosphate-

Sample	Depth	Context	Burrows	Charcoal	Phytoliths	Gravel	Intercalations/pans etc	Clay coatings	Fe mottling	Phosphate	Coal?
Ridge		Upper ridge									
M1	42-44 cm	5012		a	aa	f	aaaa	a*	a	a*	aaa
M1	44-49 cm	5015/5012	ff	a	aa(a)	ff	aaaaa	a*	aa	a*	
		Base of ridge									
M2	83-90 cm	5057	fff	a	aa(a)	ff	aaaaa	a	aaa	a	
Furrow		Upper furrow									
M3	57-64 cm	5015	ff	a	aa(a)	f	aaaaa	a*	a*	a*	

* very few 0-5%, f - few 5-15%, ff - frequent 15-30%, fff - common 30-50%, ffff - dominant 50-70%, a - rare <2% (a-*1%; a-1, single occurrence), aa - occasional 2-5%, aaa - many 5-10%, aaaa - abundant 10-20%, aaaaa - very abundant >20%

TABLE 17 SELECTED SOIL MICROMORPHOLOGICAL COUNTS

Sample no.	LOI (%)	Phosphate-P_o (mg g^{-1})	Phosphate-P_i (mg g^{-1})	Phosphate-P (mg g^{-1})	Phosphate-P_o:P (%)	Phosphate-P_i:P (%)	χ (10^{-8} m^3 kg^{-1})	χ_{max} (10^{-8} m^3 kg^{-1})	χ_{conv} (%)
xM1	1.54	0.142	0.314	0.456	31.1	68.9	6.1	320	1.91
xM2a	1.41	0.138	0.359	0.497	27.8	72.2	20.9	348	6.01
x2b	1.80	0.206	0.604	0.810	25.4	74.6	19.6	1050	1.87
xM3	1.36	0.162	0.428	0.590	27.5	72.5	3.0	238	1.26

TABLE 18 CHEMICAL AND MAGNETIC SUSCEPTIBILITY DATA

retention capacity (eg, where the soil has a low clay content), and the subsoil contains illuvial concentrations of clay and/or Fe. The majority of the phosphate present is in an inorganic form (phosphate-P_i:P_o: range, 68.9–74.6%), which is in keeping with the generally low organic matter concentration.

In terms of magnetic susceptibility, the subsoil sample stands out as having by far the highest χ_{max} value (1050 x 10^{-8} m^3 kg^{-1}). This may indicate translocation of Fe (and presumably clay) down the profile, which would support the idea of leaching of phosphate from the topsoil and its accumulation in the subsoil. It should be noted that even the subsoil χ_{max} is quite low compared with many soils in the UK (Crowther, 2003), indicating a relatively low Fe content. This could reflect either a Fe-deficient parent material and/or the effects of gleying. The χ values are low, but quite variable (range, 3.0–20.9 x 10^{-8} m^3 kg^{-1}). Only sample 2, from the base of the ridge, shows possible signs of χ enhancement, with a χ_{conv} value of 6.01%.

Soil Micromorphology

The soil micromorphological counts of burrows, gravel, charcoal, phytoliths, textural pedofeatures (intercalations/pans, clay coatings), iron mottling, phosphate (vivianite ghosts and amorphous probable Fe-P) and likely 'coal', are given in (Table 17) for each context/thin section. Soil micromorphological descriptions, soil microfabric type and soil microfacies type (SMT) are given in Table 19, alongside some integration of the chemical data and preliminary interpretations.

Discussion

The 'Furrow' Soil

Analysis of the single sample (M3, xM3) from the upper 'furrow' soil in uppermost context 5015 shows it to be a moderately phytolith-rich but poorly humic loamy sand (SMT 1). It appears to be moderately low in iron and contain very little burned material, and hence has a very low χ (3.0 x 10^{-8} m^3 kg^{-1}), although trace amounts of fine burned clay and ashes can be found. Rare charcoal is also present, one fine sand-size piece being embedded in weakly iron stained

(mottled) soil, and possibly of 'nightsoil' origin (Macphail 1998; Macphail et al, 2000). The chief characteristics of this upper furrow fill are ubiquitous broad (2–4 mm) burrows, probably by earthworms, textural pedofeatures and amorphous, probable iron, phosphate (Fe-P). The textural pedofeatures comprise very abundant fine silty clay intercalations and sometimes associated short (3 mm) pan-like features, rarely developing into (max. 200 µm thick) dusty clay coatings; and rare instances of very pale silt void infills (1mm thick). Probable Fe-P is probably in part present as rare amounts of thin (20–80 µm) brown amorphous coatings developing into diffuse hypocoatings, and impregnative nodules, and can be associated with the intercalations and void clay coatings. Pan-like intercalations can also be identified with local sorting into laminae of dusty clay.

This uppermost furrow soil seems to have formed through inwash of arable soil, partly from the juxtaposed ridge (micro-colluviation), and likely also through wash along the furrow itself. This has led to internal crust formation typical of arable soils that have undergone internal slaking (eg, Boiffin and Bresson 1987; Macphail 1992). These were penecontemporarily partially reworked by soil fauna. The furrow has also been the focus of soil drainage (cf Veneman et al 1984), with the probable loss of both some iron and clay down profile. The inclusion of high amounts of phytoliths can perhaps argue for the presence of both crop residues and organic manure here, but post-depositional soil oxidation has removed almost all organic remains apart from some root traces. Rare amounts of anthropogenic inclusions also support the view that some minor manuring has enriched this soil, although the amount of measured phosphate is low. It is therefore likely that leaching, enhanced by gleying, has removed phosphate from the furrow soil.

The 'Ridge' Soil

The ridge has been formed from a number of successive soil and depositional processes/ events. In general, compared to the furrow soil, the ridge soil is a more clay- and iron-rich sandy loam, and contains higher amounts of anthropogenic inclusions (SMT 2). Rare charcoal up to 5 mm in size and occasional burned stones present, which helps account

Material		Sample Number	Sampling depth, Soil Micromorphology (SM), Bulk Data (BD)	Phase, Interpretation and Comments
Soil Microfabric 3 over 1/2 /Microfacies 3 over 1/2	1	M1	(420-490 mm) 420-440 mm SM: as below, heterogeneous, but with many coal? fragments (10 mm), and common medium sand mixed with common (SMT 3) speckled and dotted dark reddish brown (PPL), moderately low interference colours (close porphyric, mainly speckled b-fabric, XPL), brownish orange with many blackish and occasional reddish specks; abundant amorphous organic matter and charred material, with occasional plant fragments, occasional to many phytoliths and possible diatoms present; *Pedofeatures:* textural features (intercalations) and amorphous (iron and amorphous Fe-P?) features, as below. 440-490 mm SM: *Structure:* heterogeneous (with iron mottling and layering), massive with minor burrowing and traces of fine horizontal laminae and layering; moderately compact microstructure; 10-20% voids, dominant (relict root) coarse channels (1 mm) and very coarse (6 mm) chambers; rare fine vesicles; *Coarse Mineral:* C:F (limit at 10 µm), 60:40; moderately poorly sorted coarse silt-size, mainly fine and medium sand size subrounded and rounded quartz (and feldspar), with few subangular gravel and small stones (max. 25 mm), including sandstone and quartzite; mica present; *Coarse Organic/Anthropogenic:* rare charcoal (max. 6 mm); rare relict traces of roots (0.5-1 mm) showing iron staining; rare sand-size papules/clay fragments of dusty pale textural features; *Fine Fabric:* basal layer of 8 mm thick loamy sand (leached?) SMT 1 at 122-130 mm (see M3), and at 80-122 mm, more brown, little-iron-depleted sandy loam SMT 2; *Pedofeatures:* complex textural features, including very abundant fine silty clay intercalations/sometimes short (e.g., 15 mm wide, but only 200 µm thick) pan-like features, rarely developing into 50-100 µm thick dusty clay void coatings (sometimes last phase is iron stained, with iron stained vesicle hypocoating); many weak iron impregnative nodules and amorphous iron (Fe and P?) up to 100 µm thick, and associated with partially preserved, radial and acicular vivianite nodular formations; iron stained and iron depleted panning in base of SMT 1 (base of slide); frequent infilled and partially infilled 1-4 mm wide burrows. BD:1.54% LOI, 0.456 mg g^{-1} phosphate-P; χ= 6.1 x 10^{-8} m^3 kg^{-1} and 1.91% χconv.	Upper ridge – base of 5012 Dump and cultivation of uppermost coal? and charcoal-rich layer. (Dumped in wet state, with wash of clay and iron-rich water into layer below) Upper ridge – uppermost 5015 Successive dumps and cultivation of ridge soil (as below); with evidence of likely iron-depleted loamy sand 'furrow soil' (SMT 1) being dumped as well as more iron-rich sandy loam 'ridge soil' (SMT 2). Cultivation of phytolith-rich, probably very lightly manured arable soil, with loss of some phosphate down-profile through leaching enhanced by gleying.
Soil Microfabric 2 /Microfacies 2	2	M2	830-900 mm SM: Structure: heterogeneous (with iron mottling), with burrowed (max. 4 mm wide) moderately open (channel and chamber) microstructure; 20-30% voids, dominant (relict root) coarse channels (1 mm) and very coarse (6 mm) chambers; rare fine vesicles; Coarse Mineral: C:F (limit at 10 µm). 60:40; moderately poorly sorted coarse silt-size, mainly fine and medium sand size subrounded and rounded quartz (and feldspar), with few subangular gravel and small stones (max. 12 mm), including burned quartzite and burned ferruginous siltstone; mica present; Coarse Organic/Anthropogenic: rare charcoal (max. 5 mm); occasional burned stones; rare relict traces of roots (0.5-1 mm) showing minor iron staining; Fine Fabric: SMT 2), speckled and finely dotted yellowish brown to dark brown (iron stained)(PPL), moderate interference colours (close porphyric, speckled and grano-striate b-fabric, XPL), pale orange to orange (iron stained)(OIL); many thin humic staining and amorphous organic matter, with occasional fine charred organic matter; occasional to many phytoliths; rare examples of fungal material; Pedofeatures: complex textural features, including very abundant fine silty clay intercalations/sometimes short (e.g., 15 mm wide, part biologically worked) pan-like features, rarely developing into 50-100 µm thick dusty clay coatings (sometimes last phase is iron stained); very rare instances of very pale silt void infills (0.5 mm thick); both reddish brown fine dusty clay coatings, associated with intercalations/pans, and dirty, dark grey and brown infills of dusty clay and impure clay (e.g., 1.5 mm wide with vesicle in centre); occasional amorphous iron impregnative mottles/nodular formation (10 mm size), rarely with a probable pseudomorph of radial (acicular) Fe-P vivianite (max. 1 mm); probable very rare partial ferruginisation of relict roots and organic excrements; frequent coarse burrowing; rare instances of very thin (<50 µm) organic excrements, e.g., around root traces. BD:1.41% LOI, 0.497 mg g^{-1} phosphate-P; χ= 20.9 x 10^{-8} m^3 kg^{-1} and 6.01% χconv. BD of underlying soil, 960-980 mm: BD: 1.80% LOI, 0.810 mg g^{-1} phosphate-P; χ = 19.6 x 10^{-8} m^3 kg^{-1} and 1.87% χconv.	Base of Ridge – lower 5015 Mottled (gleyed) phytolith-rich loamy soil partially homogenised by biological (roots and earthworms) activity, with intercalations/pans and associated dusty clay coatings and infills, indicative of ploughing and crops; relic phosphate features (e.g., vivianite) are indicative of manuring along with burned stones (see 6.01% χconv.). Most phosphate has been probably leached into subsoil which contains maximum phosphate-P 0.810 mg g^{-1} and χmax (1050 x 10^{-8} m^3 kg^{-1}), probably also reflecting secondary iron deposition. Biologically worked accretionary ploughsoil that was likely lightly manured.

| Soil Microfabric 1 /Microfacies 1 | 3 | M3 | 570-640 mm
SM: Structure: homogeneous, with massive and burrowed (max. 4 mm wide) compact microstructure; 10-15% voids, dominant medium (500 μm) channels and chambers and fine (200 μm) vughs; Coarse Mineral: C:F (limit at 10 μm), 70:30; moderately poorly sorted coarse silt-size, mainly fine and medium sand size subrounded and rounded quartz (and feldspar), with few subangular gravel and small stones (max. 20+ mm), including quartzite, chert and siltstone; mica present; Coarse Organic/Anthropogenic: rare charcoal (max. 1mm)(with an example embedded in yellow stained soil – nightsoil?), very rare burned clay (2 mm), burned soil and clay soil inclusions; possible rare examples of root/plant traces; very rare ashes in fine charcoal rich inclusions in burrows; Fine Fabric: SMT1) very dusty and speckled brownish grey (PPL), moderately low interference colours (close porphyric, speckled and grano-striate b-fabric, XPL), pale orange (OIL); many thin humic staining and amorphous organic matter, with occasional fine charred organic matter; occasional to many phytoliths; rare examples of fungal material; Pedofeatures: complex textural features, including very abundant fine silty clay intercalations/sometimes short (3 mm) pan-like features, rarely developing into 200 μm thick dusty clay coatings; rare instances of very pale silt void infills (1 mm thick); rare amounts of thin (20-80 μm) brown amorphous (Fe-P?) coatings developing into diffuse hypocoatings and impregnative nodules; some association between relict plant fragments/roots(?) and clay coatings; possible iron depletion; very rare instances of secondary calcite associated with charcoal-rich infills – see below; frequent very broad (4mm) burrow fills with bow-like fabrics, with very rare examples (x2) of burrow infills of fine charcoal rich organic soil with an example of blue light autofluorescent material (Ca-P?).
BD: 1.36% LOI, 0.590 mg g^{-1} phosphate-P; χ = 3.0 x 10^{-8} m³ kg^{-1} and 1.26% χconv. | Upper furrow – 5015
Moderately homogeneous accumulation of arable loamy sandy soil rich in phytoliths (with traces of manuring), characterised by disturbed/inwashed silty clay and sand (intercalations/pans) that are possibly leached (very poorly calcareous and very low χ), and which have also undergone burrow mixing, probably by earthworms; only some traces of secondary phosphate seemed to have survived probable leaching enhanced by gleying.

Biologically worked furrow fill formed by inwash of soil probably from ridge and along furrow, that shows evidence of leaching loss of iron and probable phosphate, enhanced by gleying. |

TABLE 19 MICROFACIES TYPES (SOIL MICROFABRIC TYPES AND ASSOCIATED DATA)

for the relatively high χ_{conv} of 6.01% (sample x2a). It also is characterised by both micro and macro-layering (eg, 5012–5015). In sample M2 (x2a) burrowing by soil fauna is again ubiquitous, along with textural pedofeatures. The latter have commonly been associated with cultivation disturbance of arable and horticultural soils (Gebhardt 1992, 1995; Jongerius 1970, 1983). This is likely the case here, but in addition some included very dusty clay and iron-rich textural pedofeatures, which probably arose from the dumping of wet soil, possibly from the furrow. (As an analogue, the dumping of leached soil from ditches onto banks has been recorded from other sites, such as Shaugh Moor, Dartmoor; Macphail, 1987). The former presence of phosphate is identified from ferruginous nodules that are probably partially pseudomorphic of a radial/ acicular vivianite (eg, $Fe_3[PO_4]_2 8H_2O$) crystalline formation where relict crystals are still showing traces of birefringence. This feature testifies to a former more phosphate-rich soil, and the subsequent leaching of phosphate, probably in part, into the subsoil. In this subsoil, amounts of both phosphate (0.810 mg g^{-1} phosphate-P) and organic matter (1.80% LOI) appear to be relatively enhanced, suggesting secondary deposition at the top of the subsoil beneath the ridge, with the χ_{max} of 1050 x 10^{-8} m³ kg^{-1} implying additional secondary iron deposition at this level (Crowther 2003; Macphail *et al* 2000).

The upper ridge sample (M1, xM1) shows a similar character of dumped layers, textural pedofeatures and amorphous likely Fe-P features, some probably pseudomorphic of vivianite. Anthropogenic inclusions are present in small amounts and the lower part of thin section M3 shows that leached sandy loam soil (SMT 1) was being dumped onto the ridge. The uppermost dump (SMT 3) shows coal-like material and charcoal-rich loam (5012) being dumped onto the soil (5015). Dusty clay originating from this dump has washed down profile to form dusty clay coatings and some iron-rich staining. Again, it is likely that some phosphate has been leached from this soil.

Ridge and Furrow Site Formation Processes

It is clear that although only one example of the ridge and furrow features at Great Hall, Wolverhampton, was studied, it has the expected characteristics of lightly manured, cultivated soils (Gebhardt 1992, 1995; Jongerius 1970, 1983; Macphail 1992, 1998; Macphail *et al* 1990; Simpson 1997):

- A phytolith-rich cultivation soil, although levels of organic have been markedly reduced by oxidation,

- minor manuring, although levels of phosphate are less than expected because of leaching of phosphate, enhanced by gleying, with some accumulation in the subsoil,

- biological working,

- textural pedofeatures as evidence of cultivation implement impact, although some of these pedofeatures also result from ridge construction/maintenance, as evidenced by,

- successive dumping of soil onto the ridge, sometimes clearly originating from the more strongly iron and clay depleted soils of the furrow.

It can also be suggested that the soils may have well been commonly affected by soil wetness leading to both difficulties in working and leaching of nutrients such as phosphate. Water table fluctuations (Ragg *et al* 1983) and translocation of both iron and clay down profile probably exacerbated this situation. Clearly, the employment of a ridge and furrow land management practice was in order to mitigate against a wet cultivated soil and seasonally high water table, conditions that would reduce crop yield.

CHAPTER 8: DISCUSSION

Christopher Hewitson, Malcolm Hislop and Michael Shaw

As so often with an urban excavation, attempting to arrive at a coherent narrative of the history of the site entails the assessment and bringing together of a diverse range of evidence – archaeological, documentary, cartographic, genealogical and the results of finds and scientific analyses.

The site was largely undeveloped before the medieval period, and evidence for human activity within the study area prior to this time was limited to a series of shallow features located beneath medieval deposits that were otherwise undated.

FIELD SYSTEM

Prior to the construction of the hall the site was situated immediately outside the medieval town of Wolverhampton, on its southeastern edge (Shaw 2000; Shaw above) on what had previously been agricultural land. Although the Black Country is traditionally seen as an area of heathland and woodland enclosures with a largely dispersed settlement pattern (Roberts and Wrathmell 2000, 55–6), Wolverhampton, along with many of the area's larger settlements, was surrounded by open fields (Mander and Tildesley 1960, 44), and farming would have played an important part in the economy of the medieval town. The hall site was probably taken out of the open field of Monmore, or out of an old enclosure adjacent to the field, the excavated evidence for which was a layer of ploughsoil discovered in three locations.

The morphological and micromorphological evidence supported the supposition that the soil was formed by ridge and furrow farming (MacPhail and Crowther above). The soils have been tentatively dated to the late medieval period by the presence of degraded pottery. The high level of phosphate leaching suggests the soil was commonly affected by soil wetness. Therefore there is a strong suggestion that the ridge and furrow was in place to combat high rainfall and seasonally high water table levels that were associated with the poorly draining clay subsoil.

THE POSSIBLE MEDIEVAL HOUSE AND EARLY MOAT

It has been argued earlier in this paper that historical evidence suggests the house that survived until the 19th century was preceded by an earlier house (Shaw, above). This is based on the evidence of John Leland's *Itinerary* which talks of a house belonging to the Leveson family on the edge of Wolverhampton old enough to be described as ancient by the 1530s to 1540s. This cannot have been the Great Hall, which is extremely unlikely to date from before the mid-16th century, and which would certainly not have been described as ancient at this time.

Hence, we are left with the possibility of an earlier house; added support comes from two sources. The first is the presence of the moat. Moated sites are generally regarded as being most commonly mid-12th to 14th century in date, with a particular peak in the 13th century to early 14th centuries (Le Patourel and Roberts 1978, 51). Secondly, the Leveson family possessed extensive property in Wolverhampton, perhaps with a substantial house, from at least the early 14th century (see Wisker above), and it is tempting to speculate that any such house would have been built within a moat on the site of the later Great Hall. One (secondary) source does in fact state that the hall was built on earlier foundations (Garner 1844, 177).

The excavated evidence for medieval occupation on the site is admittedly sparse. Any early house would presumably post-date the field system. The few abraded potsherds recovered from the ploughsoil, however, give only a broad *terminus post quem* (TPQ) of the 13th to 15th centuries for the construction of such a dwelling. Elsewhere, only a small amount of medieval pottery was recovered, as a residual component in later features.

The moat fills are of little help, for all of the excavated fills are late in date (18th to 19th centuries). The small amount of material recovered from the moat platform, comprising pottery and brick fragments suggest a 15th- to 16th-century date for its deposition. Hence, if the platform is made up of material from the original excavation of the moat, the moat itself would belong to the 15th to 16th centuries. It is, however, possible, that the platform material comes from a later refurbishment of the moat, associated with the redevelopment of the site and so does not date the initial excavation of the moat.

The best evidence that the site of the house was occupied in the late medieval period comes from the watching brief on the eastern section of the north wing, which yielded a quantity of late medieval/ early post-medieval pottery, apparently domestic occupation waste. This material thus differs in import from the earlier, but residual, medieval pottery, and, although the date range of the material is not sufficiently compressed to allow certainty in the matter, it does open the possibility to a late medieval, that is to say, 15th-century, occupation of the site.

Amongst the other artefacts recovered from the site, only two carry with them any suggestion of an earlier house. One is the fragment of late medieval window tracery recovered from a later feature (Ixer and Macey-Bracken above); the other is the wooden wedge, which is considered to have come from a 'substantial timber-framed structure' (Allen above). The former may have been imported onto the site as part of a consignment of building stone, but the wedge is likely to have come from a structure within the vicinity of the moated site. That no other indication of such a building was recorded during the archaeological programme is unremarkable, because the area of investigation was small compared to the size of the site, and timber-framed buildings do not always leave much trace.

While conclusive archaeological evidence for late medieval phase of occupation remains elusive, it is difficult to ignore Leland's testimony. It could of course be argued that the Levesons had moved to this site in the 16th century and that their earlier house was elsewhere but Leland's description of the house as being on the edge of the town fits very well with the present location and we must leave open the possibility that there was an earlier house on an as yet unexplored part of the site. In summary, the moat may be of medieval date, later refurbished, or, equally, it may be an unusual example of an early post-medieval moat.

THE GREAT HALL

General Layout and External Character

Taylor's map of 1750 (Fig. 4) and 19th-century engravings of the hall (Figs 8–12) show a large brick building with stone foundations, quoins and dressings. The house was aligned north–south facing west with north and south rear wings extending to the east. There was also a west projecting south wing that has the appearance of having been contemporary. It was a three-storey building with an upper storey of reduced proportions delineated by a string, and, although contemporary illustrations (Figs 9–14) suggest that it was flat roofed in the 19th century, the stylised representation of the Great Hall on Taylor's map depicts pitched roofs covering all elements of the house. Tiles were found within deposits dating from the 17th century onwards.

By the 19th century later accretions had to some extent obscured the entrance (west) front, so that there is a degree of uncertainty in attempting to phase the various parts of the building from the illustrations alone. All, however, are fairly consistent in what they show, and may, on the whole, be regarded as reliable records of the Great Hall's appearance at this time. The main focus of the west elevation was the central porch, a two-storey structure with a segmental, three-centred, or four-centred arched entrance, a mullioned and transomed window above, and a crenellated parapet. The porch supported a smaller construction, within the confines of the parapet, whose character and purpose cannot be fully discerned; it probably represents some form of architectural embellishment. The general character of the porch suggests a continuation of late medieval tradition that can be traced through such great hall porches as, for example, Winchester College (c 1382), Dartington Hall (c 1390), and Fulham Palace (c 1520).

Both to the left (north) and to the right (south) of the porch were two bays of large mullioned and transomed windows of late 16th-century character, and, between the

two left-hand (northern) bays, a narrow chimney stack with a decorative diaper pattern in the brickwork rising through three storeys and above the roofline. Diaper patterning was already much in use by the 15th century, remained in fashion into the 17th century (eg, Sudbury Hall, Derbyshire c 1613) and was revived in the 19th century. The pattern on this chimney appears to have been very definite, but that is in marked contrast to the rest of the building, which incorporates no such embellishment. The chimney therefore represents a double incongruity, firstly, for its position, whereby it breaks up the entrance front, and, secondly, for the pattern of its brickwork. It is uncertain whether this feature was part the original fabric or an addition, for although the excavation revealed that the base of the chimney was bonded into the foundations of the house (Ramsey above), that is something that might be expected in either case, and there was no definitive evidence either way.

At the north end of the front was another, much larger, chimney, to a large degree obscured by a later building in all the 19th-century drawings, but given greater exposure during the demolition (Fig. 13). Architecturally, this would have done an even greater disservice to the principal elevation, and here too there must be a supposition that the chimney is a later addition. Some evidence to support this has already been cited (Shaw above), namely, that the chimney appears to be later than one of the second floor windows, which it appears to partially block. However, the left-hand (north) side of the stack, which was only carried up as far as the second-floor string, where it was roofed, appears to have been built with stone quoins in common with the rest of the house. In addition, the base of the chimney, which seems to have been uncovered during the excavation, was built of stone blocks like the foundations elsewhere in the house (Ramsey above).

Close to the south end of the west front, though falling short of the south wall of the range, a short three-storey wing broke forward from the elevation. The second floor string of the main block was continued around this wing, which also had stone quoins. The 1845 drawing (Fig. 10) shows a north elevation comprising a single bay of mullioned and transomed windows, apparently similar in character to those of the main range. This general correspondence of the detailing suggests that the southwest wing was a close contemporary of the main block. Even so, it did not seem to enhance the aesthetic quality of the main front. The illustrations suggest that the west elevation of the wing was to a great extent blind – only in one of the drawings is a window depicted, placed centrally at first-floor level. This air of utilitarian indifference to any aesthetic considerations is bolstered by the presence of an off-centre narrow external chimney stack. There is, however, no pressing reason to suppose that this was part of the original design, and it may well be that it was a later addition. A considerable degree of modification certainly had taken place by and during the 19th century. A two-storey wing of indeterminate date had been built in front of the large chimney stack at the north end of the elevation and a succession of westward extensions to the southwest wing, in addition to which, the ground storey of the main range had been refenestrated.

The rear (east) elevation is more easily understood. Here, the building comprised central block with two projecting wings, being fenestrated with mullioned and transomed windows in a rhythm of 1:3:1 bays. Between the centre and left-hand (south) of the main block was a large external chimney stack, probably an original feature, serving an important room. Further chimneys, also external, were built against the south wall of the north wing, in the angle with the main range, and against the south wall of the main range.

While the east front, as depicted in the 19th-century illustrations (Figs 8 and 9), seems to have been intended to display a degree of balance, the extent to which symmetry might have been achieved is open to question by a study of the 1852 plan, which suggests a rather more irregular plan than is implied by the perspective views. The central positioning of the west porch, also suggests that symmetry might have been an aspiration, but the 19th-century illustrations do not supply a great deal of support for the view that such an objective was obtained. As has been hinted at in the above, it may well be that the 16th-century plan of the Great Hall, like that of Compton Wynyates in Warwickshire, was the result of an accretive development with late medieval origins. Further reason to suppose that this might have been so is provided by the disparity in height between the porch and the main body of the hall, which leads to speculation that the walls of the house had been raised, and to admit of the possibility that the original building was of no more than two storeys high.

Unfortunately, the theory that the 16th-century Great Hall was not a single phase structure can no longer be tested, but it does reinforce the intriguing possibility that has been gleaned from the archaeological evidence that the development of the site may have been a protracted process.

Internal Plan (Fig. 16)

The excavations uncovered the remains of three to four rooms of Elizabethan date represented by foundations of massive stone blocks. In no cases did the original brick walls survive, but hand-made bricks with a standard width between 2ins (51mm) and 2¼ins (57mm) were recovered during the excavations and are likely to have come from the building.

Room 1 was contained within the north wing, its approximate extent being denoted by walls F922 (north), which bordered the moat, F900 (west), which may represent the large chimney stack at this end of the wing, and internal wall F923 (east). An eastward return of wall F900 probably marked the line of the south wall. Room 1 measured c 7m (east–west) by 6.5m (north–south).

To the east of Room 1 was Room 2, which was contained wholly within a projection of the north wing to the rear (east). Room 2 was formed by wall F927 (north), which bordered the moat, wall F920 (east), and internal wall F923 (west), giving an east–west width of c 5m. The south wall was not located but was probably formed by the south wall of the east projection, giving a north–south measurement of c 8.5m. An external chimney stack is shown against the south wall on both the 1852 map (Fig. 7) and on the 19th-century illustrations of the east elevation (Figs 8 and 9).

Room 2 was divided into two unequal units by wall F924, giving a narrow cell-like room (2A) approximately 1.8m wide to the north and a much larger one (Room 2B) to the south, an arrangement that appears on the 1852 plan. The north wall (F927) of Room 2A is interesting for two reasons. Firstly, it steps out (north) from the line of the north wall (F922) of Room 1, suggesting, perhaps, that the east projection was an addition to an earlier main building, thereby adding weight to the theory of an accretive development. Secondly, there was a gap between the two sections of the north wall at the northwest corner of Room 2A, perhaps an entrance giving access to the moat, but quite possibly a drain discharging into the moat. If the latter, then one interpretation of Room 2A might be as a garderobe shaft, strategically sited to take advantage of the moat.

Room 3 lies to the south of Room 1 within the main body of the building. Its only excavated wall was the east one (Walls F911 and F913) but the remainder can be reconstructed from the 1852 map to form a rectangular room c 8m north–south by c 6m east–west. The excavation produced evidence for two western entrances which were not anticipated from the cartographic and illustrative evidence. The northernmost entrance, at the northwest corner of Room 3, would originally have given access to the exterior. However, once the northwest annexe (see below) was built in front, it may have given access into the annexe before being blocked, or was blocked at the time that the annexe was built. The other entrance, between walls F911 and F913, would have given access to the exterior. It does not appear on any of the 19th-century illustrations, and the excavation evidence confirms that it too was blocked, probably in the 19th century. A chimney stack half way along the west wall was located in the excavations (F912) and is shown on the 1852 map and on 19th-century views of the front of the hall (Figs 10–12).

The remaining rooms of the original house can only be reconstructed from the illustrative evidence. Room 4 comprised a cross passage, entered from the porch to the west, and clearly shown on the 1852 map as being accessible from the east as well. Room 5, to the south of the cross passage, is of similar size to Room 3, but was served by the large chimney stack that figures prominently in the 19th-century views of the east elevation (Figs 8 and 9). Room 6 forms a south wing and was approximately the same width as Room 1 in the north wing. The 1852 plan, however, suggests that it projected to the back of the building without any room division.

In front (west of) of Room 6 and the southernmost portion of Room 5 was a projecting wing, Room 7. The illustrations of the front of the house (Figs 10–12) and the demolition photos (Figs 13–14) suggest that this was in a similar style to the remainder of the late 16th-century building, and is therefore likely to have been contemporary.

The situation at the north end of the west front is more complicated, with evidence for a whole series of changes having been discovered during the excavation of this area, some of which are also evident on the early illustrations and demolition photographs. The demolition photograph of the west front (Fig. 13) was taken after the removal of the northwestern annexe. The photo clearly shows a tall chimney stack set against the west wall of Room 1. It is clearly later than Room 1, however, for it partially blocks the windows of the main building. Set against this chimney was a further building (the western annexe), itself of two phases. The first phase (Room 8) is formed by substantial sandstone foundations F524 and F506 and the second (Room 9) by the addition of narrower sandstone foundations F551 and F541. That the western annexe is a later addition to the main hall is confirmed both by its alignment which is eccentric to that of the main building and by early drawings (Figs 11 and 12), show a building on the footprint of Room 8 noticeably different in style to the Elizabethan Hall, with a hipped roof. Room 9 can be identified on the 1852 plan, but on none of the perspective views, and may be a mid-19th-century addition.

Taking all the evidence into account the prevailing impression is of a 16th-century house of largely Gothic character, which was, perhaps, developed in more than one stage. The core of the building was a simple rectangle, the two-storey castellated porch giving access to a central cross passage (Room 4), which in turn communicated with a pair of flanking rooms. The linear layout was derived from late medieval house plans adapted to a more modern feeling for symmetry. The southernmost of these two rooms (Room 5) was heated by a large fireplace in the east wall, and was, perhaps, the hall; the northern room (Room 3) may have formed a parlour. Servicing of these rooms would have been via the cross passage and from either the north or south wing. The construction of the north wing on the edge of the moat may suggest that this was the service block, and that the moat was made use of in disposing of the effluent consequent upon the cleaning and cooking duties of the domestics. The south wing is more likely to have been given over to superior accommodation.

The Moat

Complete sections were excavated across the moat in two locations: during the main excavations immediately west of the hall and to the south of Old Hall Street. In addition, the northern half of the moat was excavated in Trench 6 (Figs 15, 19, 21). As we have seen, the moat profile was asymmetrical, varying between around 20 to 30 degrees, and shallower on the outer edge than the inner edge. The base was flat in the main trench but more rounded in the southern trench. The moat was up to 10m in width and up to 3m in depth, and enclosed a square platform c 45m².

As we have seen the excavated sections of the moat tell us nothing about the date of its original excavation. Its earliest fills were dated to the 18th century with no deposits that could be positively dated earlier than c 1725. This suggests that either the moat was kept relatively clean throughout the 16th and 17th centuries or it was cleaned out in a single operation, possibly as part of a refurbishment of the Great Hall by the Turton family.

The waste material found within the moat typified the later years of the Hall as a high class domestic residence. The pottery located predominantly to the rear and north of the western annexe from moat sections F100 and F526 was functional and contained kitchen wares and cook wares, but also had high class wares. In particular, the glassware appeared to typify high status domestic consumption. The glassware consisted predominantly of wine vessels dating from the late 17th century through to the mid- to late 18th century. Wine at this period was subject to a monopoly granted by the crown (Brandwood et al 2004, 10) and was not, therefore, widely available, being under the jurisdiction of the wealthy elite. The survival of wine vessels from the 17th century in deposits of predominantly 18th-century date is not uncommon, as they tended to be reused repeatedly at this period. The wooden bowling ball (Plate 14) is a very rare survival. The pursuit of leisure activities, in particular bowls, was certainly a high status activity in the 18th century, particularly when the object in question was made of imported tropical hardwood. We can speculate that it was used on the lawns surrounding the Great Hall. The presence of high status vessels and objects may reflect the presence of the Turton family at the hall.

The subsequent sale of the hall and its abandonment closely corresponds with a period of poor maintenance of the moat reflected in the majority of the wares deposited in the moat dating from c 1725 with the greatest concentration of dated wares from the 1750s onwards. The spread of dates for the material suggests that the area continued to be used for deposition even after the transfer of the hall to the japanning factory. This suggests in particular that the adjacent western annexe continued to be used domestically as opposed to the industrial function of the remainder of the hall.

The final infilling of the moat occurred around 1800–10 according to pottery deposition (see Rátkai above). This suggest the japanning works were well established and the process of infilling was associated with the removal and deposition of waste from the factory and domestic premises as well as the reclamation of the moat that led to the subsequent expansion of the works. The end of the occupation of the Great Hall as a residence and its conversion to shared use with the japanning works is well documented (see below). The abandonment is also distinct in the archaeological record.

The environmental evidence from the moat fills tells us much about the surrounding area in the 18th to early 19th centuries. The recovery of evidence for fruit trees fits well with the evidence from the 1750 Taylor map which shows orchards and gardens both within and immediately outside the moat. Equally, the absence of settlement waste reminds us that the hall was still an isolated feature, surrounded by fields, until the early to mid-19th century. However, there is evidence to suggest that although the surrounding area was still used agriculturally the moat itself was poorly maintained from the later 18th century. Insect and waterlogged plant remains typified vegetation of overgrown wasteland, and weevils known to be associated with duckweed were present.

But where did the water to fill the moat come from? A late 19th-century source (Barford and Hewitt 1871, 17) says that the moat was filled with water from an artificial reservoir. Taylor's map of 1750 (Fig. 4) shows an oval patch of water on higher ground to the south of the moat and a possible leat leading down from this so this is likely to be the reservoir mentioned. We can speculate that there was a spring in this area.

The Curtain Wall

The moat around the Great Hall was bordered by a curtain wall. Evidence for this was found on all four sides of the moat in several locations during the archaeological work. The wall foundations survived as a mortared sandstone feature. Within the northwest of the site the curtain wall pre-dated the western annexe of the house as seen by its adaptation into the build of the wall.

The Taylor map of 1750 together with two 19th-century engravings (Figs 8 and 9) tell us more about the curtain wall. The engravings show that the lower courses of the wall were of massive stone blocks with buttresses at intervals. Above this the wall appears to be of coursed stone or brick with piers at intervals. A pair of small polygonal plan pavilions or turrets with conical roofs occupied the northeast and southeast corners; a late medieval or 16th-century date seems likely.

The Enclosure

The interior of the moat comprised an area of 0.45ha and was divided into four quadrants. As we have seen the hall lay in the northwest quadrant. For the use of the remaining area we are reliant on the Taylor map of 1750. At this time the northeast quadrant was occupied by lawns, the southwest quadrant by fruit trees and the southeast quadrant by gardens interspersed with fruit trees. We cannot of course be sure that these survived from the Elizabethan times although these uses would be quite typical of the period.

The Exterior

The chief feature outside the moat was the series of barns, which lay immediately to the west, and which are shown on the Taylor map of 1750. Although they lay outside the development area they were nevertheless an important part of the complex, and need to be considered. The first point to make is their size; as shown on the Taylor map they are massive, and appear as a courtyard block, c 30m

square with a further range to the south east around 40m in length. To the southwest are two further small structures. It is also important to note that they survived into the 19th century. Jones, writing of the late 1830s, says that the barns had been converted into workshops and parts of them appear to survive to be shown on the 1852 plan (see Fig. 7). Their generally loose arrangement around a courtyard recalls that of medieval manorial complexes such as Chalgrove, Oxfordshire, where a barn and other farm buildings are separated by a courtyard from the hall and domestic quarters. In the case of Chalgrove, however, the whole complex lies within a moat (Clarke 1984, 60; Steane 1985, 60).

For their function we again rely on Jones who describes them as formerly used for receiving flocks of sheep and storing wool. Given the Levesons' interests in wool this seems reasonable, although they may have been used for other agricultural purposes also. As with the interior features it should be emphasised that we do not have any dating evidence for them, except that they were in existence by 1750. It is, however, a reasonable assumption that they were Elizabethan in date given their purpose, and Jones certainly regarded them as such.

Elsewhere outside the moat the picture in 1750 is still a rural one with orchards and gardens to the north and west and fields to the south and east, explaining the environmental results. Further afield a number of brickyards are shown. Airs (1982, 59) has emphasised that bricks used in an Elizabethan building are likely to have been made on or close to the site and hence the bricks used in the building of the Great Hall are likely to have come from here. The closest – the 'Old Brickiln', 200m to the east is perhaps the best candidate as it was obviously abandoned by 1750, but there are also 'Brickiln', 250m to the southwest off the west side of Dudley Street, and 'Fryers Brickiln', 350m to the northeast. Even if none of these were the brickworks used for the Great Hall bricks they do at least demonstrate that the local clay was suitable for brickmaking.

Context

One of the earliest brick buildings in the West Midlands was the mid-15th-century house built for John of Bedford at Fulbrooke near Warwick (VCH 1945, 92; Emery 2000, 380). There are several early 16th-century examples from Warwickshire including Pooley Hall, Polesworth (1509) (VCH 1949, 187; Pevsner and Wedgwood 1966, 374; Wight 1972, 391), Wormleighton Manor House (1512) (VCH 1949, 218; Emery 2000, 210, n. 5, 343), Compton Wynyates (c 1515) (VCH 1949, 60; Emery 2000, 380–2) and Coughton Court (1530s) (Tyack 1994, 77; Emery 2000, 383, n. 17). In Staffordshire early brick buildings include St John's Hospital, Lichfield (1495), Pillaton Hall (late 15th century), and Blore Hall (early to mid-16th century).

By the time that the Great Hall came to be built, then, there was an established tradition of brick building in the region, although it should be stressed that the medium was comparatively unusual at this stage and was weighted with a particular significance, and, in the 16th century, brick buildings were important in demonstrating status (Airs 1975, 104). At this period, however, they were generally limited to the upper echelons of society, certainly in the West Midlands, where, at a vernacular level, timber remained the predominant building material down to the end of the 17th century. Hence, in a recent study of Staffordshire, Kingman estimates that there were only around 60 brick-built buildings in Staffordshire by 1660 and that they were almost exclusively located in rural areas (Kingman 2006, 25–40; 2008, 69). Hence, the Great Hall stands out as a consciously aristocratic status symbol.

Near contemporary houses include Plaish Hall in Shropshire. This is a brick building of H-plan with walls of diapered red brick and stone quoins. It was built by William Leighton who was at one time Chief Justice of North Wales, and is now considered to date from the 1570s (Newman and Pevsner 2006, 471–2).

Another close parallel, in location and date at least, is Bentley Hall, which lay around 8km east of Wolverhampton. Now demolished, it was built by Thomas Lane, around 1580. A drawing of the 1680s shows a brick building of three storeys and an E-shaped plan (Plot 1686, plate 27). The two wings, however, have stepped gables, unlike those of the Great Hall. A highly ornate banqueting house lay to the east. Recent small-scale excavations uncovered a portion of the stone foundations of the hall and its lowest courses of brickwork (Shaw and McAree 2009).

Also reasonably close by is Castle Bromwich Hall which lies around 24km to the east on the northeast edge of Birmingham. Here an E-shaped brick building of two storeys was erected by Sir Edward Devereux, MP for Tamworth, between 1557 and 1585. A third storey and highly ornamental stone porch was added in the mid-17th century (Pevsner and Wedgewood 1966, 224–5).

Moated sites are of course a common phenomenon, but it is worth pointing out that they are particularly common in the Wolverhampton area (see Larkham 1983, fig. 1), so there would have been a long tradition of regarding moats as denoting status. As we have seen moats themselves are most commonly of 13th- to early 14th -century date, and while moat building may have declined towards the end of the Middle Ages, at least one late 15th-century example is known from the Midlands, namely at Kirby Muxloe in Leicestershire, where, in 1480, William Lord Hastings excavated a new moat around his manor house and began to build a brick castle.

There is no doubt too that older moats continued in use, and often contain later buildings within them. Hence Harvington Hall in Worcestershire originated in the 14th century as a timber-framed house surrounded by a moat, but was substantially enlarged and altered in the 1580s by Humphrey Pakington, a wealthy lawyer, who made additions in red brick (with sandstone foundations, quoins and dressings) and also faced the original buildings in the

same material (Hodgetts 1991). Unlike the Great Hall, the buildings of Harvington Hall cover most of the interior of the moat, a triangular area of 0.4ha. A closer parallel, though thought to be of Jacobean date, is Ludstone Hall, near Claverley, Shropshire, an H-plan house of brick with red sandstone dressings (Newman and Pevsner 2006, 471–2). It stands in southwest quarter of a square moat, whose internal area is 0.33ha. The date of the moat is unknown. At Sheldon Hall, Birmingham, a brick central range was added to a medieval moated manor house, probably around 1610–20 (Hodder 2004, 157).

In Staffordshire itself, moats, even though they may have been refurbishments of earlier earthworks, continued to be featured in new house developments down to the 17th century. The late 15th-century brick house of Pillaton Hall was moated, but the prime example in the county, which dates, perhaps, from the early 17th century, is Caverswall Castle near Cheadle, where, in an evocation of the Middle Ages, the site of the13th-century castle was redeveloped as a mansion surrounded by a moat.

The garden features can be paralleled elsewhere. Buildings at the corner of a garden were a common Elizabethan and Jacobean motif. William Lawson's idealised garden in his *A New Orchard and Garden* (1618; reproduced in Henderson 2005, 109) shows mounts at the four corners of the garden, each surmounted by a square building with windows, finials and a banner, in a manner similar to the 'pavilions' at two corners of the Great Hall. Parterres used for lawns, orchards and gardens were common at this period, as earlier and later.

In building a new mansion house in the latest style and building material the Levesons were very much in keeping with the spirit of the times. A building date of around 1570 fits well with the Great Rebuilding of 1570–1640 as defined by W G Hoskins (1953). Although some of the details of his argument have been challenged there was an undeniable rise in building activity around this time as the disposable wealth of the gentry rose rapidly. An anonymous critic of Southampton society in 1582, quoted by Platt (1994, 2–3), summed up the prevailing mood: 'Then began costly apparel. Then down with houses, and new set in their places: for the houses where their fathers dwelt could not content their children. Then must every man of good calling be furnished with change of plate, with great store, fine linen, rich tapestry, and All other things which might make show of bravery.' (PortsRO SP12/56)

The Demise of the Great Hall

As discussed earlier (See Rátkai, and Shaw, above) there are conflicting accounts of the ending of residential occupation at the Great Hall as it transferred to the industrial use of japanning. Although the historical evidence suggests that the abandonment of the hall for residential purposes occurred from as early as the 1730s, archaeological evidence points to high status occupation up until as late as the 1770s. Much of the historical evidence relies on sources quoting at the end of the 19th century and, as such, cannot be seen as wholly reliable. The presence of a clear deposition of high status dining wares in the moat from the period of the 1750s to 1770s suggests residential occupation for a period of 20 to 30 years after the last conclusively known occupation of the Turtons at the hall (see Shaw above). Partial residential occupation is known to have continued during the halls use as a japanning works well into the 19th century. It would not be unrealistic to see this split occupation occurring from an earlier date, possibly as early as 1745, when the hall is first said to have been used for commercial purposes (Barford and Hewitt 1871, 18).

THE OLD HALL WORKS AND JAPANNING

The radical change in the usage of the hall involved a transformation from residence to factory in the space of a few short years. The heavy industrial processes involved in japanning and enamelling would be expected to leave a discernable trace in the archaeological record. In particular, the plating and drying processes would be expected to produce evidence for large scale kilns and ovens. Among the finds, there would possibly be small hand-tools, parts of larger machines such as presses, etc, off-cuts of tinned iron, discarded tinned goods (possibly showing traces of japan varnish), congealed masses of varnish and perhaps pure tin. However, little, if anything, relating to papier mâché manufacture has been recorded, except perhaps for large paste vats, small metal brads, and possibly metal moulds (Yvonne Jones pers. comm.).

As well as the waste products of the industry, adaptation, alteration and expansion of the Old Hall Works would reflect a change in the land use within the factory. The historical evidence suggests that the Old Hall was initially used for all elements of the process including packing and storage (Jones 1900, 5) but later the Old Hall was used for storage and workshops;

> ....The workshop in which the writer was placed was formerly a storeroom in the Old Hall. Inside the workshop looked like a barn open from wall to wall, the rafters and tiles were exposed to view and were black from the smoke of many winters. Rough oak boards covered the floor, while round the walls were fixed the workmen's benches...... (Jones 1900, 34).

As previously discussed these probably included the decorative elements of the japanning process.

However, the archaeological evidence adjacent to the Old Hall suggests large quantities of coke were disposed of directly into the moat within the northern section of the site, and, likewise, coke overlay many of the deposits within the main excavation area. The presence of these deposits correlates with Jones' account (1900, 5, 27f), which suggests the Old Hall contained hearths and stoves for the drying process. A number of fireplaces are visible on old photographs and their locations were recorded as chimney stacks during excavations (Fig. 16, F902, F912). These may have been reused as stoves up until the 1840s

when the purpose-built stove denoted on the 1852 Board of Health Map was constructed southeast of the hall (Fig. 7).

To the north of the western annexe there was distinct evidence for the infilling of the moat area, then excavation and subsequent use as cellaring. The presence of an infilled gap between F922 and F927 suggests waste coke may have been stoked directly into the moat. The moat itself had a series of brick walls located within it that appeared to be associated with the expansion of the hall to the north.

Town gas was first established in Wolverhampton in 1819 but this was principally for street lighting in the first instance and a reliable supply of town gas was not available until the mid-19th century. The presence of large quantities of coke would support the suggestion that the works used the local and plentiful supplies of coal provided from the Black Country mines.

Adaptation of the house was apparent in the several openings that seem to have been blocked. Jones' (1900, 5) account mentions that 'the front of the house was still occupied', which suggests that one of the wings survived for residential use. This may be reflected in the blocking of the entrance to the western annexe from the main house, which implies that the western annexe was separate from the remainder of the building, and perhaps constituted the residential element of the house suggested by Jones' account (*ibid*, 27f).

The archaeological evidence for the cartographically and historically recorded expansion to the south of the Great Hall between the late 18th- and mid-19th centuries is scarce. Evaluation and monitoring in two locations revealed little evidence of the industry within a plot directly south of the Old Hall (Breeze 2007) although the former moat line was located. The archaeological evaluation in 2003 (Ramsey above) showed evidence that the expansion of the works to the south led to a single deliberate backfilling of the moat with redeposited natural clay. The evaluation also produced 27 metal off-cuts that probably represented wasters from the manufacture of tin-plate ware. The fact that more waste material was not found may reflect the value of waste metal but also the movement of the industry to purpose built factories in the local area. Certainly important machinery would have been stripped and sold off prior to the closure and demolition of the works. The adaptation of the industry within Wolverhampton meant much of the equipment passed to alternative works such as the bicycle industry (Sunbeam Works, Niphon Works: Tyler 2007a and 2007b) and may explain the relatively clean nature of the site.

The adaptation of the Great Hall represented an unusual reuse of former domestic premises. It contrasted with the earlier growth of industry in the Black Country. Whereas much manufacturing was cottage industry, the Old Hall Works represented the transplanting of a small-scale localised industry into larger premises for large-scale production. Jones (1900) suggests the industry was adopted from Pontypool far later in Wolverhampton than in Birmingham and Bilston. It was therefore not the result of gradual growth, and the Old Hall site represented large-scale available premises where entrepreneurs such as Jones and Taylor could establish the industry on a more ambitious footing.

The importance of the works to the japanning industry was summed up by R G Hobbs in 1872: "The Old Hall' was the cradle of the tin plate and japan trade, and there is scarcely a single house in that trade, now so great, but can in some way or other trace a connection with it: there stamped iron and tin goods were first made; there the first Nasmyth's steam hammer was first used; and there the manufacture of wrought-iron enamelled goods was first started.'

ACKNOWLEDGEMENTS

The project was sponsored by The City of Wolverhampton College. Thanks are due to Andrew Brodie of The City of Wolverhampton College, and to Fabrice Vinson who monitored the project on behalf of Turner and Townsend Project Management. Thanks are also due to Jeff and Paul of Chris Sturges Plant Hire for their careful machining. Work on site was carried out by Eleanor Ramsey, Kate Bain, Helena Beak, Paul Breeze, Bob Burrows, Richard Cherrington, Mary Duncan, Emma Hancox, Erica Macey and Andy Walsh. Specialists to whom thanks are due are Stephanie Rátkai, Robert Bracken, Steven Allen, Quita Mould, Rob Ixer, Erica Macey-Bracken, Malcolm Hislop, Michael Lobb, Wendy Smith, James Greig, David Smith, Emma Tetlow, Emma Hancox, Richard Macphail, and John Crowther. Illustrations are by John Halsted, Bryony Ryder and Nigel Dodds. Michael Shaw would like to thank David Bishop and Peter Evans, the present and previous city archivists for Wolverhampton, and the staff of Wolverhampton Archives and Local Studies for their ready assistance and hospitality during his documentary researches. Thanks are also due to Professor Malcolm Airs, Dr Mike Hodder and Dr Paul Stamper for discussions of aspects of the site. Data on comparative halls was supplied by Suzy Blake, HER Officer for Staffordshire, and Emma Hancox, HER Officer for Worcestershire. This volume was edited by Christopher Hewitson and Malcolm Hislop. Richard Cuttler and Amanda Forster managed the project for Birmingham Archaeology.

REFERENCES

Abbreviations

BA Birmingham Archaeology
BUFAU Birmingham University Field Archaeology Unit
PortsRO Portsmouth Record Office
Staffs RO Staffordshire Record Office
UBEAS University of Birmingham Environmental Archaeology Service
Wolv ALS Wolverhampton Archives and Local Studies
WSL William Salt Library

Primary Sources

PortsRO SP 12/56 Criticism of Southampton Society.
Staffs RO, The Sutherland Collection D593 B/1/26/6/26/11. Contract for demolition of old steeple and building of new steeple, St Peters 1475–6.

Staffs RO, The Sutherland Collection D593 B/1/26/6/31/4 Quitclaim on tenement in Dudley Street 1524.

Staffs RO, The Sutherland Collection D593 B/1/26/6/9/6. Agreement between Henry son of Clement of Wolverhampton and Richard and Margery Leveson 1299.

Staffs RO, The Sutherland Collection D593 E/6/12, Leveson v Leveson depositions of John Terrick and Michael Nicholls.

Staffs RO D868 1/67, Account of lands sold by Sir John Leveson.

WSL S. MS. 478/20/77 Letter from J Turton on his Wolverhampton ancestors and Stebbing Shaw's proposals for his History.

Wolv ALS D-JSR/44/60 Transcript of inventory and photocopy of will of William Hollyer, Innkeeper of the Cock Inn, Wolverhampton

Secondary Sources

Airs, M, 1975 *The Making of the English Country House 1500–1640,* London: Architectural Press

Airs, M, 1982 *The Buildings of Britain – Tudor and Jacobean: A Guide and Gazetteer,* London: Barrie and Jenkins

Albarella, U, and Davis, S, 1994 *The Saxon and medieval animal bones excavated from 1985–1989 from West Cotton, Northamptonshire,* London: Ancient Monuments Laboratory report, 17/94

Allan, J P, and Morris, C A, 1984 The Wood, in J P Allan *Medieval and Post Medieval Finds from Exeter, 1971–1980,* Exeter Archaeology report 3, Exeter: Exeter City Council, 305–22

Ashbee, H P, 1969 *Index of Forbidden Books* (first published under the pseudonym Pisanus Fraxi as *Index Librorum Prohibitorum* 1877), London: Sphere

Avery, B W, 1990 *Soils of the British Isles,* Wallingford: CAB International

Ayto, E G, 1999 *Clay Tobacco Pipes,* Shire Album 37, Princes Risborough: Shire Publications

Barford and Hewitt, 1871 *Visitor's Guide to Wolverhampton*

Barker, D, 1984 18th and 19th century ceramics excavated at the Foley Pottery, Fenton, Stoke-on-Trent, *Staffordshire Archaeol Studies,* Museum Archaeological Society Report, New Ser, 1, 63–86

Barker, D, 1987 The Pottery, in M A Hodder and J G Glazebrook, Excavations at Oakeswell Hall, Wednesbury, 1983, *Trans South Staffordshire Archaeol Hist Soc* 27, 64–77

Barker, D, and Holland, M, 1986 Two post-medieval pit groups from Stafford, *Staffordshire Archaeol Studies*, Museum Archaeological Society Report, New Ser, 3, 101–17

Barker, D, and Rátkai, S, 2009 The Park Street tanks, in Rátkai and Patrick, 140–4

Bayley, J, 1992 Metalworking ceramics, *Medieval Ceramics* 16, 3–10

Boiffin, J, and Bresson, L M, 1987 Dynamique de formation des croutes superficielles: apport de l'analyse microscopique, in N Fedoroff, L M Bresson and M A Courty (eds), *Soil Micromorphology*, Association Française pour l'Étude du Sol, Plaisir, 393–399

Bradley, R, 2000 1000 years of climate change, *Science* 288, 1353–4

Brandwood, G, Davidson, A, and Slaughter, M, 2004 *Licensed to Sell: the history and heritage of the public house*, London: English Heritage

Breeze, P, 2007 *Old Hall Street, Wolverhanpton: an archaeological watching brief 2007*, BA report 1464

Burritt, E, 1869 *Walks in the Black Country and its Green Borderland*, London: Sampson Low, Son, and Marston

Cappers, R, 1996 Archaeobotanical remains, in S Sidebotham and W Wendrich (eds), *Berenike '95: preliminary report of the 1995 excavations at Berenike (Egyptian Red Sea coast) and the Survey of the Eastern Desert*, Leiden: Research School Center for Non-Western Studies, 319–36

Catherine, M, 1961 17th century nuns of Louvain, Antwerp and Lierre, *Catholic History (of Staffordshire)* 1, 17–19

Ciaraldi, M, 2009 'The plant macro remains – evidence of domestic and industrial activities at Edgbaston Street, Moor Street, Park Street and The Row, in Rátkai and Patrick, 239–58

Ciaraldi, M, 2005 The plant macros, in Cuttler and Ramsey, 21–2

Clarke, H, 1984 *The Archaeology of Medieval England*, London: British Museum Publications

Cosbert, D, 2001 *Disposal of the Cosbert black glass bottle collection: illustrated internet auction results booklet*. Available: http: www.cosbert.com/bottles/CosbertCollectionDisposal2.htm. Accessed 12 March 2010

Crowther, J, 2003 Potential magnetic susceptibility and fractional conversion studies of archaeological soils and sediments, *Archaeometry* 45, 685–701

Cuttler, R, and Ramsey, E, 2005 *An archaeological excavation at Old Hall Street, Wolverhampton, West Midlands: post-excavation assessment and research design* BA report 910

Davis, S, 1992 *A rapid method for recording information about mammal bones from archaeological sites*, London: Ancient Monuments Laboratory report 19/92

DeVoe, S S, 1971 *English Papier Mâché of the Georgian and Victorian Periods*, Connecticut: Wesleyan University Press

Dore, R N (ed), 1990 *The Letter Books of Sir William Brereton*, Record Society of Lancashire and Cheshire II, letter 707 note 1

Dumbrell, R, 1983 *Understanding Antique Wine Bottles*, Woodbridge, Suffolk: Baron Publishing

Emery, A, 2000 *Greater Medieval Houses of England and Wales 1300–1500 II: East Anglia, central England and Wales*, Cambridge: Cambridge University Press

Ford, D A, 1995 Medieval Pottery in Staffordshire, AD800–1600: a review, *Staffordshire Archaeol Studies* 7

Garner, R W, 1844 *Natural History of the County of Staffordshire*, London: John Van Voorst

Gebhardt, A, 1992 Micromorphological analysis of soil structural modification caused by different cultivation implements, in P C Anderson (ed), *Prehistoire de l'Agriculture: nouvelles approaches experimentales et ethnographiques*, Paris: Centre Nationale de la Recherche Scientifique, 373–92

Gebhardt, A, 1995 Soil micromorphological data from traditional and experimental agriculture, in A J Barham and R I Macphail (eds), *Archaeological Sediments and Soils: analysis, interpretation and management*, London: Institute of Archaeology, London, 25–40

Gibson, I, 2002 *The Erotomaniac: the secret life of Henry Spencer Ashbee*, London: Faber and Faber

Goubitz, O, 1984 The drawing and registration of archaeological footwear, *Studies in Conservation* 29, No. 4, 187–196

Graham, I D G, and Scollar, I, 1976 Limitations on magnetic prospection in archaeology imposed by soil properties, *Archaeo-Physika* 6, 1–124

Greig, J R A, 1980, The plant remains, in L Watts (ed) Birmingham moat: its history, topography and destruction, *Trans Birmingham and Warwickshire Archaeol Soc* 89 (for 1978–9), 66–72

Greig, J R A, 1982 The interpretation of pollen spectra from urban archaeological deposits, in A R Hall and H K Kenward (eds) *Environmental Archaeology in the Urban Context,* CBA Res Rep 43, London: Council for British Archaeology, 47–65

Greig, J R A, 1986 The archaeobotany of the Cowick

medieval moat and some thoughts on moat studies, *Circaea* 4(1), 43–50

Greig, J R A, 2004 Pollen and seeds from peat deposits, in M Ciaraldi, R Cuttler, L Dingwall and C Dyer, Medieval tanning and retting at Brewood, Staffordshire: archaeological excavations 1999–2000, *Staffordshire Archaeol Hist Soc* 40, 24–31

Greig, J R A, 2005 *Report on Saxon, medieval and postmedieval charred and waterlogged seed and pollen from Stafford North Walls (NWS04),* unpublished report 05.12 for BA, included as separate reports on Charred plant remains, Plant macro fossils and Pollen in E Ramsey, *North Walls, Stafford, Staffordshire: a post-excavation assessment and research design 2004,* BA report 1221

Hall, A R, and Kenward, H K, 1990 *Environmental Evidence from the Collonia,* The Archaeology of York 14/6, London: Council for British Archaeology

Hansen, M, 1987 *The Hydrophilidae (Coleoptera) of Fennoscandia and Denmark Fauna,* Fauna Entomologyca Scandinavica 18, Leiden: Scandinavian Science Press

Hayfield, C, and Greig, J R A, 1989 Excavation and salvage work on a moated site at Cowick, South Humberside, 1976, *Yorkshire Archaeol J* 61, 41–70

Henderson, P, 2005 *The Tudor House and Garden: architecture and landscape in the 16th and early 17th centuries,* London: Yale University Press

Hobbs, R G, 1872 A Midland tour, *The Leisure Hour*

Hodder, M A, 2004 *Birmingham: The Hidden History,* Stroud: Tempus Publishing

Hodgetts, M, 1991 *Harvington Hall,* Archdiocese of Birmingham Historical Commission

Hoskins, W G, 1953 *The Rebuilding of England 1570–1640,* Past and Present Society, Oxford: Oxford University Press

Jennings, S, 1981 *Eighteen Centuries of Pottery from Norwich,* East Anglian Archaeology 13

Jones, W H, 1900 *The Story of the Japan Tin-plate Working and Iron Braziers Trades, and Enamel Ware Manufacture in Wolverhampton and District,* London: Alexander and Shepheard

Jones, Y, 1982 *Georgian and Victorian Japanned Wares of the West Midlands,* catalogue of the permanent and a temporary exhibition, Wolverhampton Art Gallery and Museums

Jones, Y, 2009 *Japanned Papier Mâché and Tinware c 1740–1940,* Woodbridge: Antique Collector's Club

Jongerius, A, 1970 Some morphological aspects of regrouping phenomena in Dutch soils, *Geoderma* 4, 311–31

Jongerius, A, 1983 The role of micromorphology in agricultural research, in P Bullock and C P Murphy (eds), *Soil Micromorphology,* Berkhamsted: A B Academic Publishers, 111-138

Kent, D H, 1992 *List of Vascular Plants of the British Isles,* London: Botanical Society of the British Isles

Kenward, H K, 1978 *The Analysis of Archaeological Insect Assemblages: a new approach,* The Archaeology of York, 19/1, London: Council for British Archaeology

Kenward, H K, 1997 Synanthropic insects and the size, remoteness and longevity of archaeological occupation sites: applying concepts from biogeography to past 'islands' of human occupation, *Quaternary Proceedings* 5, 135–52

Kenward, H K, and Hall, A R, 1995 *Biological Evidence from Anglo-Scandinavian Deposits at 16–22 Coppergate,* The Archaeology of York 14/7, London: Council for British Archaeology

Kenward, H K, Hall, A R, and Jones, A K G, 1980 A tested set of techniques for the extraction of plant and animal macrofossils from waterlogged archaeological deposits, *Science and Archaeology* 22, 3–15

Kershaw M J, 1987 An 18th century pit group from Stafford, *Staffordshire Archaeological Studies,* Museum Archaeological Society Report, New Ser 4, 60–85

King, P W, 2007 Black Country mining before the Industrial Revolution, *Mining History* 16, No 6, 34–49

Kingman, M J, 2006 *Brickmaking and brick building in Staffordshire, 1500–1760,* unpubl PhD thesis, Keele University

Kingman, M J, 2008 Civic improvement and use of brick: a case study of Tamworth, 1572–1760, *Trans Staffordshire Archaeol Hist Soc* 42, 68–80

Koch, K, 1989 *Die Kafer Mitteleuropas (Ökologie Band 2),* Krefeld: Goecke and Evers

Koch, K, 1992 *Die Kafer Mitteleuropas (Ökologie Band 3),* Krefeld: Goecke and Evers

Larkham, P J, 1983 Moated sites, South Staffordshire, *Trans South Staffordshire Archaeol Hist Soc,* 24, 8–65

Leeds, E T, 1949 Glass bottles of the Crown Tavern, Oxford, *Oxonensia* 14, 87–9

Le Patourel, J, and Roberts, B K, 1978 The significance of moated sites, in F A Aberg (ed), *Medieval Moated Sites,* CBA Res Rep 17, London: Council for British Archaeology, 36–55

Lucht, W H, 1987 *Die Käfer Mitteleuropas (Katalog)*, Krefeld: Goecke and Evers

Macphail, R I, 1987 A review of soil science in archaeology in England, in H C M Keeley (ed), *Environmental Archaeology: A Regional Review II, London*: Historic Buildings and Monuments Commission for England, 332–79

Macphail, R I, 1992 Soil micromorphological evidence of ancient soil erosion, in M Bell and J Boardman (eds), *Past and Present Soil Erosion*, Oxford: Oxbow, 197–216

Macphail, R I, 1998 A reply to Carter and Davidson's 'An evaluation of the contribution of soil micromorphology to the study of ancient arable agriculture', *Geoarchaeology* 13(6), 549–64

Macphail, R I, and Cruise, G M, 2001 The soil micromorphologist as team player: a multianalytical approach to the study of European microstratigraphy, in P Goldberg, V Holliday and R Ferring (eds), *Earth Science and Archaeology* New York: Kluwer Academic/Plenum Publishers, 241–67

Macphail, R I, Cruise, G M, Engelmark, R, and Linderholm, J, 2000 Integrating soil micromorphology and rapid chemical survey methods: new developments in reconstructing past rural settlement and landscape organization, in S Roskams (ed), *Interpreting Stratigraphy*, York: University of York, 71–80

Mander, G P, 1916a The Lay Subsidies, *Wolverhampton Antiquary* 1/4, 183–192

Mander, G P, 1916b The Hearth Tax Returns 1663–1763, *Wolverhampton Antiquary* 1/4, 115–128

Mander, G P, 1921 The Lords of the Dean's Manor, *Wolverhampton Antiquary* 1/7, 212–7

Mander, G P, 1934 Mr Robert Leveson's lands, *Wolverhampton Antiquary* 2/1, 35–59

Mander, G P, 1945 The Lords of Stowheath Manor, *Wolverhampton Antiquary* 2/3, 103–7

Mander, G P, and Tildesley, N W, 1960 *History of Wolverhampton to the Early 19th Century*, Wolverhampton: W Gibbons and Sons.

Moffett, L, and Smith, D, 1996 Insects and plants from a late-medieval and early post-medieval tenement in Stone, Staffordshire, UK, *Circaea* 12(2), 157–75

Moorhouse, S A, 1983 The medieval pottery, in P Mayes and L A S Butler, *Sandal Castle Excavations 1964–73*, Wakefield Historical Publications, 83–202

Morgan, R, 1976 *Sealed Bottles, Their History and Evolution (1630–1930)*, Burton-in-Trent: Midlands Antique Bottle Publishing

Morris, C A, 2000 *Wood and Woodworking in Anglo-*

Scandinavian and Medieval York, The Archaeology of York AY17/13, London: Council for British Archaeology

Newman, J, and Pevsner, N, 2006 *The Buildings of England: Shropshire*, London: Yale University Press

Nicholas, M, 2003 *Post-medieval metalworking debris from Park Street, Birmingham, West Midlands*, English Heritage Centre for Archaeology report 29/2003

Nilsson, A N, and Holmen, M, 1995 The Aquatic Adephaga (Coleoptera) of Fennoscandia and Denmark, II: Dytiscidae, *Fauna Entomologica Scandinavica* 32, Leiden and Copenhagen: Scandinavian Science Press

Niven, W, 1882 *Illustrations of Old Staffordshire Houses*, London: Chiswick Press

Orton, D, and Rátkai, S, 2009 Glass, in Rátkai and Patrick, 178–9

Pevsner, N, and Wedgewood, A, 1966 *The Buildings of England: Warwickshire*, London: Yale University Press

Platt, C, 1994 *The Great Rebuildings of Tudor and Stuart England: revolutions in architectural taste*, London: Routledge

Plot, R, 1686 *The Natural History of Staffordshire*, Oxford: The Theater

Polak, M, 2002 *Bottles Identification and Price Guide*, Iola, USA: Krause Publications

Powell, J H, Glover, B W, and Waters, C N, 1992 *A geological background for planning and development in the 'Black Country'*, British Geological Survey technical report WA/92/33, Nottingham

Ragg, J M, Beard, G R, Hollis, J M, Jones, R J A, Palmer, R C, Reeve, M J, and Whitfield, W A D, 1983 *Soils of England and Wales, Sheet 3: Midland and Western England*, Southampton: Ordnance Survey

Rátkai, S, 1987 The post-medieval coarsewares from the motte and Keep of Dudley Castle, *Staffs Arch Studies Mus Arch Soc Rep*, New Ser, 4, 1–11

Rátkai, S, 1999 The pottery, in N Appleton-Fox *Beatties Car Park, Skinner Street, Wolverhampton*, Marches Archaeology Series 56

Rátkai, S, 2002a The pottery, in G Coates and C Neilson, *Excavations in advance of the extension to the Harrison Learning Centre, University of Wolverhampton, West Midlands: post-excavation assessment and updated project design*, BUFAU report 846, 31–3

Rátkai, S, 2002b The pottery, in J Williams, *Floodgate Street, Deritend Island, Digbeth, Birmingham: archaeological excavations 2002: post excavation assessment and updated research design*, BUFAU report 909, 12–16

Rátkai, S, 2004a Medieval and post-medieval pottery, in M Ciaraldi, R Cuttler, L Dingwall and C Dyer, Medieval Tanning and Retting at Brewood, Staffordshire: Archaeological Excavations 1999–2000 *Trans Staffordshire Archaeol Hist Soc* 40, 1–55

Rátkai, S, 2004b The pottery, in K Nichol and S Rátkai, Archaeological excavation on the north side of Sandford Street, Lichfield, Staffs, 2000, *Trans Staffordshire Archaeol Hist Soc* 40, 58–121

Rátkai, S, 2004c 'The Pottery', in N Tavener, *The Former Century Cinema Site and land adjacent to the south, St Julian's Friars, Shrewsbury, Shropshire: report on a programme of archaeological fieldwork*, Marches Archaeology Series 349

Rátkai, S, 2006 The Pottery, in J Adams and K Colls, *Out of Darkness, Cometh Light: life and death in 19th-century Wolverhampton*, Birmingham Archaeology Monograph Series 2, BAR British Series, Oxford: BAR Publishing

Rátkai, S, 2009 The pottery, in Rátkai and Patrick, 92–171

Rátkai, S, forthcoming The pottery, in N Taverner, *Excavations at 15, Sandford Street, Lichfield*

Roberts, B K, and Wrathmell, S, 2000 *An Atlas of Rural Settlement in England*, London: English Heritage

Roberts, F, 1963 The Society of Jesus, *Catholic History (of Staffordshire)* 3, 1–23

Schweingruber, F H, 1982 *Microscopic Wood Anatomy: structural variability of stems and twigs in recent and subfossil woods from Central Europe*, 2nd edn, Teufon, Switzerland: Internationale Buchhandlung für Botanik und Naturwissenschaften

Shaw, M, 2000 Mapping the town, medieval Wolverhampton and Walsall, *West Midlands Archaeology* 43, 29–32

Shaw, M, and McAree, D, 2007 The rediscovery of Bentley Hall, Walsall, *West Midlands Archaeology* 50, 2–5

Shaw, S, 1801 *The History and Antiquities of Staffordshire*, Volume 2 of 2, London: J Nichols

SHC 1883 The visitation of Staffordshire made by Robert Glover, Somerset Herald AD 1583, *Collections for a History of Staffordshire* 3rd ser, 3(2), 1–55

SHC 1907 Staffordshire suits in the Court of Star Chamber, *Collections for a History of Staffordshire*, 3rd ser, 10(1), 71–188

SHC 1908 A review of the recent publications of the deputy record keeper, *Collections for a History of Staffordshire*, 3rd ser, 11, 271–83

SHC 1911 Inquisitions post mortem *1242–1327*, *Collections for a History of Staffordshire*, 3rd ser, 13

SHC 1912 Star Chamber Proceedings, *Collections for a History of Staffordshire*, 3rd ser, 14, 1–207

SHC 1941 Some letters of the Civil War in South Staffordshire, *Collections for a History of Staffordshire*, 3rd ser, 137–47

SHC 1958a The Committee at Stafford, 1643–1646, *Collections for a History of Staffordshire*, 4th Ser, 1, 90-157

SHC 1958b The Gentry of Staffordshire, *Collections for a History of Staffordshire*, 4th Ser, 2, 22

Simpson, I A, 1997 Relict properties of anthropogenic deep top soils as indicators of infield land management in Marwick, West Mainland, Orkney, *Journal of Archaeological Science*, 24, 365–80

Smith, D N, and Tetlow, E, 2005 *The insect remains from Old Hall, Wolverhampton*, UBEAS report 111

Smith, D N, 1996 The insect remains from the Abbey Ditch and other contexts at Long Causeway, Peterborough, unpubl report to BUFAU

Smith, D N, 1999 *Banbury town centre: an assessment of the insect remains*, UBEAS report 4

Smith, D N, 2003 *The insect remains from the land to the south of Edgbaston Street and Park Street, Birmingham city centre*, UBEAS report 41

Steane, J M, 1985 *The Archaeology of Medieval England and Wales*, Beckenham: Croom Helm

Toulmin-Smith, L, 1964 *Leland's Itinerary in England and Wales*, 5 volumes, London: Centaur Press

Tyack, G, 1994 *Warwickshire Country Houses*, Chichester: Phillimore

Tyler, R, 2007a *Niphon Works, Lower Villiers Street, Blakenhall, Wolverhampton, West Midlands: historic building assessment*, BA report 1669

Tyler, R, 2007b *Sunbeamland Works, Paul Street, Blakenhall, Wolverhampton, West Midlands: historic building record and assessment*, BA report 1728

VCH 1945 *The Victoria History of the County of Warwick* III, Oxford: Oxford University Press

VCH, 1949 *The Victoria History of the County of Warwick* V, Oxford: Oxford University Press

Veneman, P I M, Jacke, P V, and Bodine, S M, 1984 Soil formation as affected by pit and mound relief in Massachusetts, USA, *Geoderma* 33, 89–99

von den Driesch, A, 1976 *A Guide to the Measurement of Animal Bones from Archaeological sites*, Peabody Museum Bulletin 1, Harvard University

Watson, P, 2002 Richard Leveson, in E Cruickshanks, S Hanley and D H Hayton (eds), *The History of Parliament: The House of Commons 1690–1715*, volume IV of V, Cambridge: Cambridge University Press, 618.

Watt, S, 2000 *Old Hall Street, Wolverhampton: an archaeological desk-based assessment: phase II,* BUFAU report 734

White, H, 1996 *The Old Hall site, Wolverhampton: a desk-based assessment*, West Midlands Joint Data Team, Archaeological Report, New Ser, 7

Williams, J, 2001 *Old Hall Street, Wolverhampton: an archaeological evaluation*, BUFAU report 734.01

Wisker, R F, 1995–6 The estates of James Leveson, *Trans Staffordshire Archaeol Hist Soc* 37, 126–9

Trade Directories (in date order – all in Wolv ALS)

Sketchley and Adams 1770 Tradesman's *True Guide for the towns of Birmingham, Wolverhampton, Walsall and Dudley*; copy of Wolverhampton portion only reprinted as *The Wolverhampton Directory*

Pearson and Rollason 1780 *The Birmingham, Wolverhampton, Walsall, Dudley, Bilston and Willenhall Directory*

Bailey 1783 *Western and Midland Directory*

Holden 1805 *Holden's Triennial Directory for 1805, 1806 and 1807* 1805

Bridgen, 1833 *Directory of Wolverhampton*

Bridgen 1847 *Wolverhampton Post Office Directory, including Bilston, Willenhall, Wednesfield, Sedgley, Gornal, Tettenhall*

Hulley 1880 *Hulley's Directory of the Hardware District (includes Bilston, Willenhall and Wolverhampton)*

Cartographic Sources (in date order)

Taylor, I, 1750 *Plan of Wolverhampton*, copies in Wolv ALS

Godsons of Brailes, Warwickshire, 1788 *A plan of the township of Wolverhampton in the County of Stafford*, original in Lichfield Joint Record Office, copy in Wolv ALS

Wallis, G, 1827 *Map of the town of Wolverhampton*

Bliss, 1828 *Map of Wolverhampton*, copy in Wolv ALS

Dewhirst, 1836 *Map of the town of Wolverhampton*, copy in Staffs RO

Tithe 1842 *Wolverhampton tithe map and schedule*, copy in Wolv ALS

Bridgen, 1850 *Map of Wolverhampton*, copy in Wolv ALS

Haggar, R S, 1852 *Health of Towns Map*, large scale 1:528 version, original and copy in Wolv ALS

Steen and Blackett, 1871 *Plan of the town and borough of Wolverhampton*, scales 1:528 and 1: 2640, original in Wolv ALS

Ordnance Survey 1886 1:500 *Plan of Wolverhampton*

Ordnance Survey 1903 County Series 1:2500 map, 1st revision

Other graphic sources (in date order)

Wolv ALS N2/OLD/E1 Old Hall from Bilston Street. The original date of this drawing is uncertain. It is reproduced in Jones 1900 (opposite page 26), see note 5, and said to be of 1839. A crude version of it does, however, appear in the margins of the Bliss map of 1828 (note 32), while a copy in Wolv ALS, reproduced here, is annotated 1830

Buckler, J, 1837 South west view of the Old Hall at Wolverhampton. [Despite its title the view is actually from the southeast], WSL *Staffordshire Views* XII, 123a,

Wood, T P, *c* 1838 Wolverhampton Old Hall, in WSL *Staffordshire Views*, XII, 94b

Buckler, J, 1845 Remains of the west front of the Old Hall, formerly the residence of the Leveson family, in WSL *Staffordshire Views* XII, 124

Wolv ALS DX/6/76 This drawing is titled 'The Rise and Fall of an Art Industry'

Wolv ALS N2/OLD/E/10 Photograph of the demolition of the hall showing the southwest corner 1883

Wolv ALS N2/OLD/E/11 Photograph of the demolition of the hall from the northwest 1883